TURNING
THE FUTURE
INTO
REVENUE

TURNING THE FUTURE INTO REVENUE

What
Businesses
and
Individuals
Need to Know
to Shape
Their Futures

GLEN HIEMSTRA

WILEY

John Wiley & Sons, Inc.

Published by John Wiley & Sons, Inc., Hoboken, New Jersey.
Published simultaneously in Canada.

For general information on our other products and services please contact our
Customer Care Department within the United States at (800) 762-2974, outside
the United States at (317) 572-3993, or fax (317) 572-4002.

Wiley also publishes its books in a variety of electronic formats. Some content that
appears in print may not be available in electronic books. For more information about
Wiley products, visit our web site at www.wiley.com.

Library of Congress Cataloging-in-Publication Data:
Hiemstra, Glen, 1949–
    Turning the future into revenue : what businesses and individuals need to
know to shape their futures / Glen Hiemstra
        p. cm.
    Includes bibliographical reference and index.
    ISBN-13: 978-0-471-79293-2 (cloth)
    ISBN-10: 0-471-79293-4 (cloth)
1.   Business forecasting.   2. Stock price forecasting.   3. Economic
forecasting.   I. Title.
    HD30.27.H54 2006
    330.01'12—dc22
2006004852

Printed in the United States of America.

10   9   8   7   6   5   4   3   2   1

To Ed Lindaman
Who inspires still.

To Dr. Tracie Hiemstra
Who makes the future inviting.

And to David, Cat, and Erin
Who make the future worthwhile.

CONTENTS

CHAPTER 2
How to Profit from Five Key Technology Trends   28

CHAPTER 3
How to Profit by Increasing the Knowledge Content of Your Product or Service   54

CHAPTER 4
How to Profit from the Next Energy Wave   74

PART II
HOW TO PREDICT THE FUTURE OF YOUR BUSINESS OR CAREER—AND PLAN FOR IT NOW   91

CHAPTER 5
Plan for the Future—But Hedge Your Bets   97

CHAPTER 6
Be Your Own Futurist and Focus Your Organization on the Future   111

CHAPTER 10
Planning Activities for You and Your Enterprise   168

CHAPTER 11
Tailoring Your Career to the Future   179

PART IV
WHERE AMERICA IS FAILING THE FUTURE   185

CHAPTER 12
Environmental Imperatives   187

CHAPTER 13
The Great Divides   196

ACKNOWLEDGMENTS

I am often asked how I became a futurist. My process was simple. From an early age I had an interest in the future, reading Tom Swift books and other science fiction as a youth, devouring news of the space race as a young adult. Then, when I was a third year college student in 1970, the college I was attending hired as its president Edward B. Lindaman. Dr. Lindaman came to the college straight from the Rockwell Corporation, where he had been director of program planning for building *Apollo*, the final assignment of his 25-year career at that company. A founding member of the World Future Society, Lindaman became a personal mentor in the classic sense, suggesting things I ought to read and seminars I ought to attend. Over the next decade, ultimately as a faculty member, I learned from Lindaman a particular approach to the future, which is reflected in this book.

Ed died prematurely while on a trip to China in 1982. No person I have known before or since approached the future with such enthusiasm, nor possessed such a magnetic ability to communicate that enthusiasm for the future. Decades after he left us, people still occasionally tell me they attended a seminar with Ed, and, they say, he changed their life. Lindaman once told me the simplest of things, "You can do it." Ed was one of a kind, and with gratitude this book is dedicated to his memory.

Writing a book is both a challenge and a joy. No one has encouraged me more, for many years, to get to it than my wife Dr. Tracie Ryder Hiemstra. An accomplished author and businesswoman, she cheered and cajoled and advised, until here we are. She edited, too, and without her, there is no book. Thank you.

When I started this project, I claimed that the entire text would flow from memory. It was not so. A great deal of fresh research was required, and four able research assistants were critical to the project. Michael

Vassar, brilliant young scientist and futurist, proves that reverse mentoring is possible, as he, a digital native, advises me, a much older digital immigrant, on future science and technology, energy, and economy. In a family affair, our three adult children, Erin Hiemstra, Catherine Ryder, and David Ryder spent many hours combing the net and the library for material on the environment, China and India, and the great divides, and offering editing advice as well. Each is supersmart and dedicated to a sustainable future, and it was a thrill that they were willing to help.

Brenda Cooper, science fiction author, futurist, and colleague since the beginning of Futurist.com, pushed me for years to write more. I am pleased to have been associated with her excellent work. Bill Hainer collaborated closely for more than a decade on concepts of futuring and planning as we worked together on a variety of creative projects. Bill will recognize the roots of much of what I say, and I am always grateful for the work we did and the friendship we share.

Reverend David Brown, lifelong friend and frequent muse on religion, politics, baseball, and the future pushes me regularly, and I am happy to call him friend and colleague.

Mark Anderson, publisher of the Strategic News Service, contributed his thoughts, and I thank him for that. Jin Lan, founder of Octaxia, provided valuable insight into the future of China in many e-mails and phone calls, and his generous assistance is deeply appreciated.

Through the many years that I have been at this, there have been guides I have known who deserve recognition. They include Sohail Inayatullah, the best futurist in the world in my opinion, Bob Jacobson, Tom Furness, Barbara Hubbard, and Robert Theobald. Other guides I have known at a distance, through their books and seminars. I recommend you seek out the work of Peter Drucker, Buckminster Fuller, William Irwin Thompson, Russell Ackoff, Ray Kurzweil, Hazel Henderson, and Karl Weick.

Most futurists stay away from science fiction, a big mistake in my opinion. In fact, if you want to understand the future, read some science fiction. I have the pleasure of knowing and interacting regularly with some of the best, David Brin, Greg Bear, Bruce Sterling, Louise Marley (and Brenda Cooper, of course), and I only wish I knew the future like they do.

Thanks to my agent Peter Rubie for taking this project on so quickly and well. Finally, thanks to editor Richard Narramore and assistant editor Emily Conway of John Wiley and Sons. I appreciate that you found me and took the chance.

When Ed Lindaman died, I described him as a window on the world for all who knew him. My hope is that this book will serve you as a new window, and that what you see inspires you to discover your own preferred future.

ABOUT THE AUTHOR

Glen Hiemstra is the founder of Futurist.com, an internationally respected consultant, and a speaker for business, government, and professional associations. A former award winning educator, he is a full-time futurist, and a Visiting Scholar at the Human Interface Technology Lab at the University of Washington. His past and present clients include Microsoft, Adobe Systems, Boeing, Northern Telecom, Apax Partners, and Ambrosetti—the European House. Strategic partners include the Club of Amsterdam.

Glen lives in Kirkland, Washington, with his wife Tracie. They travel widely and love to meet their three adult children in farflung locales. If pressed to name his favorite place, Glen will usually respond with the name of an alpine lake high in the Cascade Mountains or a beach on the Baja.

INTRODUCTION

You cannot substitute agility for strategy. If you don't de-velop a strategy of your own, you become a part of someone else's strategy. . . . The absence of strategy is fine, if you don't care where you're going.

—Alvin Toffler, n.d.

Any student of the rise and fall of cultures cannot fail to be impressed by the role played in this historical succession by the image of the future. As long as a society's image is posi-tive and flourishing, the flower of culture is in full bloom. Once the image begins to decay and lose its vitality, however, the culture does not long survive.

—Fred Polak

THE FUTURE CREATES THE PRESENT:
WHY YOU SHOULD CARE HOW YOU SHAPE IT

The future creates the present.

How can that be?

The Olympic athlete stands on the diving board. The eyes close for a few moments. Then the eyes open, the athlete moves forward, springs from the board, and completes a perfect dive. What was going on prior to the dive? The athlete was mentally rehearsing the upcoming dive, creating a positive self-fulfilling prophecy of the immediate future. In other words, the athlete was creating an *image of the future* intended to impact the present.

The principle of the self-fulfilling prophecy is well established. The mental image that a person has of him or her self in the future exerts a powerful influence over behavior and even over the biological processes of the body.

If you want to change what you are doing today, change your image of the future. Change the future and the present will follow.

THE FATE OF THE DINOSAURS

In 1993 *Fortune* magazine did a cover story that featured three dinosaur shapes, each of which had a name—Sears, IBM, and General Motors. The *Fortune* writers were asking whether these three companies had become dinosaurs, in danger of going extinct. What was interesting about this question is that the same three companies had been named by Peter Drucker 30 years earlier as the best managed companies in the history of the world. What had happened?

The most critical factor had been their images of the future. Each had an image, and each focused on business strategies that would make them successful in that imagined future—of the future of retailing, of computing, or of the automobile business. But while they were focused on implementing those strategies, the world went somewhere else. Perhaps this happened before they noticed the world was changing, but more likely they noticed the changes around them, but ignored them.

Your business is in danger of ending up shaped like a dinosaur on the cover of a business magazine. How do you avoid this fate? You begin with your image of the future, of your organization, or of yourself. What is it? Does it make sense given what we can see happening in the world? How do you change it?

The image of the future in any enterprise—whether that image be the future that you expect and are getting ready for, the future that you fear and are attempting to avoid, or the future that you prefer and are trying to create—is the most potent leverage point for change in the enterprise. Change the image in a way that is shared and believed, and new strategies and actions will automatically appear.

WHY STRATEGIC PLANNING ISN'T WORKING

What future images are dominating your own business? What if your image is wrong and the world is moving in a new direction? Do people in your company, your division, your office have any idea what direction you are headed in? Do you?

Gary Hamel and C. K. Prahalad in their book *Competing for the Future* argued that leaders in organizations have a critical responsibility that they are not very likely to fulfill, at least in U.S. companies. That responsibility is to develop a shared image of the long-range future. The authors suggested, amazingly, that senior leaders ought to devote one day a week to this task.

Contrast that to what passes for typical long-range planning. You have an annual two-day retreat to do "strategic planning," which includes a couple of rounds of golf. With the information presented and discussed in the retreat, various people are assigned to update company goals and objectives, and to outline the initiatives planned for the coming year to achieve the goals. This gets rolled up into the strategic plan, with a horizon of three years. The next year the process is repeated. Outside of this, company leaders spend little or no time on long-range planning. Little wonder that about 65 percent of the time the words in the strategic plan make little or no discernible difference in the behavior of the company.

In the late 1990s I assisted the King County (Washington State) library system in developing a long-range vision and strategic plan, as they prepared to build a number of new libraries in this rapidly growing county. One of the sessions engaged the library board and management team with a panel of experts to explore long-range trends. On the panel, besides myself as the futurist, were the architect hired to oversee the building designs and the director of the Microsoft library project. As the panel progressed, I cited the Hamel and Prahalad notion about the value of company leaders devoting 20 percent of their time to developing shared long-range vision. "Interesting," said the Microsoft director, "because I would say that is approximately the amount of time that Bill Gates and his senior leaders spend doing just that. Sitting around and developing shared perspectives on what technologies, competitors, and consumers will be doing and wanting several years down the road."

HOW LONG IS LONG RANGE?

No question is more frequently asked of me, as a futurist business consultant, than, "How far out should we look when doing long-range or strategic planning?" The tendency in the past decade has been to shorten the horizon or to eliminate strategic planning altogether. We began living in Internet time, the life cycle of products and jobs and companies decreased, the world flattened, and flexibility came to be seen as more important than strategy. We can't know the future anyway, it was argued, so why even bother? Just get efficient, get fast and agile, and the future will take care of itself. Thus, strategic planning, if it happened at all, looked at three-year horizons at most.

There are deep problems with this approach. The chief problem is that in spite of rapid change, fundamental, discontinuous change typically takes longer than three years. If your view is that limited, you cannot see the big picture. A long-range and wide-angle view allows you to see new opportunities when others do not. Strategic planning as usually practiced will not afford you this long-range, big picture view, and without that view you may spin your wheels forever.

Strategic Planning Is an Oxymoron

Strategizing and planning are such different activities that "strategic planning" is almost an oxymoron. True long-range planning involves three interrelated but distinct stages or activities: strategic thinking, strategic decision making, and strategic planning. Unfortunately as commonly practiced the three stages are mixed together and done badly. Very often what happens is that senior executives, assisted perhaps by planning staff or consultants, re-write the previous year's plan, producing a report that is then sold to company employees to get their buy in so that they will implement the plan. Strategic thinking, if it happens at all, is rudimentary, narrow in scope, short-range, and aimed at developing a single view of the future that reinforces past assumptions. It is little wonder that when external events result in rapid and discontinuous change, the only alternative for the company is to shift into crisis management and try to survive.

A better approach is to follow a three-stage process for preferred future planning. The first stage of this process is developing foresight. The second stage involves choosing a future direction. Taken together, these two stages are what we call futuring. The final stage is deciding on a web of strategies to shape the future and to respond nimbly to surprises along with the routine but difficult task of turning vision and strategy into action. The problem comes when you do only this final stage and think that you have done adequate long-range planning. In fact, you have only set yourself up for failure and the need to fall back into reactive, crisis management. Your competitors who are doing effective futuring will see the opportunities that you do not, and will respond more flexibly to apparent surprises. The good news, if it is that, is not many of your competitors will be doing effective preferred future planning, so you have time to learn and use the methods.

Long-Term Is at Least 20 Years

The long-term view must be at least a couple of decades into the future. Through years of experience working with enterprises of all kinds, private and public, I have found that taking a long-range view of about 20 to 25 years, as a part of the process, is best. We can allow ourselves to believe that things can and will be different and thus give ourselves permission to imagine making fundamental changes in our organizations. We know we will be wrong more than we will be right, but we also know that the creative act of thinking strategically this far ahead will enable us to see opportunities that a three-year horizon will surely miss. Finally and importantly, 20 years is a short enough time that we can, allowing for some luck, suppose that we will still be there to see what happens. Thus we have a personal stake in the outcome.

TWENTY TO TWENTY-FIVE YEARS? YOU'RE KIDDING

We are not talking about making a plan for 25 years. We are not talking about deciding a business strategy for 20 years from now. That would be a waste of time. Plans are made on a shorter, even very short horizon. But the short-term plan leverages what can be learned from a long-term view.

The principle can be called "future before you plan." This terminology was coined more than two decades ago by my mentor Edward Lindaman and his colleague Ron Lippitt as they collaborated. Lindaman and Lippitt, pioneers of futuring as a business practice, argued that planning ought to be preceded by futuring. This is both an effort to expand our thinking about the possible and probable future and to deliberately create a description of the preferred future. Working backward from these future images, their research demonstrated, led to more creativity and better strategic thinking than did traditional problem solving or strategic planning.

If you want to change your present reality, if you want to position your company today for success, begin in the future. Change the future, and the present will follow.

This is a book about how to shape the future in order to change the present. The essential process is called preferred future planning, a process that ties together futuring and strategic planning. It is a process that takes you more deeply into the future than does traditional strategic planning, although each approach shares certain concepts and terminology. By creating shared images of the future, the process you learn here has the potential to transform your situation.

PREVIEWS AND PREMISES

We want to accomplish two things in this book. First, expand your images of the future. Second, learn better how to future and how to plan. As we do these things, you will discover how to profit from the future and how to protect yourself. You will see how to create a positive future and how to avoid potential catastrophe. We examine the long-range and the short-range future, often simultaneously. We apply our thinking at a variety of levels, individual, business enterprise, and societal. Some of our thinking will be far out, but all of it will be as practical as it gets.

Part I—What Your Future Will Look Like: Four Powerful Trends and How You Can Profit or Protect Yourself. These four major trends—demographics, technology, economics, and energy—are combining to revolutionize our businesses and our world. We look at:

Chapter 1: *How to Profit from Demographic Tidal Shifts.* The biggest news is this: Population growth is ending, and businesses may face a future of declining customer bases.

Chapter 2: *How to Profit from Five Key Technology Trends.* The fundamental arenas of science and technology are making the unimaginable become our daily life.

Chapter 3: *How to Profit by Increasing the Knowledge Content of Your Product or Service*. The twenty-first century economy depends on knowledge-value. It turns out that it is what you know that counts. The most important trend may be this: China and India are becoming knowledge intensive economies.

Chapter 4: *How to Profit from the Next Energy Wave*. Cheap oil is disappearing for good. What will emerge from an historic shift in energy use is the biggest business opportunity in history.

The second purpose of this book is to offer some guidance about how to create a long-term perspective, and then how to turn that into actionable ideas in your company or in your life. Exploring images of the future can be enlightening, but doing so can be mere entertainment. The purpose for such future exploration is to discover what you should be doing or learning right now.

Part II—How To Predict the Future of Your Business or Career. We outline basic principles for becoming your own futurist so you can better design your career, or your enterprise, by following these guidelines:

Chapter 5: *Plan for the Future—But Hedge Your Bets* reveals why planning fails more often than it works and suggests simple steps to assure success.

Chapter 6: *Be Your Own Futurist and Focus Your Organization on the Future* explores what it means to be future oriented, vision driven, collaborative, and strategic.

Chapter 7: *Ten Key Practices of the Future Oriented Enterprises* examines what is required to position your business for success in the twenty-first century.

Part III—Preferred Future Planning Exercises, Tools, and Activities. This section offers specific tools for shaping the future of your business or career, with an emphasis on turning strategic decisions into practical steps today.

Chapter 8: *Forecasting the Future—Activities for You and Your Enterprise* offers several strategic thinking techniques including environmental scanning and scenario planning.

Chapter 9: *Choosing a Direction—Activities for You and Your Enterprise* asks what future you prefer. Vision and values come together as strategic decisions.

Chapter 10: *Planning Activities for You and Your Enterprise* focuses on turning strategies into action and managing the change that follows.

Chapter 11: *Tailoring Your Career to the Future* explores specific growth opportunities for future revenue and work.

The future is not child's play or something that would be nice to pay attention to if only we had the time. The fate of the planet, the fate of your enterprise, your own fate and that of your family depend more on what we do over the next couple of decades than on what we have done up to now. What should you do? Put your feet up on the coffee table, open a can of beer, and say, "The heck with it; nothing I can do about it anyway." Or do you have other options?

Part IV—Where America Is Failing the Future. In the final section of the book, we begin with the premise that here in the United States where I live we have, in many ways, put our collective feet on the coffee table. This response, or rather nonresponse, is no longer sufficient. Instead we have responsibilities to the future and to explore:

Chapter 12: *Environmental Imperatives.* The weather is getting wild. Yet the possibility exists to create a sustainable future in which everyone on the planet could live comfortably.

Chapter 13: *The Great Divides.* We are divided across race, religion, access to technology, education, health, longevity, gender preference, wealth, and access to resources. These divides must be closed if we are to have a future.

Chapter 14: *A Vision for the Twenty-First Century* suggests that if you want to lead the crowd, you might want to adopt a planetary business vision. In the end, the future is up to you.

TURNING THE FUTURE INTO REVENUE

Whether you are in business, the title of this book probably caught your eye. The future is indeed about revenue.

In the early 1980s I was an academic. The research that I pursued at the time was focused on this question, "How will emerging information technology change both organizations and human communication?" In conducting this research, I gained access to transcripts of conversations on the ARPANet, the military and government network that became the public Internet. Specifically I focused on team projects that were conducted, in part, via interaction on this computer network. I studied similar group work on a university-based scientific network known at the time as EIES, or Electronic Information Exchange System, created by Murry Turoff and Roxanne Hiltz. In addition, I sat in and observed teleconferences of various kinds, both audio telephone conferences, and early videoconferences.

A few years later I left higher education for business consulting and the life of a professional futurist. As I left I possessed a significant asset from my earlier studies—foresight into what was coming—the Internet and later the World Wide Web. I was not the only person who knew, of course, but this foresight put me far enough ahead that when the opportunity arose to establish Futurist.com, I was the first to think of it or to follow that vision with action. This book is a result of that long-ago foresight. The editors at Wiley, considering a book on the future, wandered into Futurist.com, contacted me, invited a proposal, and off we went. Once again, the future had turned into revenue.

Am I actually that visionary? Not really. I merely attempt to leverage our unique human ability to learn from the past, live in the present, and anticipate and dream the future.

You can, too. In the pages that follow we take every opportunity to discover ways in which you might profit from future opportunities, or protect yourself from future risk. We name some business ideas and suggest strategies for shaping the future, whether that future is your own or that of your enterprise. But the future is full of surprises and individual discoveries, and my hope is that what you get from this book is not actually in these pages. Rather, it is more likely that you will create a new idea, based on what is here in combination with your own experience. From that idea, revenue can flow.

IS THE FUTURE ONLY ABOUT REVENUE?

No. It is quite legitimate to suggest that to make the future about revenue is to focus on the wrong thing. The future is actually more about sustainability and saving the planetary environment for future generations. It is about economic justice and confronting inequality. The future is very much about human relationships and love for one another. The future is about each of these things and ultimately, at the end of our days, they will count for more than any revenue that we accumulated.

But we live in the world that we live in, and in this world individuals seek to make a living, businesses seek to make a profit, and revenue is necessary to accomplish great goals, most if not all the time. Whether I am keynoting an international investment conference in London, a tourism convention in Costa Rica, or a technology event in the United States, this topic always arises.

This was brought home to me most clearly in the year 2000 when I facilitated a think tank event aimed at assisting the development of a national vision for transportation in the United States in the year 2050. Attending the think tank was a representative of the Rocky Mountain Institute, which was then and is now pushing for initiatives to reinvent automobiles. This person made the following argument, simple in its expression, profound in its meaning. The Institute is primarily interested in sustainable communities. Like many others with that interest, they had focused on strategies and initiatives to get people out of cars, since the automobile culture has been so damaging to the environment in so many ways. The Institute was pushing a huge rock up a hill, the top of which would never be reached.

Then an insight came. Since cars were a major problem but the entire culture depended on them, the fastest way to make progress toward sustainability would be to *change the cars*. In this insight we see the makings of future revenue, huge future revenue. The current rush to hybrids is a clear step along this path. The leader of the Institute, Amory Lovins, has called the shift to the next energy era not just the right thing for a sustainable future, but the greatest business opportunity in history.

In titling this book *Turning the Future into Revenue*, I am not saying that revenue is the only important aspect of the future. At the same time revenue is essential if we are to create preferred futures.

BECOMING YOUR OWN FUTURIST

When I speak to groups of people on futuring and planning, I often say that one of my goals is for people to walk out at the end of the event defining themselves as futurists. The challenge is to learn how to anticipate the future, to consciously imagine and dream it, to suffuse it with hope even when reality seems bleak, and to act. This is not as easy as it sounds, especially when you will have to get up and do it again when things have gone wrong and surprises have overwhelmed what we expected and imagined. The approach is well summarized in these words from Ed Lindaman's seminal work, *Thinking in the Future Tense* (1978): "We have the awesome responsibility of being *able* to construct our own future and having to choose *whether to* and *how to* participate in that creative process; then we have to *decide what options* we prefer."

Each of us has this opportunity and responsibility. If you can tap your innate ability to future and grasp the power that exists in knowing that the future creates the present, you may discover opportunities you never suspected were there.

WHAT YOUR FUTURE WILL LOOK LIKE: FOUR LONG-TERM TRENDS AND HOW YOU CAN PROFIT OR PROTECT YOURSELF

OUR FUTURE: A SOCIAL-ECONOMIC-TECHNOLOGICAL REVOLUTION

There is a lodge in the Columbia River gorge in Washington State, about 30 miles upriver from the small town where I lived in my youth. Now and then a company or association will hold a strategic planning retreat at this wonderful lodge and invite me to come speak about how the future will be different from today.

To get there, on the last leg of the trip I will drive the Interstate highway up the river from Portland, Oregon. As I drive, I pass by a field of hay and a barn, alongside the freeway. It is the same field in which nearly 40 years ago I would, as a summer job, help to harvest the hay and put it into the barn. Though a little worn out, the field and the barn look much the same today as they did then.

A paradox of the future always strikes me when I drive by that field. I am on the way to tell a group of businesspeople that "everything is changing" in the future. But alongside the road is evidence that nothing changes.

So it is with the future. It will look quite different from today, even startlingly different. The future consists of very rapid change, change that we see and comment on all the time. Yet we know that the future also consists of continuity. Some things change very little, or very slowly. Twenty years from now people will need food to eat and clothing to wear and shelter to live in. This has always been true. Only the ways of providing these needs change. Twenty years from now people will be born and they will die. They will get sick and need to be cared for. Products will be made, and they will break or wear out and need to be repaired or replaced. People will get into relationships and fall out of them. People will want to be entertained, and some people will want to entertain. The list of continuities is very long.

But things will also change, as we will see, at an accelerating rate. This is the second paradox of the future, that change is fast and slow. This paradox hits home when the future that we expect fails to appear—where are our flying cars, where is the leisure society? The paradox may appear when something that appears stable "suddenly" shifts—the Berlin Wall comes down, the sale of music CDs comes to a halt.

There is a third paradox to the future. The future is a combination of danger and open-ended possibilities. You have probably seen a well-known Chinese language character for "crisis," the weiji, a two-part language symbol, which means "danger" plus an "incipient moment, when something begins or changes." In other words, a crisis. The weiji, in conveying that danger means the future is opening up into something new, captures the third paradox. When faced with danger, an instinctual response is to close up and defend territory. An alternative response is to find a new way through.

Continuity, change, paradox. The future also consists of choice. The further out we look, the more "choiceful" the future is. What the world will look like three years from now has largely been decided. Some sudden paradigm shift may occur in that time span and we can adjust, but we cannot change everything in so short a time. On the other hand, what the world will look like 20 or 30 years from now will depend as much or more on the choices made between now and then, than on all the choices made up till now.

The critical long-term trends shaping our future—demographic shifts, technology advances, economic discontinuities, the next energy wave— each create opportunity and danger and provide choices to be made. We might assume that life has never changed this fast before. But rapid change has happened in the past.

My paternal grandparents emigrated from the Netherlands to Montana in the first decade of the twentieth century. Born in the 1880s, they were a young couple who had dreamed of the big-sky country. In Montana my grandfather built a first house consisting of a wooden wall fronting a cave, and they joined a small Dutch community to begin their lives as dry-land wheat farmers. Montana turned out not to be a picture postcard existence, however, and in the mid-1920s one last hail-storm wiped out one last wheat crop. Giving up, the family, now including six children, loaded their belongings into a truck and headed for Oregon where they had heard the farming was better. The truck broke down in Idaho, however, and so the family stayed there, eventually leaving farming behind.

About the time they settled in Idaho my guess is that my grandparents sat one evening at the kitchen table, looked at each other and said, "You know what? Life is completely different from when we were little kids back in the 1880s." For them, this was true.

What had changed in the years from 1890 to 1920? X-rays, use of electricity, the movie camera, and radio were new. Telephone use became common. The Wright brothers and others flew airplanes. Albert Einstein proved that E = MC squared. World War I was a crushing global event.

Most importantly, this was the time of the second and final industrial revolution. In 1900 most U.S. workers were still farmers and ranchers. The next largest category was live-in, household servants. Two decades later the agricultural age had ended and a majority of workers were employed in wage-based jobs, in factories and offices, and people were flocking into cities and the beginnings of suburbs as we know them.

In 1900 the horse was still the dominant means of transportation in the country, so dominant that it took one-fourth of the nation's farmland just to feed all the horses. Then Henry Ford built the Model-T and the assembly line. By 1920 more than half of U.S. households owned an automobile.

What my grandparents had lived through was a rare historical transition, a social-economic-technological revolution (Snyder 1999). Such revolutions happen periodically but infrequently through history. Today we are past the midpoint of our own revolution that future historians will compare to previous such shifts through history. We are reliving the lives of my grandparents.

Understanding the nature of such revolutions, the lessons we might learn, and the probable course of the next 25 years, is the first step in turning the future into revenue.

NATURE OF THE REVOLUTION

What is a social-economic-technological revolution? In a nutshell, technologies are invented that are powerful enough in time to change the social economy. When the revolution is over, the lives people live are different.

The revolution of 1890–1920 can be labeled the "electromechanical" revolution, as it involved primarily the invention and deployment of electric motors and internal combustion engines. In addition, the communication technologies of the telephone and the radio played key roles. Most fundamentally, this revolution was based on cheap oil.

As they began to be used, certain of the new technologies were capable of being combined into integrated systems, which accelerated their development and spread their impact. For example, combining variable speed electric motors with internal combustion engines gave rise to modern transportation and industry.

Eventually the new integrated industries emerged as dominant in terms of income generated and people employed. Meanwhile, older industries stagnated and some became obsolete, withered, and died.

PATTERNS TO REVOLUTION

Five patterns are worth noting. The entire process from initial inventions to domination of the social economy took about 50 years, or two and one-half generations. Second, during the first half of the revolution personal incomes went flat or declined, as older industries died while new industries were not sufficiently developed to compensate. People wondered what had gone wrong with the world. Third, at some point, when the new industrial technologies were sufficiently developed and integrated, economic growth accelerated sharply producing an avalanche of the new. Fourth, the technological, economic, and social changes were accompanied by or contributed to political upheaval including, most notably, the communist revolution of 1917. Finally, the gains that occurred in the new economy and the losses in the old economy were not evenly distributed, either in time or geographically.

There are many parallels today to the electromechanical revolution. We are 35 years into the digital-biological-nanotech revolution. We can precisely pinpoint when it began, in 1971, when Intel sold its first microprocessor, the 4004. It accelerated with genetic engineering, Apple, Microsoft, and the IBM PC, fiber optics, the fax machine, cell phones, the evolution of the early Internet into the World Wide Web, and finally the beginnings of nanotechnology research and development. By the turn of the century the biological, nano, and digital information industrial complex were emerging worldwide as dominant in the social economy.

The key image is this. We are a little more than 30 years into our own revolution. The groundwork has been laid and the new industries have emerged as dominant. If this revolution happens like the last one, then *the most fundamental changes are just beginning* and will occur over the next two decades. When it is over we will sit at our kitchen tables and say, "You know what? Life is completely different from when we were so young back in 2006."

WHAT WILL CHANGE?

Not everything will change in the next two decades, but a great deal will. Specifically, when we look back from the perspective of 2025 or so, we will notice things like the fact that retirement came to an end, that jobs changed to stints, that homes went back to the future and became the center of life, that learning moved well beyond schools, that processes for making things and buying and selling them transformed. How and when and where we work will change, as will how and where we live in relationship to our work, how and when and why we travel, how and when we communicate, how we relate to and integrate with the rest of the world, how we view family and how we raise families, how we govern ourselves, and more. In fact, we will probably note that the past couple of decades saw as much change economically, socially, politically, and technologically as the entire twentieth century.

Such a revolution may involve new and powerful technologies, but eventually the social and economic changes themselves begin to call forth further technological development. A virtuous cycle develops in which technologies lead to economic changes that lead to additional technologies that lead to social changes, and so on. The changes thus will be primarily social and economic but will have been driven by key technologies: nanotechnology, biotechnology, information technology, robotics, hypertransparency. It is people who are impacted profoundly by a social-economic-technological revolution, and it is with people that we begin.

CHAPTER 1

How to Profit from Demographic Tidal Shifts

It is change, continuing change, inevitable change that is the dominant factor in society today. No sensible decision can be made any longer without taking into account not only the world as it is, but the world as it will be.

—Isaac Asimov, 1995

Demography is destiny. It is an old saying. There is no doubt that the most predictable aspect of the future is the shape and nature of the population. Yet, strangely, we get it wrong all the time. In the twentieth century, we did not anticipate the Baby Boom, nor the extent of the rise of global population as death rates declined. We only began to forecast these developments after they were well underway.

Now we look around, we see people much like ourselves, we occasionally read about a key trend such as the aging population, yet we blithely assume that the future will resemble the past. In this first quarter of the twenty-first century, major demographic tidal shifts are underway. Some we see, but we underestimate the implications. Others we fail to see, though the evidence is right before us.

SO MUCH OLDER

Let's begin with something we do see, the aging population. Imagine walking down the street in any U.S. city or town. Notice that as you walk about 1 in 10 people whom you see is over the age of sixty-five. With the exception of Florida, where 20 percent of the population is over sixty-five today, in most of the United States the average is about 10 to 12 percent. Now, travel in a time machine to the year 2025. Take the same walk. Notice that about one in every four people whom you see is over sixty-five. The U.S. Census Bureau predicts that there will be about 27 Floridas by 2025. This is a different world.

Ken Dychtwald published the seminal book *The Age Wave*, in 1990. Yet 15 years later I could still spend a day with the staff or city council of most any U.S. city and ask the following question: "What are you planning for the day when 20 to 25 percent of your community population is over the age of sixty-five, rather than the 10 to 12 percent of today?" And what would be their answer? "Nothing. We haven't thought about it."

If I asked senior leaders of a company what they were planning for the day when 25 percent of their potential customer base will be over age sixty-five, their response would tend to be, "I had no idea it was going to be that many." Worse, their human resources departments are still focused on moving people over age fifty-five out of the work force as soon as possible, when the real agenda ought to be considering how to keep them longer, using whatever creative employment arrangements that can be thought of.

Living to be age sixty-five is not new. Benjamin Franklin lived to age eighty-four, after all. But what is new, and I mean historically new, is that so many are living to age sixty-five and beyond. In fact, of all the people who ever lived to be sixty-five in the history of the world, two-thirds of them are alive today. And when you consider people over age seventy-five, three-fourths of those who have ever lived that long are with us today.

The numbers are truly staggering. It is a global phenomenon as people are aging all over the world, with elders generally comprising the fastest growing population cohorts even in developing nations with vast youth populations. Worldwide, it is estimated that in 1900 there were about 10 million persons over sixty-five. By 2005 nearly 400 million persons were over sixty-five globally, a 4,000 percent increase. Estimates are that about 2 billion of the world's population will be over sixty-five in the year 2050, nearly a quarter of the total population.

In the United States, as in other industrial nations, the numbers are impressive. In 1900 the average life span was age forty-seven, and about 3 million persons were over age sixty-five. This was four percent of the total population of 76 million. By 1950 there were 12 million over sixty-five, eight percent of the population. By 2005 some 36 million of a total population of 296 million were over sixty-five, 12.5 percent of the population. The average life span was up to seventy-seven. To sum it up, between 1900 and 2005 in the United States the number of persons over sixty-five had increased twelvefold, while the under sixty-five population had merely tripled.

What of the future? It is obvious that we are living longer and longer, due to factors such as better hygiene, better nutrition, better safety from accidents, and better heath care. Given just routine advances in these factors, longevity will increase. A consistent trend in the United States since 1840 has been an increase in life expectancy of five years every two decades. When we take into account the anticipated breakthroughs in medical science and the science of life extension, it is clear that we will live longer and longer. This is despite a current epidemic of obesity that is contributing to growth in diabetes and causes some demographers to downshift predicted longevity by a couple of years.

We will cross a critical threshold on January 1, 2011. On that day the first Baby Boomer to turn sixty-five will celebrate a birthday. We've all heard that, right? Ho hum, big deal.

But off we go, into a national environment in which every 8 seconds someone else turns sixty-five . . . for the next 18 years. We will see a 50 percent increase in the over sixty-five age group by 2015 to a total of 55 million, then another jump to 72 million by 2030, which will be 20 percent of the total population. This number may be too small, if life extension science enables people already elderly today to live super-long life spans. And even then, compared to people in some parts of the world, we will still be young.

In Japan 19 percent of the population was over sixty-five by 2005. In Italy, 20 percent of the population is aged today. By 2050 it is expected that the median age in Italy will be fifty-eight, with more than 40 percent of the population over sixty-five. How is that going to work? Aging is just as dramatic elsewhere in Europe, in China, the rest of Asia, and on their heels Central and South America. When *BusinessWeek* took on the aging issue in a 2005 article, they summarized the issue with a money quote: "The aging workforce is the biggest economic challenge policymakers will face over the next 20 years," says Monika Queisser, a pension expert at the Organization for Economic Cooperation & Development" (Engardio and Matlack 2005).

The bottom line is this. We are embarking on a grand global experiment. The experimental question is: How shall we organize societies and economies when so many people are over the age of sixty-five. No one knows the answer, because it has never been attempted before. And we are the experimental subjects.

DISRUPTIVE DEVELOPMENT

Perhaps the most critical thing to understand in order to grasp the challenges and the opportunities is that we are talking about a *discontinuous change*. The aging of the population on this scale is a disruptive development, not a continuation of business as usual. Further, and perhaps more important, this trend is not merely a matter of numbers. The explosively growing elder population is big, but it is also qualitatively different from any previous elder generation. Up to the final years or even months of life, the elder of today is less likely to be ill or disabled than previous generations. They live not just longer, but in better health. At the same time many of them live many years with chronic but not disabling medical conditions, a fact not lost on the pharmaceutical industry.

They are more educated and more technologically savvy. Some 26 percent of U.S. elders use the Internet, the lowest percentage of any age group. But women over age sixty represent one of the fastest growing segments in Internet usage and each new set of elders will be more familiar with the net. They are less likely to be poor than previous generations, owning about 70 percent of the nation's assets, and generating about 40 percent of the national income. Television aims its advertising and programming at the young, as though they were where the money is, but the money is with the elders. BMWs may be driven by the young and sexy on TV, but the average age of a BMW purchaser is fifty-one. Cadillac may attempt to appeal to the young, but it is the sixty-four-year-old who is most likely to buy.

Today's elders are achievement oriented and adventurous compared both to previous generations and even to the general population. They flock to hands-on experience and adventure travel. Grand Circle Travel, for example, is a leading global travel company offering "insider" tours of countries led by local hosts, as well as offering the largest variety of small ship and river boat experiences in the world. The average age of their "adventurer?" Seventy-eight.

As we ride this wave into an elder society, where do we suppose people may choose to live? In the United States, the easy and obvious answer is Florida, Arizona, and other Sunbelt states. Easy and obvious, but wrong. What actually appears to be occurring is that marriage, mortgages, and memories keep most people at home, or near their adult children. Instead of mass migration to retirement havens, the real action will be in naturally occurring retirement communities (NORCs) (Coughlin 2005). If people move it will tend to be toward university towns, small cities, and rural towns so long as they are close to cities and children. For many, who have no need of a half-acre of labor-intensive lawn and a rusting basketball hoop on the garage, the move will be into high-rise developments in the center of larger cities, where they will have access to transit, commerce, and entertainment.

RETIREMENT IS DEAD

As we face a time when a quarter of the population is of retirement age, the most important lesson from that future is that we are at the end of retirement. The modern concept of retirement, it turns out, is a recent invention and historically will turn out to have been a passing fad. Prior to the twentieth century people did not retire, not in the modern sense. They slowed down, they worked less, but most worked until they dropped, and as we have seen they dropped relatively young. Early in the twentieth century the notion of retirement took hold as the final industrial revolution changed the nature of work and society. Germany was the first nation to officially adopt retirement as a social policy, in 1889, when Otto von Bismarck designed the first old-age social insurance program.

He was motivated by a desire to keep the German industrial revolution humming, and to stave off any radical socialist proposals. Originally, the retirement age was set at seventy, but it was lowered to sixty-five in 1916, and ever since age sixty-five has been generally accepted as the age to shift from work to retirement. However, as late as 1950, more than half of men age seventy in the United States work force were still on the job. In recent decades there has been a major push toward earlier retirement, though the official age remains at sixty-five.

So why will retirement die in the next couple of decades? When it was first invented, not many workers lived long enough to see retirement. Thus it did not take much money in societal terms to sustain a small group in a leisure-based retirement. But more and more people began to reach retirement age, and many of them had not accumulated sufficient savings to last for many years. Social Security and corporate pensions were designed to account for this, but either did not provide sufficient funds in the case of the former or fell short of covering everybody in the latter case. In those nations with universal old-age pension systems, the financial challenge of paying for everybody as they live longer while fewer young workers pay into the system has become ever more daunting and now borders on the impossible. As for corporate pensions, even a cursory level of attention to twenty-first century news indicates that worker pensions are being phased out. Thus pure leisure-based retirement as classically conceived will not be affordable in the future. Despite monthly business magazines with blaring headlines about "How to Retire Young! And Rich!" most people will simply have to earn money in their later years.

But there is a more basic reason why retirement will die. Consider this story. My brother spent time as a financial advisor for a national firm. One day in 2003 he received a call from an old high-school basketball teammate, who had spent his career as a public-sector firefighter. The old-age pension system in that career has been historically quite good, and now at age fifty-five the friend was ready to retire. His question was how to manage his one million dollars of accumulated benefits to enable him to play golf each day for the rest of his life. My brother traveled to meet him, armed with two issues. The first was how to assure that a million dollars would last not for 15 or 20 years, but for 30 or 40 years, a reasonable expectation for a life span given current trends in longevity. This challenge was difficult, but conceivable. The second issue was more significant, and that was to ask the friend whether he really wanted to simply play golf every day, *for 40 years!* Most people, when contemplating retirement, still imagine a time span of 10 or maybe 15 years. But simple actuarial statistics suggest that if you've made it to sixty-five in relative health, you will live another 20 years at least, and in the future there is every chance that the average postretirement life span will be much longer.

WORK IS ALIVE

So if retirement is dead, what of work? This is the second great lesson from a future populated by elders. Work is alive. A critical task for business in the next quarter century will be to devise ways for people of retirement age to stay in the work force. This will require changes to Social Security law and pension policies, as well as creative approaches to employment beyond full-time work.

Individuals are well into the project of reinventing the third phase of life formerly called retirement (the first two phases being education and career). They are looking to do things they have always dreamed of, finding ways to earn income with home-based or small businesses, combining travel, leisure, and income generating work in new combinations. The leading Internet job search company Monster.com has a special section devoted to the return to work after retirement called Careers at 50+ (Monster.com).

A national survey of U.S. workers in 2005 found that 7 in 10 expected to work full time or part time after retirement. Only 13 percent expected to live a classic leisure-based retirement life style (Reynolds, Ridley, and Van Horn 2005). Work after retirement will become not just a matter of individual choice but of social policy in the coming decades.

SOCIAL SECURITY IS ALIVE, TOO

Social Security is the federal government's most successful attempt to provide society with a safety net. In 2004, Social Security paid out more than $471 billion in benefits to more than 46 million individuals, including nearly 7 million disabled workers and 4 million children. The underpinning of the framework of Social Security is exemplified in remarks made by James Roosevelt Jr., grandson of the creator of Social Security, Franklin D. Roosevelt. In a *Boston Globe* editorial, Roosevelt Jr. explained that the Social Security program had been designed by his grandfather to be "simple, guaranteed, fair, earned, and available to all Americans" (January 31, 2005).

Since its inception in 1935, the Social Security system has been publicly financed by current workers' payroll taxes to pay benefits to today's retirees. Payroll tax surpluses are placed into the Social Security Trust Fund, the balance of which Congress often uses to pay for other federal programs. According to the 2005 Social Security Trustees report, beginning in 2017 Social Security will not bring in enough money through the Social Security Tax to pay 100 percent of benefits to all retirees and will be forced to begin drawing on the Trust Fund to pay benefits. The Trustees have calculated that the Trust Fund has enough reserves to cover all benefits through 2041. In 2041, with the Trust Fund depleted, the payroll tax revenue will be sufficient to pay 74 percent of promised benefits on a pay-as-you-go basis.

Social Security is not, contrary to popular belief, in crisis nor is it "facing bankruptcy." Social Security was designed for long-term sustainability. The program's financial solvency can be adequately extended to cope with the Baby Boom and overcome Congress's tendency to raid the system, two phenomena that were not predicted in 1935. This can be done with simple and modest adjustments to the retirement age as people live longer, increasing the upper income limit on taxation, and if necessary a very small adjustment in the tax rate itself. Employer based pensions are rapidly disappearing. Policy makers must simply make the decision to protect future generations by ensuring the availability of the invaluable support from Social Security benefits.

GOING DIGITALLY NATIVE

At the same time the world is getting old, it is getting young. There is a new generation in our schools and entering the work force. They are the generation born between 1980 and 2000. They are a large group in the United States, about 60 million strong. This is almost, but not quite, as big as the Baby Boom generation, who are their parents. Globally, they are a huge group, particularly in South America and Central America, Africa, and Muslim countries such as Egypt or Indonesia. Here as much as 50 percent of the population is under age twenty-five.

There is one thing about them that stands out above all other characteristics. They are the first Digital Native generation. This term, attributed to Marc Prensky (2001), captures the essence of their experience growing up, and is more descriptive than other terms usually applied to this group, such as the millennial generation. What does the term mean? That they grew up digital, even in developing nations, with computers, cell phones, the Internet and now iPods. If you have children of this era, you know what I mean. Watch them as they constantly multi-task, always connected via their cell phones and instant messaging, notice how quickly they seek and obtain information, notice how they approach buying consumer goods, notice how they seek out the ATM and avoid going inside a bank, notice how they purchase virtually everything with electronic money, even a $3.00 Latte.

The rest of us, older than digital natives, will always be digital immigrants, no matter how skilled with computers and the Web that we might be. For us, the digital world is always new, always novel, and we question whether the old ways might be better. But for the natives, such a question makes no sense, because they do not know the old ways.

Get ready for this generation, as they are your incoming employees, and your future customers. Just behind them will come the Futuristic generation, born since 2001.

IMMIGRANT NATIONS

In 2000 the percentage of foreign-born members of the U.S. population hit 10.4 percent, up from 7.9 percent in 1990, and the highest since a century earlier. Half were from Latin America (14 million) while one-fourth were from Asia (7 million). Regionally, the West and South absorb more of current immigration than do other regions. But most striking is that the foreign-born population is especially concentrated in metro areas, with 54 percent living in nine metro areas with populations of 5 million or more, compared to 27 percent of the native-born population.

Globally, we are witness to global migrations as work shifts around the planet and local demographic dynamics demand an opening of borders. The Islamic Diaspora into Western Europe to fulfill the need for workers, and the tentative openings of Japan to immigration for the same reason are but two examples.

GENERATIONS

So the population is young and old and immigrant. There is an additional way to view potential customers and employees. The last decade or so has seen a spate of books on the topic of "generations." Each describes the characteristics of several generational cohorts of about 20 years or so. Key to the concept of generations is that the two decades you grow up in play a major role in determining your outlook on life and your behavior. With today's long life spans, for the first time in history we have six generations living simultaneously, from the GI generation now in their eighties to the Futuristic generation born since 2001. Between them are the Silent generation, the Boomers, Generation X, and the Digital Natives each with their unique characteristics.

THE POPULATION BOMB ENDS—IN A WHIMPER

In the spring of 1970 I was an undergraduate college student. I received the assignment to drive to the Spokane, Washington, airport to pick up Paul Ehrlich, a guest lecturer coming to our campus to speak on the topic of his best-selling book, *The Population Bomb* (Ehrlich 1968). It was the title of that book, as much as anything else, that seared into the public consciousness an image of the future of unending, exponential population growth, an explosion that would overwhelm the capacity of all earth resources and eventually lead to civilization's collapse and even population die-off.

At the dawn of agriculture 8,000 years ago, it is estimated that there were five million people on earth. Population grew steadily, though relatively slowly for the next several thousand years, to perhaps 500 million by the fourteenth century, when the great plague was ravaging Europe and killing up to one-third of the population. Since then, despite local interruptions for war or disease, humans have known nothing but accelerating population growth. In our era the concept of a population bomb certainly seems to confirm what we see with our own eyes, as housing developments, shopping centers, roads, and automobiles crowd around us. Indeed, the twentieth century was the century of explosive growth in population, as the global total soared from 1.7 billion people in 1900 to 6.5 billion people in 2005. Currently the global population increases by a net of 141 people every single minute.

And so, if you ask most anyone to name a few long-term problems, "overpopulation" is quite likely to be among the top issues cited. But what most of us do not know is that the population bomb is coming to an end with a whimper, not with a bang.

We are, in fact, on the verge of a historical trend reversal that will represent one of the most profound changes in human history. We stand on the threshold of an impending decline in human population. Sometime in the next four decades, and I believe sooner than later, humanity will go over the top of the population curve, and start down the back side. The backside ride may be steep, and it will be challenging.

Population growth is caused by three interrelated factors, which are death rates, in-migration versus out-migration, and fertility. As people live longer and longer, death rates slow but, of course, do not disappear. Longer life spans are often cited as evidence for continued population growth, despite what may happen to the other factors. Living longer merely time-shifts the impending population implosion a couple of decades ahead. (This does not take into account the possibility of stupendous increases in life spans of hundreds of years, but that is a subject for Chapter 2.) Living longer will delay but not prevent the inevitable.

Migration of population groups is meaningful for local areas, but is, of course, a net zero when it comes to global population. The United States is an example of a nation that grows more from immigration than from natural births versus deaths. Japan, on the other hand, as a nation that traditionally has allowed little immigration, faces immediate population decline unless their borders are opened much more widely, something that is not likely. Globally, patterns of population migration actually are likely to slow population increase, and speed up population decline. Why? Because at the current time, for obvious reasons, population migrations tend to be from poorer, less-developed regions where birth rates are relatively high, to more affluent and developed regions, where birth rates are lower. It does not take long, it turns out, a generation at most, for immigrants to adapt to the customs of their new homeland, and birth rates fall accordingly.

So living longer will shift an impending population decline into the future. Migration is a net but temporary gain for some nations. At the same time migration is a wash globally and may even speed the day when we go over the top of the growth curve. But it is fertility rates that are the key.

Fertility rate is defined as the average number of children per woman in a given population group. Birth rates are falling all over the world, including the United States. It takes a fertility rate of 2.1 children per woman to maintain a steady state in the population. The birth rate in the United States is 2.08, in Canada 1.52, and Mexico has fallen from 7 to 2.1 in the past two decades. All countries in the world, save four, have seen declines in birth rates since 1980.

All of the former Soviet Union, all of Western Europe, Australia, Japan, Canada, and now the United States have birth rates below that required for replacement. Japan's population was projected to begin to decline in 2007. In 2005, deaths in Japan exceeded births by 19,000, suggesting that the decline may have begun two years earlier than predicted. If so, Japan's population will have peaked at 127 million, and is forecast to decline to 100 million by 2050. Russia declined by 10 million in the past 10 years. Italy, a population bellwether, declined by 40,000 people from 1995 to 2000, and is expected to decline by six million by 2025, although immigration is providing some offset. This mirrors the anticipated overall decline for European population of between 40 million and 80 million people over the next 40 years.

In fact the developed world as a whole may go over the top of the population curve and begin our ride down the backside as early as 2013. By the end of the twenty-first century, Europe and Japan could lose up to two-thirds of their current population. The United States will lag. The Census Bureau still confidently predicts an increase in U.S. population of nearly 100 million by 2050, to a total of 390 million. But they are quite likely wrong in this forecast, despite our relatively open border policies. The U.S. population will peak by mid-century, and possibly much earlier, at something like 325 to 350 million. Fertility, again, is the key.

Average fertility in the developed world has fallen from 1.7 in the early 1990s to about 1.5 in 2005, and appears headed to 1.4 in the coming decade, according to the United Nations. Meanwhile, in the developing world fertility is assumed to have been about 3.3 in the 1990s, and is projected to decline to 2.0 by 2020, and then to 1.6 by 2050. As fertility falls, population does not just approach decline; it changes in character. The age ratio switches from a large proportion of youth versus a small proportion of elders to the opposite. By 2050, for example, Italy is projected to have a population in which only 2 percent are kids under age five, while 40 percent of the population is over age sixty-five, with obvious implications for continued population decline.

Median age increases as we live longer and have fewer kids. Globally, the median age in 1900 was probably about twenty. Today it is about thirty-seven in the developed world, and just over twenty-eight in the much younger developing world. By 2050, the median age may rise to fifty or more.

If an aging population is a disruptive change, then a shift from population growth to population decline can only be doubly disruptive, like a break in the space time continuum, so significant will it be. What could possibly explain this impending population decline, a decline caused not by plague or disease or environmental collapse, but rather by the very benefits of modern civilization?

WHY POPULATION DECLINES

Improved global communication, thus better information about family planning, is an obvious factor. Global economic development has for decades been correlated with declining birth rates. Grow the economy, birth rates decline. Improved global health care is another factor. Africa, the continent that currently maintains the highest birth rates, is also the continent with the least economic development and the worst access to health care, not to mention the highest rates of AIDS. Thus, the best form of insurance of species survival is to have kids, as it has always been. And birth rates remain high, though declining.

Male fertility, this time defined as the potency of sperm, has also been falling. A variety of explanations related to environmental factors are assumed to play a role, and lower male fertility will obviously contribute to an overall decline in population birth rates.

The economic emancipation of women is another very significant factor. As women have gained access to the paid labor market, a phenomenon primarily of the past half century, two things happen. They have less time for multiple children, and more importantly they achieve a level of economic independence that makes delayed marriage more feasible, not to mention the possibility of no marriage at all. And families shrink. Thus, when you look at the fertility map of the world, you will notice lower fertility rates where women are most economically free, and higher birth rates in areas where the culture still dictates little or no direct involvement for women in the moneymaking economic system. This is one of the great divides between the non-Muslim and the Muslim world, in fact, though participation in the economy varies widely among Muslim nations. In Iran, for example, after the 1979 revolution, women entered the education and economic system as never before, and birth rates fell from 7 in 1979 to 1.8 in 2005, confounding conventional thinking about Islamic culture.

There is one deep demographic trend contributing to population decline, seldom mentioned but perhaps critical. It is the move of human beings from rural areas to the cities. In terms of where and how we live, no trend is more dominant today than the shift to cities. Through all of history we have been mostly country people. In 1800 only 3 percent of people lived in cities, in 1900 just 14 percent. In 2005 we crossed yet another threshold, with 50 percent of global population living in cities. By 2030 it is expected that 61 percent will be city dwellers, and by 2050 perhaps 75 percent or more. This is despite the fact that some old cities continue to see their centers empty out, cities like Detroit or Milan or Frankfurt.

What we are seeing is the emergence of mega cities, vast metro areas with huge populations. Soon there will be nearly 60 cities with populations above 5 million, of which 21 have populations greater than 10 million. And, counterintuitively, with huge cities come fewer people.

When people move to the city several things happen. Space is limited, so there is less room for children. Greater economic opportunity in cities for women encourages smaller families. While children in the country-side can be an economic asset, helping on the subsistence farm for example, in the city they can be a liability. In the city, work for children is prohibited, or where not prohibited, scarce. Cities have always been associated with fewer kids, and as we all move to cities, we will have fewer kids still.

Let's be clear. Global population is growing today, and will continue to grow for some time, from 6.5 billion today to a peak of 9 billion by 2050, according to standard forecasts. Even this level of growth puts tremendous strain on earth systems, particularly given our profligacy with energy and waste. And no one can be certain that today's declining fertility trends will continue.

However, it looks increasingly likely that the standard forecasts are wrong and a population implosion is near. Once underway, it will accelerate. We will, I think, go over the top of the curve much sooner than 2050, and peak at some number closer to 8 billion. Like going down the back side of a roller coaster, a decline will be difficult to stop once it is in full motion and going faster. This disruptive change raises the most interesting questions. Should we stop it, if we can? Or would it be a good thing to allow the human population to decline by 20 or 30 percent or more? After all, was California more pleasant to live in and to visit in 1950, when the population was 10 million, or in 2005, when the population was 36 million? Is the earth's environment in need of fewer people, or more? If you attended a conference (and there will be many such conferences to come) and one side of the room argued for policies to increase family size, while the other side advocated allowing population decline to continue for some time, which side would you be on?

The initial response of nations and governments is predictable. Japan began developing policies to encourage larger families as early as 2002, as did Germany and Russia. Both Greece and France announced plans in 2005 to offer straight cash bonuses to families that have more than two children. Nation after nation will face this issue in coming decades. Such a knee-jerk reaction—"What, our population is declining? Get women to have more kids"—is not, in the long run, the only or the best response.

Instead, population decline may offer a unique opportunity to reconceptualize both economy and environment, and to develop new forms of sustainable civilization not dependent simply on more, always more.

From the perspective of business and the economy, the issues become especially dicey. How will you sustain your business, when every year there are fewer customers than the year before? We have no models for this. You can simply raid customers from your competitors, but what if you already have an 80 percent share, and each year the 80 percent is smaller? What happens to housing and property values as populations begin to literally shrink? Prices drop of course, but suppose the decline becomes a way of life for decades and more? How can we design a system for that?

It is not that the impending decline is going unnoticed. UN population experts made their first comments on it in 1996, and futurists such as Sohail Inayatullah and I began writing about it in the late 1990s. But the presumption of ceaseless population growth feeding ceaseless economic growth continues to dominate both the popular and the intellectual culture, even though the assumption is obsolete. The timing of when to change our assumptions is challenging, to say the least, as parts of the world begin their decline even now, while the globe as a whole grows for decades before we all begin to decline. But change our assumptions we must.

FUTURE INTO REVENUE

Understanding and responding to demographic changes will always provide a path to new business ideas. Each generation needs different products and services. Elders today are not the elders of yesterday, and the same services do not fit. Nor will the elders of tomorrow be the same as those today. Just take a moment to daydream of a walk through an assisted living facility, circa 2025, the Rolling Stones blaring from the speakers, or circa 2065, 50-Cent blowing out the joint as ninety-year-olds bob their heads.

When it comes to youth, some have argued that the concept of generations is being turned on its head. The pace of change means that generations no longer last for a couple of decades, but a decade, even a half-decade at most, before styles, attitudes, and basic life experiences become unique.

Then there are the two big discontinuities, aging and the historical shift to declining rather than growing population. These are paradigm shifts, when all kinds of things change, foreseen and unforeseen, predictable and unpredictable. They suggest a need for creative thinking and great flexibility, as we try to imagine the business of tomorrow.

OLDER FUTURE INTO REVENUE

There is money to be made in an older future. It is not in the classic retirement industry as exemplified by the retirement investing columns prominent each week in daily papers, none of which ever seem to recognize that retirement is dead. Rather there will be opportunities for employment and investment in businesses such as drugs for hypertension and diabetes, assisted living real estate developments, as well as new kinds of companies devoted to non-institutional assistance to both active and chronically ill elders. Leisure and travel activities such as adventure travel, spas, and casinos will boom. The insurance industry, especially long-term insurance will flourish.

Medical treatments such as orthopedic and other implants, lasers and advanced cosmetic surgery techniques, natural and complementary medicines and medical practices will be good plays. More exotic stem cell and systems biology research, development and applications to life extension will see major growth. Dental implants and re-growing teeth via stem cells will boom. Upscale natural foods will be popular, while at the same time discount stores will serve the large proportion of elderly with limited resources. Fitness centers to offset the current obesity epidemic will continue to offer opportunity. Retiring Baby Boomers, having grown up with Earth Day and the environmental movement, and living in their later years on a planet stressed by climate change, are likely to be increasingly "green" and products and services that speak to this will win. Finally, a booming business in offering third-phase life advisory services may emerge.

This is just a short list. Think of day-to-day life. Consider passing through our gigantic airports with their vast distances to get from plane to plane when you make a transfer at a regional hub. Visualize the few elders currently being carried on carts or chairs. Now envision nearly a quarter of the passengers requiring such assistance. Who is going to reinvent airports and the services within them? Or notice that in Dustin, Florida, there were 14 licensed drivers over the age of 100 in 2005, and then begin to think of all the reinvention to come in automobiles, transportation infrastructure (think size of the font on traffic signs), and alternatives to driving, and more ideas will come to mind.

We are embarking on an experimental journey to reinvent society for a time when 25 percent or more of us are old. We are the experimental subjects.

A YOUNGER FUTURE INTO REVENUE

Each generational cohort suggests a variety of market opportunities, as does the fact that nations are going immigrant. Think for example of all the multilingual and native cultural businesses that are springing up in neighborhoods worldwide, even as the corporate world goes homogonous.

But the most significant opportunities to turn the future into revenue have to do with the digital natives and the even more digital generations to follow. No one is more adept at tapping into the digital native than Steve Jobs and Apple Computer. Beginning really with the first Apple machines, then the Mac, and then the iPod, each generation of technology from this inventive company seems to mainline directly into the digitally wired brains of the digital native generation.

Those in charge today in the typical company or community are digital immigrants. They are adept with technology perhaps, but always view it as the new thing rather than the normal thing, even the boring old thing, as digital natives see it. Thus, we tend to underestimate the degree to which the future will be digital, not as a result of spectacular technology developments, but as a result of simple generational change. Every business, large and small, needs to reassess its digital future for a time when the technology is more robust, but more so for the time when the primary customer base, and the primary workers will have always been digital.

"Will we do X online in the future?" we like to ask. The problem is that in answering, digital immigrants think of themselves, when they should be thinking of the digital natives. Their answer may be different by orders of magnitude. What may digital natives already be doing online, for example? How about this list from Prensky (2004, 4–12):

- Communicating
- Sharing
- Buying and Selling
- Exchanging
- Creating
- Meeting
- Dating
- Collecting
- Coordinating
- Evaluating
- Gaming
- Learning
- Searching
- Analyzing
- Growing up
- Evolving

Finally, while I have argued that the elder generation will contribute to growth in city living, it is also clear that digital natives, in general, seek urban life. Thus, the future will certainly be urban, and urban business and services are likely to flourish.

POPULATION IMPLOSION INTO REVENUE?

Fewer customers year by year. How is this going to work? We can begin by saying that there is fertile ground in the next couple of decades to develop economic theory and models for sustainable economy in the face of declining population. There is policy to be decided regarding whether to encourage or try to stop the decline. Japan and Europe will be the early test beds.

The same resources available to fewer people ought to, if managed well, lead to greater per capita wealth creation. This is particularly true when combined with prospects for ever doing more with less and less, as Buckminster Fuller used to say. He believed that it was possible for the first time as the twentieth century came to a close to imagine a world of relative wealth, in which half the population did not have to subsist on a dollar or two a day. Instead, if we tapped our intelligence and behaved more cooperatively, the vast majority could approach a reasonable standard of living.

But what does this mean in practical opportunities? Let's look at real estate development in the metro areas of developed countries facing nearer time peak population. Recent years have seen two countervailing pressures. One is an effort to rein in sprawl, usually via social policy that encourages in-fill in central areas, while discouraging development in surrounding rural areas. The other pressure is prices, as expensive prices in central areas push the young and the poor to settle farther and farther out, where land is cheaper. One of two things will happen as the decline hits in region after region. Either the central cities will empty, or the surrounding suburbs will. We ought now to develop both policy and market mechanisms to favor the center over the burbs. We can even begin to imagine, decades hence, a return of some previously developed land to a more natural or agricultural state, and quite obviously this ought to occur in what was the surrounding countryside rather than the city center.

A second fundamental opportunity will be increasing worker productivity. With fewer workers in developed countries, which are also aging the most rapidly, their only choices for work are outsourcing work, immigration, and increasing productivity. Each will play a role in varying degrees, region by region, but increasing productivity is most attractive because it has the potential to increase per capita wealth.

Developing immigration policies and more diverse societies will become an imperative around the world, and consulting businesses will spring up to assist in that transition. It will not be easy. Business development in the developing world where the populations will still be growing and relatively young is also an obvious arena for growth. Balancing this global activity while sustaining national economies will be the challenge, as we explore further in Chapter 3 on economies of knowledge.

Finally, we are approaching a time to reconsider the whole life structure of work/leisure/family that we have developed in the past several hundred years of industry. The four-step life sequence of learn—work—retire—die is up for reexamination. As currently practiced, this pattern and the structures that accompany it do not, for example make child rearing easy, nor does it account for the need to shift jobs several times in a lifetime.

A better approach may be something like significant leisure breaks during the primary child rearing years to allow more time for family. As for retirement, why not institute a policy of allowing for two to five years of retirement when one is age fifty to fifty-five, paid for by retirement benefits, without early withdrawal penalties? During this time one would be expected to consider the question of What do I want to do with the rest of my life? and to reeducate accordingly. Then, back to work until age seventy or seventy-five or more depending on how longevity and health research plays out. This mid-life retirement, obviously a kind of universal sabbatical, would be one meaningful way to respond to the demographic tidal shifts that we face.

CHAPTER 2

How to Profit from
Five Key Technology Trends

It is such an amazing time to be alive. Everywhere you turn, you can find some opportunity, in ways and amounts that go far beyond what was true 30 years ago. The next 20 years will see a logarithmic increase in businesses to create, in new discoveries, and in things that can be done that could never be done before.

—Mark Anderson, 2005

THE REALLY SMALL IS REALLY BIG

Untold thousands of years ago, human ancestors sat together and worked. They were the first manufacturers in history, as they held stone fragments in either hand, and chipped away at the stones to produce cutting tools and spear points. Thousands of years later other humans advanced the manufacturing process when they placed some ore taken from the earth into a container on the fire. When the ore was melted it was poured into a mold, perhaps pounded with hard tools as it cooled, producing the desired shape, a sword or a plow. Still later, manufacturing processes combined ores to make alloys, huge furnaces were built and assembly lines erected.

In the late twentieth and early twenty-first centuries, processes were refined further. Water jets and lasers made precise cutting feasible. Computerized design and robot assembly became routine. Microscopic transistors were etched onto computer chips using chemical lithography. Fabrication plants cost billions of dollars. But no matter how sophisticated the twenty-first century manufacturing process, it has more in common with those early human ancestors than it has differences. We still take pieces of matter and chip away at them until they have the desired shape, or we melt various kinds of matter together in big pots, and pour it into molds.

What if, instead of manufacturing things by chipping or melting them, one could grab an individual atom or molecule, chemically or mechanically, and place it precisely, then grab another and place it so that it bonds with the first, repeat the process with a third, and so on? This is the burgeoning field of nanotechnology. The word *nanotechnology* means, simply, "the ability to see and manipulate matter at the scale of atoms and molecules." Literally, the nanoscale means from 1 to 100 nanometers, or about the size of 10 atoms.

Nanotechnology may be the next and greatest industrial revolution. Yet as recently as 2005 I could address a conference of business or government leaders, even manufacturers themselves, and find that 75 percent or more, by a show of hands, had at best only a vague knowledge of nanotechnology.

It all began in 1959. In an oft-quoted speech entitled "There's Plenty of Room at the Bottom," physicist Richard Feynman said, "What I want to talk about is the problem of manipulating and controlling things on a small scale. . . . It is a staggeringly small world that is below. In the year 2000, when they look back at this age, they will wonder why it was not until the year 1960 that anybody began seriously to move in this direction" (Feynman 1960).

In the 1980s scientist Eric Drexler laid out a conceptual vision for nanotechnology in his book *Engines of Creation*. The consensus view at the time was that the idea of nanotechnology was intriguing but not likely to advance much beyond the realm of science fiction.

Two developments occurred at about the same time to spur the field along in the late 1980s. One was the perfecting of the atomic force microscope, the other the discovery of a new molecule, Carbon-60. Richard Smalley was the first to discover that when he zapped some carbon powder with a laser, under the right conditions unique molecules were formed. They took the shape of hollow soccer balls, the outer walls of which are arranged in chemical bonds that mimic the famous triangular structures of geodesic domes. Thus the material came to be known, in honor of the geodesic dome inventor Buckminster Fuller, as Buckyballs, Buckminster fullerenes, or simply as fullerenes. Carbon-60 became the third form of carbon known to exist along with graphite and diamond. The discovery of fullerenes led to carbon nanotubes, elongated tubes of Carbon-60, which now generate the most research and development. Nanotubes are ultrastrong, fireproof, capable of conducting electricity, insulating, glowing, dissipating heat, and, being hollow, being loaded with other molecules. Nanotubes can be 100 times stronger than steel and one-sixth the weight. As Bruce Sterling puts it, "Buckytubes are voodoo."

Smalley, along with Robert Curl and Sir Harold Kroto, received the Nobel Prize in chemistry in 1996, for their early work with Carbon-60, which had occurred in the mid 1980s. Now, in the early years of twenty-first century, at least 60 industrial companies are producing commercial quantities of carbon nanotubes, in amounts of tons per year. Nanotubes can be grown at the rate of a trillion a minute, grown by vapor deposition, and teased into self-assembly by pulling them into a ribbon.

Potential applications range from the very small to the super-large. Memory applications appear to be the easiest of initial nano-computing products, and Moore's Law suggests that carbon nanotube electronics will begin to replace silicon for memory around 2010–2015. For example, Nantero is developing a nanoscale memory product, aimed at replacing memory types such as DRAM and flash memory. A key advantage of their technology will be instant on-off computers, no waiting for boot-up, in addition to major increases in memory capacity.

On a large scale, mattes of nanotubes or other nano-engineered materials are envisioned as super materials for cars or airplanes, or a variety of engineered structures such as bridges. Imagine structures made of nanofabric that are more capable of withstanding earthquakes and hurricanes, not to mention being fireproof and able to produce their own electricity.

On the massive scale lies the dream of an elevator to space. Envisioned by Arthur C. Clarke and succeeding writers, the idea is very simple. Suspend a large weight beyond geosynchronous orbit above Earth, attach a cable from the weight all the way to Earth, and run elevator cars up and down it. Suddenly, one would have cost-effective, even cheap access to orbit and beyond. Current NASA studies suggest that nanotubes bound together may provide the high strength and low weight ratio needed for such a cable. The cable may be 3 feet wide, thin as paper, and 63,000 miles long. In 2006 NASA and the Spaceward Foundation are sponsoring a second annual challenge research competition on the elevator, with competitions to demonstrate a high strength tether and a power beaming technology. The Foundation has dreams of a functioning elevator within a decade, but a more realistic expectation would be an established elevator in space by 2022. The chief application would be placing and repairing satellites.

Down here on the earth nanotechnology is already becoming big business. Since 2001 research funding by governments has increased globally by about 30 percent per year on average, to $4.6 billion. Business investment is on a similar scale at about $4 billion annually. So much progress was made in the field between 2000 and 2005 that researchers now feel that what appeared decades off may in fact be possible in less than 10 years.

Robert Frietas, leading expert in nanomedicine, has conducted detailed studies of self-replicating machine systems and is close to completing an analysis of the chemistry of diamond. NASA studies have concluded that self-assembling nanosystems do not depend on any exotic chemistry and are within current capabilities. The ability of instruments to see nanosystems has expanded far beyond what were believed to be physical limits over the past five years, enabling the visual examination of individual molecules, atoms, and small nanosystems.

Over the next decade, we can expect to see applications on the market to include:

- Fast recharging batteries with 1.5–3.5 times current battery capacity. Toshiba wants to aim them at both laptop computers and hybrid cars. They recharge to 80 percent of capacity in a minute.
- Nano-fluidics for biotech applications such as cell sorting and DNA synthesis.
- Nano-sensors for antiterror applications and security in general.
- Active and smart materials with internal actuators and sensors to sense strain and other potentially hazardous conditions and to adjust to the environment.

- Ordinary materials with antimicrobial, dirt resistant, tear resistant, stain resistant, conductive, and structural properties. Fabric from Nanotex has been incorporated into clothing for several years already.
- The cool chip, a means of using thermotunnel technology to deliver cooling in settings from autos to buildings to electronic equipment. While conventional refrigerators operate at only 45 percent efficiency and current thermoelectric cooling systems at only 5–8 percent efficiency, the cool chip is projected to work at 55 percent efficiency.

In the longer-term, applications will appear everywhere.

Materials—Nanotechnology is leading to the development of new and exotic materials. At the same time it is transforming mundane and familiar old materials. Nano-concrete is already being used in experimental construction of highway bridges, allowing for bridge decks that are only three inches thick yet strong enough for all standard traffic, including trucks.

Medicine—Opportunities begin with a simple need, clean water. Applying nanoscale engineering to water filtration holds the promise of reducing disease and death from waterborne pathogens. Research is also underway on more powerful nanofilters to act as implantable artificial kidneys within a decade.

There are many possible applications for disease detection and treatment. In 2005 a femtosecond laser was shown to be capable of correcting eyesight, and paves the way for nanolaser medicine. Gold nanoparticles can be engineered with an antibody that attaches to cancer cells. When bathed in light by an external laser, the particles reveal previously undetected cancer cells. In recent experiments at UC San Francisco and Georgia Tech the gold nanoparticles, when illuminated with an argon laser, heat in such a way as to kill the cancer cells without harming surrounding tissue. Similar results have been achieved at Rice University using silicon nanoshells and gold nanoparticles. Other experiments have used nanotubes combined with monoclonal antibodies to successfully detect breast cancer.

Electronics and Computing—Development of single molecule logic gates and memory devices is one focus. Possibilities under investigation include nanotube lattices, cascades of single molecules, and using quantum states or electron spin. All the major labs from IBM to Bell plus academic and government institutions are in the hunt. Hewlett-Packard (HP) has formulated a strategy for moving from silicon to molecular computing and does some of the leading work on molecular scale logic gates. Many small firms will come and go as the search for nanotech computers continues. Success will come in fits and starts rather than in a smooth development curve. This work is still at the level of basic science but getting closer to commercially viable solutions.

Displays—Among the first commercial nanotech computing products will be a variety of displays. Recent success by Motorola in developing nano-emissive display technology, suggests the possibility of near to market applications in brighter computer and HDTV displays. The most interesting display advances at the nanoscale will probably come in variations of e-paper. Among the most mind-catching scenes in nanotechnology literature such as Neal Stephenson's *The Diamond Age* (1995) or movies like Steven Spielberg's *Minority Report* is when a character reaches into their pocket and pulls out a sheet of folded plastic, unfolds it, and reads the daily paper or a magazine as the "nanopaper" changes pages one by one.

This smart paper is under development at many companies and labs, including Parc labs, Gyricon, and eInk. While their technologies are not yet in the nanoscale, their demonstrations of flexible and changeable computer displays are partway there. Five years from now we ought to see electronic paper in a variety of applications and by 10 years from now it may be as common, affordable, and readable as real paper, and may refresh fast enough to be used for video as well. Eventually e-paper will be ubiquitous and used for most forms of display.

Weapons—There are many potential military and police applications of nanotechnology, and military labs are among the chief research institutions and funders. Primary areas of development involve improving armor and personal uniform fabrics with nanomaterials and nanostructured smart materials, reducing the weight of carried gear, nuclear-biological-chemical (NBC) protection gear and sensing equipment, and medical technologies. Additional research concentrates on information technology and high density energy storage. When combined with advanced forensics and ubiquitous monitoring equipment, future crime may be curtailed. Nonmilitary spin-offs should be substantial.

Manufacturing—A holy grail that is being sought by nano scientists and technologists is the creation of molecular manufacturing devices that can become self-operating. In one version imagine a box the size of a microwave oven. Every home may have one some day. Into one end of the box you feed some raw material, perhaps a slurry of carbon or preformed nanotubes, hydrogen, and oxygen, or perhaps boron or aluminum. Inside the box, a nanotechnology fabricator, the raw material is rearranged according to a pattern you have programmed in. Such programming may be as simple as selecting a design in a catalog and keying the correct code number into your assembler.

After an appropriate wait, perhaps overnight, you open the other end of the box and remove your manufactured product. It may be a pair of sandals or a set of dishes. Such a device may produce most things currently made of polymers, along with decent substitutes for many biological materials except for foods and pharmaceuticals. A large fraction of industrial goods, but not a comprehensive set of such goods, may be manufactured in this way.

In another version of molecular manufacturing, raw material is fed into a machine more akin to an ink jet printer. The "paper" is a prefab substrate made of polymer, perhaps created by molecular manufacturing methods or perhaps made more conventionally. Onto the substrate you spray a thin layer of nanoscale semi-conducting material capable of converting light into electricity, solar cells in other words. Because the material is so inexpensive and you can produce so much of it, you are going to paper the exterior walls of your home, turning it into one giant solar energy collector. Konarka, already a manufacturer of printable polymer solar cells, has on the drawing boards such nanotechnology cells that could be printed or woven into fabric. The jacket you wear tomorrow could charge your cell phone as you walk down the street.

However actualized, a molecular or nanoscale manufacturing capability has the potential to transform the world economy in a year, so dramatic would be the development of true molecular manufacturing. Until then, it is nearly as transformative to imagine the advances in both what is manufactured and in manufacturing techniques that will come from the mere ability to see and manipulate matter at the scale now possible.

One institution that shares this vision is the recently created Center for Bits and Atoms at MIT. They describe a key part of their vision this way:

> One of CBA's grand challenge goals is quite literally to create "it from bit," seeking to realize von Neumann's vision of a universal assembler. Analogous to the earlier results in communications and computation, if logic can be introduced into the process of physical assembly then perfect macroscopic structures could be built out of imperfect microscopic parts.

Currently the Center uses computer-aided design and desktop computer-aided fabrication units that enable the lab to, in their words, "accessibly emulate the functionality of a Personal Fabricator . . ." A key feature of their FabLab program is that they are working with students in developing countries around the world, demonstrating that the design revolution that personal fabricators will provide need not be limited to the wealthy.

There is one other form of nanoscale manufacturing that is possible, and it could be the biggest nano revolution of all. Consider the concept of "programmable matter" (McCarthy 2003). More than a decade ago scientists succeeded in isolating individual electrons within a confined space, and thus became able to manufacture what are commonly called "quantum dots." These dots have unique properties and are extremely effective as a diagnostic tool in medicine. A company called Quantum Dot, purchased in late 2005 by Invitrogen, was a pioneer in creating and using quantum dots for medical imaging. But the use of quantum dots for imaging may be only the beginning.

The tools for confining electrons and creating quantum dots can be used to essentially create artificial atoms, by manipulating the number of contained electrons in a way that mimics actual atoms but without the protons or neutrons. Theoretically, artificial lead can be created, turned into artificial gold, and back again. The challenge is developing ways to build macroscopic materials from artificial atoms, and to connect them to one another and to external electrical leads in such a way that the resulting matter can be programmed. Among the more mundane products that may result would be programmable paint that changes color on command. Beyond that are super-displays, batteries, and capacitors, even programmable walls and ceilings that become solid or clear upon command and act as both heating and cooling systems.

Nanotechnology will be applied to virtually all areas of life. Studies by both the U.S. and European Union (EU) governments forecast that within a decade a large minority or even a majority of consumer products will incorporate nanotechnology in some way. Much of this will be imbedded electronics, and either smart or highly durable materials. Stainless clothing, sunscreen, sports equipment, and displays are only the beginning.

The bottom line of the possible future with nanotech is this. If and when we succeed in creating the first independently functioning and intelligent molecular manufacturing systems, whatever the form it takes, humanity will face about a two-week revolution. Many forms of manufacturing will become obsolete as will many manufactured products. Eventually the entire world system of raw material distribution, manufacturing, even recycling will be changed. Most of all, should molecular manufacturing reach its ultimate potential, humanity will face as never before the question of what are we here for, if it is not to make things ourselves?

The whole idea of scarcity would be challenged as well. If almost anything can be disassembled into its constituent molecules, and then the molecules can be reassembled (note that this is precisely what we do whenever we eat food), then material goods become abundant. Social and political assumptions are overthrown.

A stop nano movement has also begun, based on environmental and human health concerns. Nanotubes are, after all, indestructible. Organizations from Greenpeace to the Action Group on Erosion, Technology and Concentration (ETC) have raised legitimate cautions regarding nanotechnology. Fears center on four potentials. First is the likelihood that second-order consequences of most nanotech applications will be little understood in advance. Second is the potential of molecular scale substances and devices unintentionally getting into the bloodstream, and either accumulating in harmful ways or carrying with them other harmful contaminants with potential health effects. Third, there is concern over the creation of nonbiodegradable pollutants, and their use in what may be considered throwaway devices. Finally, there is the technically unlikely possibility of the "grey goo" scenario, in which nanomachines capable of self-replicating go out of control and destroy some large swath of the environment. The latter is the stuff of science fiction, but about as likely, according to Frietas, as automobiles suddenly driving off by themselves, collecting tree sap for fuel, and taking over the world without being designed to do so. Still, even this unlikely scenario will be worth study.

ENGINEERING YOUR LIFE

In 1972 Paul Berg at Stanford University became the first to successfully create a recombinant DNA molecule by combining the DNA of two different organisms. In combining a gene from a monkey virus with a molecule of DNA from a bacterial virus, Berg had, for the second time in the history of human beings, discovered fire.

Realizing the potential benefits and dangers of his discovery, Berg proposed a one-year moratorium on recombinant DNA studies until safety issues were addressed. In 1980, Berg was awarded a Nobel Prize for his groundbreaking work in genetics. His initial experiment became the foundation of the fields of genetic engineering, the biotechnology industry, and in more recent times, systems biology and important aspects of the probable future of health care.

Not quite 30 years after Berg made his breakthrough, I was helping to conduct a series of retreats involving Nobel Prize-winning and other scientists, for a project called Humanity 3000. The question addressed by these distinguished thinkers was, "What will it take for humanity to survive for another 1,000 years?" At the beginning of each retreat those participating introduced themselves. I will not forget the words of introduction used by one participant, Dr. Gregory Stock, director of the Program on Medicine, Technology and Society at the UCLA School of Medicine.

"Who in the group," he asked, "has a child or grandchild under the age of one?" A few hands went up. "That child may be the first person to live . . . forever!" he exclaimed.

As we noted in the previous chapter, huge gains in eliminating infant mortality combined with much improved sanitation and medicine has enabled an increase in average life span of five years every two decades. This is dramatic enough, and simply continuing the trend line will take us to average life spans of around one hundred by century's end. The possible future however holds more dramatic promise.

The human genome project of the 1990s, boosted by the independent efforts of Craig Venter succeeded more quickly than had been hoped for in sequencing the human genome. This has led to worldwide efforts to first, understand the genome and how it functions, and second, to begin to manipulate or modify the genome in ways that lead to improved health.

Gregory Stock, however, was thinking of something far beyond current research in order to make such a bold claim. As he explains in his book *Redesigning Humans* (2002, 3), "The arrival of safe, reliable germline technology will signal the beginning of human self-design. We do not know where this development will ultimately take us, but it will transform the evolutionary process . . ."

Among the first lessons learned as the genome was decoded is that things are not simple. Huge numbers of genes appear to have no function, but perhaps do. While some diseases and conditions seem to have single genes that control them, other diseases have multiple genes that seem to be involved, and most diseases cannot yet be reliably connected to genetic makeup at all. Moreover, genes provide the instructions for the creation of proteins that themselves are more numerous and complex than the genes, and it is the proteins that seem determinative of most of what happens in the body.

This complexity has led to the new fields of genomics, proteomics, and finally to systems biology. It is from systems biology that most actual medical and health-related advances that trace back to the genetic code are expected to come. The focus of this twenty-first century science is to study the complex interactions of genes, proteins, and biochemical reactions as an integrated network or system. Obviously, information science and computing becomes a fundamental resource for dealing with such complexity. One of the leaders in this effort is the Institute of Systems Biology, which describes their purpose as "analyzing biological complexity and understanding how biological systems function . . . [by bringing] . . . together a multidisciplinary group of scholars and scientists, from biologists, mathematicians and engineers, to computer scientists and physicists, in an interactive and collaborative environment."

Currently well over 1,500 diseases have been associated with particular genetic variations, including propensity for heart attack, atherosclerosis, asthma, vascular disease, schizophrenia, Type-2 diabetes, obesity, and many more. A leading company in this search is deCode, based in Iceland. Targeting 50 diseases, to date they have isolated 15 genes and drug targets in 12 common diseases and have mapped the genes for 16 more. The research process is simple enough in concept: Conduct a population study to learn if a particular genetic variation is associated with a particular disease. Determine which proteins are expressed by the gene. Develop therapeutic compounds that will bind to and alter the effect of that protein. Actually turning that knowledge into useful medicine is a painstaking process.

If the promise of genetically based systems biology is realized in the next decade or two, then according to Leroy Hood, founder of the Institute for Systems Biology, we will see emerge a new approach to medicine that is predictive, preventive, and personalized. Medicine ought to be able to move "upstream" from its current approach to treating disease after it has occurred, to using advanced information science to anticipate health problems that you may experience, devise ways to prevent them from occurring, and do this in a way that is personalized to your unique genetic makeup. Revenues derived from gene related therapy products and treatments are expected to grow from $125 million in 2006 to $6.5 billion in 2011, according to *Gene Therapy News* (November 2005).

Genetic medicine is only one aspect of biotechnology. There is a great deal of high-level engineering data contained within biology, data that we are now beginning to access and to apply elsewhere. The field of biomemetics, in which the attempt is made to make machines that mimic biological systems, is an example.

Research with stem cells is well-known and the possibilities are tantalizing. The remarkable ability of these cells to become virtually any cell in the body will hold the promise of rejuvenation and bodily repair until such dreams are conclusively disproved. Today more than 75 different cancers, blood disorders, and immune diseases are being treated with stem cells. Stem cells can regenerate blood and immune system cells after radiation treatments for cancer. Heart and liver cells can be regenerated, as can cartilage. Parkinson's disease, muscular dystrophy, multiple sclerosis, stroke, AIDS, Alzheimer's, leukemia, other cancers, diabetes, and osteoporosis are all the subject of research with stem cells.

Stem cells from embryos and from adults are all being tested. Adult stem cells may hold promise for the creation of a kind of personal repair kit, if these cells can be coaxed into regenerating your own organs when they have been damaged by disease or accident. People have begun to bank cord blood stem cells, which though specialized just to regenerate various blood cells, could be used if the child (or adult) ever develops a blood disease or needs a skin transplant or other treatment where donor rejection is a problem. And of course the first company to use stem cells to treat baldness will likely be the biggest revenue generator of all.

In 2005 researchers reported the successful use of stem cells to treat spinal cord injuries. Working with mice and rats that had spinal cord injuries, the injection of human stem cells enabled them to walk again, and subsequent tests showed conclusively that the stem cells had generated both spinal cord and related cells. As is always the case with such reports, a variety of problems must be addressed before human trials are attempted. By late 2005 at least one company, Geron, had applied to conduct human trials in 2006.

The spinal cord experiments use embryonic stem cells. Recent technology advances have suggested that it may be possible to obtain embryonic stem cells without harming the embryo, as compared to standard techniques, which destroy the embryo. Most readers will be familiar with the raging ethical controversy in the United States and in other countries about the morality of obtaining and using embryonic stem cells. In the United States at the current time this controversy has led to a policy in which government funding is not available for research unless it involves lines of stem cells already being worked with when the relevant policy was enacted. In response some states, led by California, have established state funded research programs that do allow for new embryonic cell use.

Other countries have taken a more liberal approach, including South

Korea, which by the end of 2005 was establishing itself as a global leader in embryonic stem cell research. Because it is a culture in which the arcane question of when life begins—at conception, at quickening, at birth—is simply not an issue, and in which science and scientists are revered, the research in question is strongly supported.

Research in biotechnology will continue, worldwide. Should research or medical treatment based on embryonic stem cells or even cloning be outlawed in one place, the pace of research will be little slowed. The day that a previously paralyzed citizen of a country that outlaws such research walks off the plane only to be arrested "for walking again," political opposition to such research will simply melt away.

The ultimate potential of this research takes us back to Gregory Stock and his introduction regarding the prospect of living forever. That seems farfetched, though Stock himself is confident. At the same time, it is the impact not only on our health but on longevity that make the various fields of biotechnology so alluring. Leroy Hood believes that a jump of 20 years in average life span is reasonable. Forecasting that a life span jump of 20 to 40 years in this century seems likely, Ronald Bailey (2002) concludes:

> Physical immortality may not be in the immediate offing, but the day may come when death is radically postponed, if not fully optional. The barriers to this goal are not just biological but political. Believe it or not, some of our most influential contemporary intellectuals are opposed to the idea of long, healthy lives.

A BIT OF INTELLIGENCE

Odds are very good that everyone reading this book uses a computer and probably owns several when you consider desktops and notebooks and iPods and cell phones and PDAs and Xboxes, not to mention your automobile, a package of computers on wheels. This is unlike nanotechnology and biotechnology, which we mostly read about, though you might be wearing some pants made with Nanotex while you do that reading. In other words, the computing revolution has already become a ubiquitous part of our lives, just as was forecast a couple of decades ago.

Futurist.com was founded in the mid 1990s as the result of a story that I have already told. When I was introduced to audiences as the founder of Futurist.com people would be suitably impressed, mostly by what they assumed this meant in the hot market of the time. Following the bursting of the Internet bubble and the crash of the stock market in 2000, I began to receive a different response. At first, people would look concerned. "How is it going?" they would ask, as they watched dot-com company after company crash and burn. Then, the reaction changed to horror. "Oh, that is too bad," they would say on hearing that I owned "Futurist.com." Finally, when I persisted with the name while everyone else was dropping the "dot com," people's reactions changed to bewilderment that a futurist would use such an anachronistic term.

When the market crashed and, in particular, when most of the retail Internet pioneers disappeared, people began to think, "Well, that was fun while it lasted; too bad that whole Internet thing didn't work out." But it did work out. The pioneers, as pioneers tend to be, were just a decade ahead of their time.

Witness the stunning revival of web-commerce in 2004–2005, as sales growth far outpaces the growth for other retail channels. In the 2005 Christmas season a stunning 27 percent of U.S. gift purchases were made online, and online sales were up 30 percent over 2004. Witness also the shift in advertising dollars from traditional media to the Internet, dollars that once wandered away after the crash, but now are back and growing. Finally, notice the numbers when you see them of the declining hours that the Digital Native generation devotes to traditional media—television declining, radio declining, and newspapers almost no attention at all. It turns out that the Web is going to change everything; it is just taking a little longer.

SIX KEY IT DEVELOPMENTS WILL DOMINATE THE NEAR FUTURE

First, and no surprise, is ubiquitous wireless access. Sales of laptop computers, with built-in wireless cards, exceeded desktop computer sales in 2005 for the first time. This trend will only continue, and it is likely that we are at the beginning of the end of the desktop computer except for certain specialized applications. In addition, the ability of cell phones and other handheld devices to access information from the net is now a fixed expectation. In fact the move of many municipalities and rural jurisdictions to provide free or very low-cost wireless as a public utility in the same way that roads are provided is a recognition of where we are headed and of the necessity of being connected in order to be economically viable in the twenty-first century.

Now, more powerful and longer-range wireless systems are coming. WiMax, which has a range of up to 30 miles, was installed in New York, Boston, Los Angeles, Dalian, Chengdu, and other cities in 2005, and revenues grew at 10 times the rate of 2004. By 2007 more than half of U.S. wireless Internet service providers are expected to be offering WiMax; for rural providers the numbers will be nearer 100 percent. Applications that will grow as a result of this robust access will include:

- Always on ICQ to your phone or perhaps your glasses (ICQ is a software that enables you to know when friends and associates are available online).
- Biomonitors to measure certain health parameters during exercise or rest, to alert authorities in case of emergency, or perhaps just to suggest improvements in your diet.
- Context sensitive cell phones that know they are in a restaurant or theater and thus ought not ring out loud.
- Wearable sensors that can transmit context via your cell phone to those considering calling you.
- Storage of all sensory data, enabling life recording if you wish, leading to voice and text searchable records of all life events.
- Extremely audience sensitive advertising, as in the personal messages sent by billboards in science fiction movies as characters walk by.

At the same time, growth in broadband speed and access in the United States is expected to continue to lag behind much of the world. Current estimates place the United States between thirteenth and eighteenth in broadband access, a distinct competitive disadvantage. This becomes more evident when we consider the second key IT development, the emergence of Web 2.0. While the term may have disappeared by the time you read this, the concept will be dominating the Web. Web sites are migrating toward a highly interactive model in which web site owners and users, merchants and consumers, can engage in substantially more interaction than with original web site designs. Blogs, feedback systems, online reviews, instant recording of opinions, podcasts, RSS feeds, Wikis, tagging, and vastly increased use of video and sound are all mechanisms to bring greater life into formerly static Web interactions.

A third major IT development is radio frequency identification (RFID) and ubiquitous global positioning systems (GPS). By 2007 most hand-held computing devices will have built-in GPS locators, as will, it might be assumed, laptop computers and all new vehicles. Virtually all manu-factured products will have RFID tags, at least at the time of shipping and purchase. When these devices and products are location aware, a variety of possibilities emerge. For example, simply knowing where you are will be advantageous for the easily lost. But when your communica-tion devices know where they are they can create a map of your current surroundings, let your friends know you are there, find out whether friends are in the vicinity, access information from the Web relevant to where you are, tell you another location where you can find something you need, and so on. Services like these are just now being developed and even imagined, but will be common and generating revenue in a few years.

Grid computing is the fourth key IT development for the near- and medium-term future. When connected via the global Internet individual computers can become, in effect, individual nodes within a single ma-chine, a vast "global computer" to quote Mark Anderson. Various projects have tapped the unused computing time on idle machines in the past few years to, for example, search for extraterrestrial intelligence. This is only the beginning.

The Grid Computing Information Centre, run by Dr. Rajkumar Buyya in Australia defines grid computing as "a type of parallel and distributed sys-tem that enables the sharing, selection, and aggregation of geographically distributed 'autonomous' resources dynamically at runtime depending on their availability, capability, performance, cost, and users' quality-of-serv-ice requirements." Simply, it means a way of combining the power of computers around the world in appropriate combinations for appropriate purposes. Even more simply, it means access to supercomputing power on an as-needed basis.

Up till now the power of a limited number of actual supercomputers has been applied mostly to forecasting the weather or calculating how to blow things up. With grid computing, supercomputer power can be applied to all kinds of scientific and business questions that needed the power but never had the access. Questions like molecular modeling for drug design, high energy physics, modeling brain activity in real time and producing a working mirror of the brain, simulations of the environment, or of consumer behavior, or of market behavior. This ability placed in the hands of enterprises of all kinds and sizes, and even individuals, at low cost or even for free will lead to applications limited only by imagination.

Ubiquitous biometric applications are the likely fifth key IT trend. The ability to measure biometrics exists, in the form of iris and retina scans, finger and palm print scans, voice recognition, and so on. It is just a matter of wanting enhanced safety and security, and making biometric measures and communication cheaper. A combination of several scans offers the greatest reliability and security, and thus is likely. Face recognition systems become more feasible as data banks grow more robust and processor speeds enable fast pattern matching. Over the next decade or so, most forms of ID including licenses, passports, and credit cards will be replaced by biometric systems. This has obvious application for travel and building security. The shift to doing most average computing on wireless portable devices, whether laptop, phone, handheld, or wearable means that data security will become a more significant issue, and built-in biometric ID will become the norm. Look into the camera on your phone and the phone will confirm that you are who you say you are and authorize use. Consumer transactions will also shift toward the biometric, until we reach a point where a fingerprint and iris scan may be all that is required to complete a purchase.

The sixth key IT development is in some ways related to grid computing, in that it involves many computers dispersed geographically communicating with one another. This is the enterprise of massively multiplayer online role-playing games, or MMORPGs. Perhaps the best known such game in 2005 is World of Warcraft, which celebrated its first year anniversary as the year ended, and became the number one game, with more than 4.0 million subscribers, including 1.5 million in China. The Matrix Online, various Star Wars and Middle Earth games, and a variety of Dark Age of Camelot games are but a few others that attract a total of 20 million worldwide players. At an average of $40–$50 for software and $15 a month for a subscription, the potential revenue is tremendous.

These games are beautifully produced and so highly immersive that they are often referred to as virtual reality when they are not quite. The games can even move beyond imagination and the virtual world and become in some senses real. For example, one MMORPG game, Second Life, involves its 60,000 worldwide players in both a fictitious world and a real economy. The players use game currency, convertible to real U.S. dollars via PayPal, to buy products such as virtual clothing for their virtual bodies in the game. Other players act as haute couture designers, selling a fabulous limited edition dress for, say, $5, while everyday duds sell for a dollar. Thus the game of Second Life proceeds, with all kinds of products and services being designed, bought, and sold. The players exchanged $2 million in real dollars per month in 2005, making the economy of Second Life equivalent to that of a small island nation in the real world. Some players even make their entire real living within the game now, which supports about 100 virtual jobs according to the game developer, Linden Research.

Beyond these six primary IT trends and developments are two additional IT potentials. One is true virtual and augmented reality, and the other is mind-reading technology for control of robotics and lie detection. Virtual reality (VR) evolved from the U.S. Air Force virtual cockpit project led by Tom Furness. It involves total immersion within a computer-generated world but has never taken off commercially. Full immersion VR will eventually become affordable for smaller enterprises and average people. Imagine the games just described if one could be inside the game with other players all around them, as compared to seeing them on a beautiful but still two-dimensional screen.

Augmented reality is available today. Here, a person wears some kind of device such as a virtual retinal display that paints a computerized image onto the eye, while allowing simultaneous vision of and interaction with the real world. Microvision, a Bothell, Washington, company is among the first to sell commercial systems for augmented reality. While future prototypes look like cool sunglasses, a current model aimed at auto repair technicians features a virtual retinal display built into a baseball cap with a drop down monocular reflector, connected by wire to a small computer on the hip. This system can hold all relevant repair information for various makes and models of vehicles, and as a technician works it can superimpose instructions or diagrams over their view of the real work. Another developer, Mark Billinghurst, director of the Human Interface Technology Lab in New Zealand, has invented software called Live 3-D, which, using normal desktop computers and the Internet, enables remote users wearing augmented reality glasses to see each other in full three dimensions. Literally, you can get up and walk round behind another person and see how they look from the back, though they are not in the room with you. Eventually this, too, will become normal as a means of teleconferencing and remote communications.

Finally, work is being done on mind reading. Actually, the work is on brain scanning techniques, searching for ways to measure and record the electromagnetic activity of the brain in real time as it performs various functions. Techniques include functional magnetic resonance imaging (fMRI), which is most common, along with magnetoencephalography, which measures weak magnetic activity, positron emission tomography (PET) scans, transcranial magnetic stimulation, and others. Each of these is increasing in spatial and temporal resolution at an exponential rate, doubling every year. Should nanotechnology sensors ever be available and capable of being used inside the brain, scanning results will improve accordingly. Such scanning has been able to detect lies better than standard methods, but the real goal is to simulate and reverse-engineer the brain. Doing so would lead to more robust parallel processing computers, and, some believe, even to the ability to download the brain and create a backup of your memories.

Before that capability is fully realized, computers themselves will have to evolve. In order to sustain Moore's Law beyond the next decade, computing will either become three-dimensional or move beyond silicon and into the realm of molecular or even single electron transistor computers using techniques taken from nanotechnology. Debate continues about the likelihood that we will sustain a century of exponential growth in the power and speed of computing accompanied by regular declines in cost. Kurzweil (2005) is most persuasive in making the case that exponential doubling will likely continue even as specific technology solutions hit walls and new solutions emerge. It appears that not only computing power, but DNA sequencing, telecommunications speed and cost, nanotech capabilities, and other technology arenas are also developing at exponential rates. This is in part because information technology builds on the base of all that has come before, is now connected globally, works continuously, and amplifies human intelligence. Thus each technology generation is likely to accelerate the doubling time of its own development.

ROBOT LOVE

In 2004 DARPA, the Defense Advanced Research Project Agency, sponsored the DARPA Grand Challenge. Seeking to develop technology for autonomous, that is driverless vehicles, the grand challenge offered $1 million to any team who could deliver a vehicle that negotiated a 144-mile course over dirt roads, desert terrain, and a variety of obstacles. The vehicle had to be the size of a car or jeep, and all were modified road vehicles of some kind. Twenty-five teams entered. On race day, off they went. Or not. The winner made it a total of 7.7 miles before breaking down, and many of the robotic cars barely made it out of the gate.

Skeptics laughed and were reassured that the ability of artificial intelligence had once again proven to be exaggerated. DARPA decided not to award the prize.

The following year, 2005, DARPA issued the same challenge, and raised the prize to $2 million. One hundred ninety-five teams entered and twenty-five teams made it though preliminary rounds to the finals. On race day they lined up on a grueling course similar to that of 2004, this time totaling 131 miles. At the end of the day, an entry from Stanford University, a modified Volkswagen Touareg, finished the entire course in less than the required 10 hours and was awarded the prize. Four additional teams joined the winner in traveling the entire 131 miles autonomously, and many other teams traveled substantial distances before succumbing to problems.

Few images are more associated with the future than the personal robot. Looking like a mechanical human, in film and television they clunk about endearingly or occasionally dangerously, serving trays of cocktails. It is one of the images that leads people to wonder why the future never arrived.

But it is arriving, of course. Today there are nearly one million industrial robots worldwide. They generally look more like mechanical arms than people, but they are robots nonetheless. A robot is essentially any machine that can perform tasks automatically and in a humanlike way, usually replacing a human for the given task, and that can also operate independently of human control once programmed. Increasingly robots are also able to move about independently rather than staying in a fixed location.

We can add to standard industrial robots an increasing variety of service robots and personal or domestic-help robots. The former may perform services in many environments, from businesses to battlefields to Mars. Service robots may clean windows, milk cows, assist in surgery, deliver mail or tools or parts, act as military observers, conduct bomb disposal and security sweeps, clean hazardous waste, rove around Mars. Unmanned vehicles on the ground, in the water, in the air are service robots, performing a service on behalf of humans but without humans.

Personal robots are multiplying rapidly, and they vacuum floors, mow lawns, sort laundry, provide entertainment and education, monitor security, and provide rudimentary care for elderly or ill persons. When you add up all the numbers, from the one million industrial robots to the more than 600,000 Roomba and Scooba vacuuming and floor scrubbing robots, to entertainment bots, to the DaVinci Intuitive Surgical Robot, a safe estimate is well over two million robots in use today, this despite relatively flat sales for classic industrial machine tool robots. By 2007 total robot sales are expected to reach $17 billion, up from about $5 billion in 2004. It was this growth along with his knowledge of future technology that led Rodney Brooks, founder of a leading robot company, iRobot, to conjecture that personal robots are about where personal computers were in 1978 . . . being developed, still pretty basic, and owned only by early adopters. Others compare what is coming in robotics to household appliances. Nearly a century ago electric household appliances such as refrigerators made their appearance, and over time became part of the background of our lives. Essential. Normal. As Don Kara, editor of *Robotics Trends* put it in 2005, it is rare to "find a market change so profound that it will radically alter the way we live our lives day-to-day. The emerging personal and service robotics market, or mobile robotics if you prefer, is one such market."

Ten years from now robots will begin to take over the military skies, as UAVs (Unmanned Aerial Vehicles) the size of today's fighter jets begin flying. On the very day this was written, Boeing unveiled a mockup of its full-size unmanned combat aerial vehicle, the X-45C. The test flights will begin in 2007 and end in 2011. The X-45C looks like it leapt off the screen of a space adventure movie.

Some years ago I lead a major university department of astronautics and aeronautics in strategic planning. As they listed probable future developments, they wrote that by 2010 airplanes would fly themselves. "Seriously?" I asked. Easily, was their reply, except for passenger jets, since passengers would at this time still be too uneasy to get onto a plane with no pilot.

But smaller and gentler robots will be the norm, and many will not look like robots to us. In fact, we already interact with versions of them . . . the ATM, the automatic fuel pump at the gas station, the self-service check-out line at the store. These are rudimentary robots, fixed in one place but performing work formerly done by humans and doing it with little human intervention except for occasional servicing.

There is an old joke about the factory of the future, which will employ a single human and a dog, along with countless robot machines. The human's job will be to watch the machines. The dog's job will be to keep the human from touching the machines.

Marshall Brain, founder of the web site *howstuffworks.com*, has become fascinated with the future of robots, and writes about them frequently in his *Robotic Nation* series and blog. He is concerned that the story of the human and the dog might be too prophetic. If you really draw the technology and robot trends out for two or three decades and begin to ask what are the human jobs that could be done by smart robot machines, the list becomes very impressive very quickly:

Manufacturing.
Cashier sales.
Cleaning.
Repair of all kinds of things,
    including robots.
Restaurant service.
Construction jobs of many
    kinds.

Baggage handling.
Checking you in for flights (already
    there!).
Flying airplanes.
Providing public transit.
Entertainment.
Farming.
And so on.

What makes Brain's thesis provocative is a bottom-line question he raises. Doing some simple calculations, he imagines that 50 million jobs could be done by robots in 2015 or 2020. He notes that we are told not to worry, that the economy will invent 50 million new jobs, to compensate. It is true that this has happened historically. But, asks Brain, since we can see this coming, why is the economy not inventing more new kinds of jobs now?

The full application of robots to complex jobs is closely tied up with IT and artificial intelligence (AI). People in the field refer to weak and strong AI. Robots today have intelligence, in that they can make simple decisions based on their programming. They can learn and can even solve some problems. But their intelligence is limited, and novel problems generally cannot be dealt with. But this is improving. Strong AI will involve the ability to reason, to solve problems, and at its strongest to be self-aware in some sense. Such a paradigm breakthrough could happen next week, or decades in the future, and some doubt that strong AI is even possible. If it is not possible, we will never see the fully humanoid robot of science fiction fame.

KNOWING EVERYTHING ABOUT EVERYBODY

To conclude this overview of some driving technologies, it is important to acknowledge a social and cultural phenomenon hidden in plain sight within all of this technology change. This is the inherent tension between privacy and transparency. In a 2005 scientific poll of Washington State citizens, home of Microsoft and many other technology companies, 64 percent said they believed that 20 years from now the amount of privacy and freedom that Americans have will be lower, while only 14 percent believed there will be more privacy and freedom.

Stories of identify theft are a staple of the news business, and ID theft is in fact on the rise. We have already reviewed the likelihood that personal security biometrics will be a growth field. The U.S. Department of Homeland Security gave $800 million to 50 cities in 2006 exclusively to install surveillance cameras. Night vision goggles are a popular gift item. Google yourself, and see what interesting things turn up. Someday cameras may literally shrink to the form of "smart dust," so small that you may barely be able to see them, but they will see you just fine.

Is this a problem, an opportunity, a threat? Or merely interesting? David Brin was among the first and most authoritative to tackle the subject. In *The Transparent Society*, he argued that transparency is not only inevitable but ultimately may be to our advantage as individuals and societies. That is, transparency might be a terrific opportunity.

The modern concept of privacy is mostly a result of industrialization and urbanization. A friend who spent time with the Masai in Kenya noted that among the most interesting features of their culture was that an individual was almost never alone, that in fact the whole concept of aloneness was foreign to them. Today, as this book makes plain, key underlying assumptions of Western civilization such as privacy are being challenged. As Brin summarizes at the end of his book (334), "It was fun while it lasted, living on these city streets amid countless, nameless fellow beings, not knowing any of them unless you chose to, being able to walk away from any embarrassment or petty discourtesy, just another forgotten face in the crowd. It was also lonely."

But what is the opportunity? My eighty-five-year-old mother lives alone, in a distant city. When she got on the net, she became more connected. When she got a cell phone, she became more accessible. When in the not too distant future our phones are location aware and voice activated and the network is much smarter, I expect to be walking down the street and hear her voice in my earpiece saying, "Glen," and it will be my mother, who will know where I am because her phone told her. And I will know where she is. Or perhaps I will get up one morning, and my computer will say to me, "You know, it is past 9:00 A.M. at your mother's house, and the coffeemaker has not been used. Perhaps you ought to call and see if everything is okay." This is less private, but better.

If we try to cling to the past, we will miss many potential benefits of a true information society, but we will not prevent the powerful or the deadly from using such technologies against us. One of the best defenses of freedom may in the future be the ubiquity of cameras and instant communications. Who would have known about the torture at Abu Ghraib prison in Iraq in 2004 had not some unwitting participants taken digital photos of themselves and sent them around the Web? How would we know what happened on the famous hijacked airplane that crashed in Pennsylvania in 2001 had the possibility of listening in on cell phones not existed? In fact, how would those passengers have learned of what was happening in the world had they not been able to make the calls in the first place? Millions of cameras, no probably billions of cameras, sending pictures around the planet on the Web are more likely to add to our security than to challenge our freedom. More information rather than secrecy has always been a more effective tool against tyrants and oppressive governments, and this is likely to continue to be the case.

CHAPTER 3

How to Profit by Increasing the Knowledge Content of Your Product or Service

On Mondays, Wednesdays, and Fridays I think that we are experiencing a discontinuous transition from one world-system to another, a 'catastrophe.' On Tuesdays, Thursdays, and Saturdays, I feel better and think that it is going to be a transition with continuity, one like the previous transition from medievalism to modernism. On Sundays I try to rest and seek a contemplative detachment.

—William Irwin Thompson, 1985

Years ago I spoke to a Congressional summit on the future. Quoting another futurist, I noted that demography might be anticipated accurately a generation, or about 20 years into the future, technology might be anticipated a couple of computer generations, or about 36 months into the future, while the economy, with so many variables, can at best be anticipated 6 months into the future. Afterwards the chief economist of Wells Fargo commented to me, "If you can actually anticipate the economy six months out, you can make me a lot of money." Well, of course it is not so easy to anticipate economic performance. At the same time, the shape and nature of the future economy is quite foreseeable, and in this chapter we take a look.

Five dynamic forces are shaping the future economy. They do not represent the whole picture, but if you grasp these five, you will have a better chance of shaping your own economic future. The five key forces are rapid innovation and technology convergence, knowledge value, the spending wave, the global free market, and perhaps most of all, the surging development of China and India.

RAPID INNOVATION AND TECHNOLOGY CONVERGENCE

When the technology stock market crashed in 2000, many casual expert observers thought that it was not just a market bubble that had burst, but that in fact a bubble of technology development itself had come to an end. The news was full of breathless accounts of the end of the information economy. Experts fell over one another to say, "See, the idea that there is a new technology driven economy with different fundamentals was all a big mistake, and incidentally we were right about this all along. The new economy is dead. So there." They could not have been more wrong. What they were actually seeing was the end of the beginning, and mistaking it for the end. Technology development and convergence continued apace though a bit beneath the radar.

The real story was that the new technology led and web-based economy was barely underway. Even today it is still a frontierlike economy, and thus we continue to see speculation, mistakes, wins and losses, starts and stops, experiments that work and experiments that do not. But it will continue to grow. Why? Because of something called the S-Curve, a staple of economic theory regarding innovation.

The S-Curve says that an innovation that catches on will grow slowly until about 10 percent of the market has adopted it. At that point a takeoff is reached, and the market quickly expands to about 50 percent penetration. As this happens, the excitement is incredible, and lots of players jump in, too many in fact. A shakeout ensues, and market growth pauses. The whole thing seems to have come to an end. But for powerful and even vital innovations, the real market will eventually reach 90 percent. That is, during the pause, there is nearly half the growth yet to happen.

When the technology market paused in 2000, adoption of personal computers was nearing 60 percent, but the Internet and cellular phones were at about 50 percent in developed countries. Broadband, the actual key to the technology driven future economy, was just getting started, and it was not yet at 10 percent in consumer adoption. It was no wonder that a web-based economy was limping—the whole thing was too slow!

The development of multiple Internet devices was just beginning. As high bandwidth was built out, the use of the net for transactions began to grow rapidly. The idea that retail sales on the net were not going to work was sillier than the idea that every retail.com would succeed automatically.

As a retail channel, the Internet is growing now, as we have noted. The ultimate stage may arrive when most rooms and all handhelds have a screen and each screen has a voice. When you open the dresser drawer in the morning to grab some socks and see just those old ones, you can simply say, "On screen, go to Nordstrom . . . pause . . . Order five pairs of casual socks, varied solid colors," and be done with it. Then commerce on the Web will expand further. How soon is this? The next 10 years, some think sooner.

IT'S WHAT A PRODUCT OR SERVICE KNOWS THAT COUNTS

In the past 25 years a new recipe for commerce emerged. The ingredients were no longer confined to raw materials, labor, and capital. The new ingredient began to make the major difference in success or failure. Intelligence. Not the intelligence of the people involved, but rather, the intelligence of the product or service itself.

Peter Drucker pointed out decades ago that it was knowledge applied to things rather than to being that created the industrial revolution. Keynoting the Summit on the Future 2005 in Amsterdam, I was asked to focus on what the new Europe needed to do to become a knowledge based economy. A knowledge society then is nothing new. What is new is that knowledge is now applied to everything, even to itself, so much so that people, goods, and services compete based on their knowledge value. As prescient as Drucker may have been in seeing this first, no one described it better than Taichi Sakaiya (1991). He pointed out that while knowledge contributed to the emergence of industrial society, it was cheap energy more than anything that was key. What emerged through that era was a cultural esthetic in which the goal became standardized products and services consumed in as much abundance as possible.

Now that esthetic is dying, as the limits to cheap energy are reached, as information technology enables rapid expansion of information and knowledge, and indeed as industrial society itself transforms into the next stage. What Sakaiya believed was coming next was an era in which the economic value of knowledge itself would become the driving force of commerce, an era he labeled the 'knowledge value revolution." The past decade and a half have borne out his "history of the future," and understanding knowledge value has become fundamental to success in business.

Knowledge value is deeper than popular conceptions of the knowledge society. A knowledge society emphasizes an educated population, which is vital to be sure. However knowledge value refers to the knowledge that we may imbed *within products and services themselves*. Any automobile today is not only more complex and more expensive than a 1970s era Chevy Nova. It is the vehicle itself that is smarter, that has vastly more knowledge value built into it. Yet the people who built today's car may not actually be any smarter than those who built the Nova. A new car with built-in navigation is smarter than one without it, but an auto with built-in navigation and active collision avoidance is smarter even yet. A hybrid is not just a gasoline motor and electric motor combined in a neat package. It is a brilliant computing machine, making continuous observations of its external and internal environment and constant calculations of what is required to operate at peak efficiency. It has superior knowledge value.

The same principle applies to services, where we frequently assess the potential value of a service based on its perceived knowledge value. Neural network modeling software used to predict the failure of concrete in stress tests, or used to forecast stock prices may be judged to have higher knowledge value than simpler tools. As with products, services that contain higher knowledge value will tend initially to be more expensive and more specialized. Greater differentiation and specialization of products and services is a fundamental characteristic of a knowledge value economy. However, the rapid production of new knowledge means shorter and shorter life spans for products and services as competitors rush in with smarter products, a phenomenon we are clearly seeing. Because greater knowledge goes into new product development as well as into more efficient production, prices tend to actually decline over time, despite enhanced knowledge value.

A knowledge value economy has several characteristics that distinguish our time from the past.

- Information is the primary commodity, not land, not raw materials, not even manufactured products or services themselves.
- Knowledge is the element of greatest value, and ability to survive and flourish depends more and more on ability to learn new knowledge and apply it quickly.
- Communicated knowledge increases value the most, and those companies that enable such communication will be dominant.
- The competitive advantage of all products and services increasingly resides in the knowledge value of the product or service. How much knowledge went into its production? How much knowledge is contained within it? To what extent and how easily can the customer perceive or access the knowledge value?
- When a physical product such as land or a manufactured item is sold, the seller no longer has the product. In contrast when knowledge value is sold, the seller retains the knowledge value after the sale. Knowledge value is thus never lost, but only increased through transactions. Hence there can never be scarcity of knowledge value, and without scarcity there will always be pressure to lower prices.
- The pace of technological change quickens. Integrated communication systems, which enable collaboration and quickly communicate new discoveries, quicken this pace even further.
- The shelf life of knowledge value decreases continuously, thus putting a premium on speed. Design and production cycles taking years, even months, are obsolete.
- Uncertainty in a rapidly changing environment suggests caution but requires experimentation. There is a tendency to want to wait for things to "settle down" before deciding what to do next, but the environment will not wait.

What this all means is obvious. If you want to competitively position your product or service, make it smarter. There is little question that an iPod is perceived to be smarter, both in functionality and appearance, than its competitors. You will probably need to become smarter yourself to do something like that, but the key is to put the intelligence into the product or service.

SPENDING WAVE WANES

A false security has lulled the U.S. economy in this century. Riding the momentum of decades of technological leadership and demographic advantage, we've been able to weather external events and reckless economic and tax policy. But the ride is in a house of mirrors. Economic growth statistics have masked an underlying decay, as the middle class is squeezed into multiple jobs to keep even and the number of people living in poverty grows year by year, even while the percentage of wealth that flows to the top two or three percent skyrockets. Savings as a percentage of disposable income fell to negative rates in 2005 as people spent everything they had to survive. Rosy pronouncements about GDP growth ignore all of this. Meanwhile monetary policy is designed to enable people to draw wealth from home equity and pour that into consuming, something which is happening to the tune of billions of dollars per year. It keeps the masses relatively happy. But deluded.

Looming on the horizon is a critical tipping point. Little attention is paid to it though it is one of the simplest and most profound economic drivers. It is the spending wave. Popularized initially by demographer and economist Harry Dent (1995, 2004), the spending wave is the answer to the question, When in your lifetime do you spend the most money? The answer is about ages 42 to 50, time-shifted forward or backward a bit depending on when you have children, if you have a family. It is in these years that the kids are most likely to be teenagers, and thus you are buying the biggest house you will ever live in, and extra goods of all kinds from cars to computers and clothing. This is common across cultures and around the world, by the way.

The performance of the consumer driven U.S. economy has been highly correlated to the percent of the population who are in their peak spending years. Thus, in the first years of this century, as the nation lived through a recession, consumer spending went up quarter by quarter. How could this be? The answer is that the final wave of Baby Boomers is in the peak spending years. They had no choice but to spend.

The spending wave has just a few more years to run, between now and 2010, as the first Baby Boomers prepare to retire and the last Boomers move through their peak spending years. This mini-boom time is one of the mirrors, creating an illusion. The next few years are actually likely to be very good, even great, according to Dent. But the generation that follows, Generation X, is smaller by millions of people. Thus, other factors being equal consumer spending is likely to begin decreasing in about a half-decade, and joining the decline will be the stock market and housing prices. A reasonable scenario then is a few years of terrific opportunity for business creation and career enhancement, followed by prospects for a downturn after 2010. Anticipating this gives you an inside edge to profiting from the next few years, while preparing for what comes after. Pay attention.

GLOBALIZATION—CHARTING NEW TERRITORY

Our ability to avoid the economic downturn forecast by the spending wave depends heavily on the performance of the global economy 5 or 10 years hence. We have not much time to get there. A robust global economy appears to be a way through.

The global economy is often cited as a new economic factor, but it is as much the past as it is the future. It has become the way the world works now, as simple as that. Thomas Friedman (2005) calls it the flat world. Indeed it is. Two years ago my spouse left a career in business consulting and opened a small retail fine gifts store. It was eye-opening to discover how 700 square feet of retail space in Seattle, Washington, can be so thoroughly imbedded in the global economy. Because of her desired product mix, she was immediately dealing with suppliers from *all over the world*.

In Italy in late 2005 I taught a seminar to a group of Italian business leaders, primarily CEOs. We discussed Starbucks and how that company had taken an essentially Italian approach to coffee and globalized it. How had this happened? Italian companies traditionally have not considered themselves to be global enterprises, focusing instead on local customers. This, the CEOs believed has to change, if Italy is to flourish in the new economy. This view was amplified in a survey of EU senior executives on future competitiveness by the sponsoring company, Ambrosetti. They found that, on the whole, EU business executives expected to lag in competitiveness for the next decade for a variety of reasons, chief among them a lack of European integration (Cohen 2005). They also cited unfair competition from abroad, along with illegal product imitations.

In the developing world globalization of the economy may be described as a mixed blessing. Even that is being charitable, according to some. John Perkins (2004) described his ultimately terrifying experience in global development in which he had played the role of an "economic hit man." His job was to produce inflated estimates of the benefits of development, in order to create such a debt load that developing nations could not escape the debt. This was all imbedded within a process involving the most cynical exploitation of developing nations, with minimal benefit to local populations.

Domestic agriculture subsidies in developed countries are an example of exploitive globalization. Such subsidies mean that U.S. grown rice can sell more cheaply in Thailand than locally grown rice, and the same goes for U.S. corn sold in Mexico. Thus, local farmers cannot compete even in their own country against foreign suppliers supported by large subsidies. To be fair, U.S. farmers make the same complaints about others, for example certain products and crops in Europe. This issue has been constantly broached in the various rounds of World Trade Organization negotiations, but not successfully dealt with to date.

Others argue that the development of an increasingly free global marketplace has been the most important and beneficial economic project since World War II, a process that accelerated in the 1990s with the shift of the former Soviet Union and China toward market economies. The Internet now assures that business will globalize even more, as information integration and cross-border communication is continuous.

William Knoke (1996) described both the current and future dynamics of the global economy with keen anticipation when he named it the "age of everything-everywhere" in which nations would become anachronisms, terrorism would flourish, religion would resurge, business strategies and economic theories would need re-thinking, and old labor skills would become irrelevant. He mistakenly anticipated the fragmentation of large corporations and doom for labor unions. Instead, as the global economy has unfolded over the past 10 years the power of large corporations has increased, and labor unions, while down at the moment, are poised for a global comeback.

Our purpose in highlighting the global nature of the economy here is not to do a thorough analysis of it, nor is it merely to call attention to the obvious. Instead, we want to emphasize three critical ideas. First, globalization is both positive and negative as a driving force. Which predominates depends heavily on how it is approached in the coming decade. If we move to rationalize global labor, build wages toward the middle instead of the lowest possible, and develop international approaches to sustainability and climate change, it can be, on balance, positive. Cultural disruption and loss may occur but can be outweighed by positive benefits. Benjamin Friedman (2005) persuasively argues that the moral value of rising standards of living is often overlooked. History demonstrates that when living standards are increasing and people can reasonably expect their future life to be better off compared to their past, they will care less about comparing to others, and will in general become more tolerant and more willing to settle disputes peacefully. The opposite is true when living standards have stagnated or are perceived to be likely to decline. This seems vital. If globalization proceeds in a way that increases living standards compared to the past, it will be positive. If it is exploitative and living standards are flat or declining, social strife will ensue.

The second critical idea is that outsourcing is a fundamental part of globalization. If the economy stays global, outsourcing of jobs will happen, and the impact is probably underestimated. More total jobs and more kinds of jobs will be outsourced. The number of U.S. jobs outsourced remains murky, and difficult to calculate. U.S. agencies, for example, do not keep official statistics on outsourcing, a strange fact given the detailed statistics kept on most everything else. Numbers cited range widely from tens of thousands of job exported per year to hundreds of thousands or more. No one actually knows the real story, or is not telling if they do. Estimates are that from 13 million to 20 million U.S. jobs will be offshored in the coming decade, half in manufacturing and half in service and high technology. If we are talking about existing jobs that are literally picked up and moved, the numbers may tend toward the lower range. But if we are talking about those plus jobs that would traditionally have been created locally but now are created overseas, the numbers certainly hit the higher range. In any case, I believe, as does Ted Fishman (2005) that the typical estimates are off by at least 100 percent. As high skill jobs continue to become vulnerable, the migration of work will accelerate. There is no getting around this, save protective legislation or extreme goodwill on the part of employers. Becoming as high in quality and low in cost as possible is the only bulwark for the individual business. Reforming the U.S. tax code to discourage rather than encourage offshoring would help. But if the economy is to be a global one, then in the long run we are talking about a process in which labor will seek its optimum level and where work and production will become, to use Knoke's term, "placeless."

The inevitability of job outsourcing, barring an end to globalization or the creation of protections against job movement, brings us to the third and most critical point. We appear to be in for a several decade leveling process. We hear bland assurances that plenty of higher paying new jobs will appear to replace those outsourced. But where are they? Unblinking global trade supporters claim that more jobs are insourced than outsourced. We also are assured by political leaders and intellectuals who support globalization that there is nothing to worry about, we can just send fifty-five-year-olds back to community college, and that value-added jobs are in any case not going anywhere. There is a kind of blind faith that it will all work out in the end. However, it seems more likely that we are looking at an adjustment process that could take up to a couple of generations, with significant downward pressure on wages for that entire time. Two generations is too long and the disruptions too severe.

It is vital to become much more deliberate about this whole process. A realistic examination of the deep and long-lasting impact on wages would be a start. Relieving U.S. employers of the burden of health care costs, via a national health insurance program, would be a critical step to take. Major improvements in adult education are needed, as are programs to teach people to actually become international entrepreneurs. Moving soon to revise the U.S. tax code would help, in particular Subpart

F, which governs the taxation of foreign subsidiaries controlled by U.S. companies. These tax provisions encourage offshoring by relieving the company who moves jobs overseas of significant taxes on the portion of profit now generated overseas. Finally, steady insistence on a level playing field in labor practices and environmental protections can act to counter low-wage advantages.

CHINA GAINS, INDIA RACES

Boeing a few years ago began offering high-level management education to executives of Chinese airlines. The intent was twofold, to incentivize the executives to prefer Boeing products, and in any case to increase the likelihood that Chinese airlines would be profitable in the long run because the executives had been trained in global business practices. It happened that my spouse was part of the creative team who designed and managed these intensive one- to three-month schools, which took place in Seattle and in St. Louis. As part of the education program I had the opportunity on occasion to spend a day with the classes of 30 very smart, very ambitious Chinese businesspeople exploring the long-term future. Even better in some ways, my spouse and I were able to invite entire classes over for parties at our home. Arriving by bus, they might be there to attend an American style barbecue, or in one case a Halloween costume party complete with apple bobbing.

Three things stand out in my impressions of these classroom sessions and social gatherings. One was the very high level of education and ambition displayed. Second was an interest in the long-term future but not yet a great deal of knowledge about future trends either technological or social-cultural. But most of all was the intense level of curiosity about how everything worked. I remember in particular the first barbecue, when the guests gathered around the gas barbecue, looking beneath it in order to see how it all worked, asking where the gas came from, how much the device cost, and so on. Here they are, I thought, learning how to do financial modeling of future passenger loads, and their greatest excitement appeared to be over the simple engineering of a gas barbecue.

This story is valuable, I think, because it taps into some contradictory yet simultaneous truths about the Chinese. Although they have been growing economically at breakneck speed for 30 years, doubling the size of their economy three times, they still struggle to meet the basic needs for food and clothing for many of their people. Millions of Chinese even today would find a gas barbecue a welcome technology, even as millions of others are already living middle class lives with cell phones and cars and high-speed trains. Second, the Chinese are eager now to be a leader in the global economy, not merely an entrant. Finally, they are racing ahead technologically, still building dams by human labor and wheelbarrow while simultaneously developing global airlines, computer software, and spacecraft.

The latter development was brought home in a recent interview with Jin Lan (2005), founder of Octaxias Company LLC, the China Connection boutique consulting company offering services to U.S.-based companies wishing to do business within China. A native from China who came to the United States to study in the 1980s and stayed on to work and found his business, Lan has a unique perspective on the crossroads of Chinese and U.S. business. His experience ranges from having facilitated the visit of President and Mrs. George W. Bush to the Great Wall in 2002, to leading a training session for 25 Chinese mayors with U.S. mayors in Portland, Oregon. When I asked Lan to name the most significant developments to watch for in China in the coming two decades, his short list included:

- Breakthroughs in agriculture, from hybrid high-yield crops to genetic modifications, to "space agriculture," which involves a very active space research program to discover if hybridizing crops in space can improve them, a project that Lan suggests has led experimentally to a tenfold increase in yield.
- Nanotechnology, where although China is five years behind the rest of the world, the Chinese are pouring tremendous amounts of money into research and development.
- Information technology, where four developments stand out. First is the huge user base in China for both "beyond 3G" cell phones and for computing, which portend a major role for China in setting global standards. Second, local production of software in the

three-dimensional Chinese language will lead to future breakthroughs in three-dimensional computing. Third, the increasing dominance of the Chinese in manufacture, with China now producing 70 percent of desktop computers, 60 percent of laptop computers, and by 2010 20 percent of chips. Finally, these last two are combining into a fourth, the local engineering ability to produce, for example, a new computer chip to run with the Chinese language and Linux, combined with cheap manufacture, to produce a $50 to $80 computer, vital to bringing computing to the whole population.

- Research biotechnology, involving both DNA and RNA, to be combined with traditional Chinese medicine, leading to potential medical breakthroughs.

According to Lan, then, China's future has little to do with gas barbecues and everything to do with leading-edge technology development. There is no more important fact about China to absorb than that. They intend to be technological leaders, and as we see later, they are developing the capacity to be such leaders.

"Once China comes into view, it is hard not to see it everywhere" (Fishman 2005, 6). But there is also India. India is very similar in potential impact on the global economy and is often described as the next China (though some call China the next India!). In general, less attention has been paid to India because it has not become the manufacturing center that China has. Thomas Friedman remedies that by focusing very much on India in *The World Is Flat* (2005), as he tells story after story about how India is becoming the model for placelessness. Information and intellectual capital know no place, need no place because of technology, and thus Bangalore is a city in which all the technology and information trends can come together and produce a thriving local global information industry. "Countries like India are now able to compete for global knowledge work as never before—and America had better get ready for this" Thomas Friedman notes (7).

The forces discussed so far in this chapter as drivers of the future economy are important, but they pale in the face of Chinese and Indian economic development. We have never seen anything like it, massive populations, ambitions for global development and leadership, full of pent-up energy and demand, and, crucially, with access to twenty-first century technology, global networks and education. Thomas Friedman (265) sums it up, throwing in a developing EU country for good measure:

> One cannot stress enough: Young Chinese, Indians, and Poles are not racing us to the bottom. They are racing us to the top. They do not want to work for us; they don't even want to be us. They want to dominate us—in the sense that they want to be creating the companies of the future that people all over the world will admire and clamor to work for.

This may sound alarming, coming from a recognized authority, and Friedman obviously intends to sound an alarm. The United States is lagging now in many areas, and if you simply draw trend lines a couple of decades out, you have to ask how the United States maintains its leadership. The same applies to other advanced industrial counties accustomed to economic leadership. To the extent that the United States needs to wake up, the alarm may be welcome. But it is also important to look at the mutual benefit that can come from Chinese and Indian development, and in this section we attempt to do that, while at the same time pointing out some important challenges.

KEY DRIVERS OF CHINESE AND INDIAN DEVELOPMENT

Sheer Size

The two countries are, as we all know, massive. If current trends hold, India will surpass China in population in 2030, as a result of India's 2005 fertility rate of 2.78 versus a fertility rate of 1.72 in China. The UN currently forecasts an Indian population in 2050 of 1.6 billion people, going steady state then, but up from a billion today. China's population with 1.3 billion people today, is forecast to be at 1.4 billion in 2050 and declining at that time, making India then the most populous nation in the world.

Rapid Growth, Huge Demand

China's annual GDP growth rate of 9.5 percent is followed closely by India's 8 percent. By 2050, China is forecast to have an economy 75 percent larger than that of the United States. If China achieves a per capita income half that of the United States, a reasonable goal, their economy will actually become two and one-half times larger. India, with its population growth and level of technology education will likely be competing with China for global leadership. Already India's market for automobiles is catching up, with a 2005 sales growth rate nearly double China's, though total sales were half as much at more than one million units.

Education Leadership

Education is where the contrast between the United States and India and China becomes the most telling. India graduates 2.5 million from college per year now, and 350,000 engineers, five times the United States annually. This compares favorably with China, which currently produces 3.4 million college graduates, 60 percent of whom graduate in science and engineering, and also produces about 350,000 engineers. Only five percent of the U.S.'s 1.4 million college students graduate in engineering, although another 25 percent complete science degrees of some kind. In basic education, China is shifting from six years of compulsory education to nine. English has the status of an official language in India, which has been critical to the positioning of India in computing and telecommunications. While 50,000 U.S. students learn Chinese, in 2005 there were more Chinese studying English than those who speak English as a first language in the United States, Canada, and the United Kingdom combined.

Shift to Technology Leadership

Providing manufacturing and services cheaply is still the entry to the global economy. Japanese companies can hire three Chinese programmers for the cost of one in Japan. Manufacturing workers may still work for 25 cents an hour. But other Asian and African labor can be cheaper yet, so that is not the key any longer. Thus, both nations are well down the road in shifting from being purely suppliers of cheap labor to technology leadership, first in production of technology, and now to the design and management of such technology.

Research and Development Support

While combined private and public research in the United States still leads the world, trends are not promising. Federal spending on basic science in the United States has stayed flat for 30 years, while spending on physical sciences has decreased. Chinese government support for both science research, and as we have seen for science and technology education, grew 22 percent between 1995 and 2002, and more in recent years.

Poverty

This is one of the two most critical competitive advantages for China and India. When a Chinese industrialist or Indian telecom pioneer goes to the country to recruit for a new operation, the pitch is something like the following: "Move to the city, come to work in my operation, and you can eat well every day." In the United States or in the EU the same pitch would be something like, "Come to work in my operation and you can have a bigger television and another iPod with more memory." The incentive is not the same, cannot be the same. According to Benjamin Friedman after a certain point the pursuit of more wealth may actually be "futile and morally innervating" (*The Economist* 2005). He advocates for the United States a reversal of its current course, and instead a decrease of the federal deficit, limits on spending and a reversal of recent tax cuts, and full accounting of environmental costs, along with improved schools. These and other steps he believes are vital to finding the energy to sustain a growing but already wealthy society.

Freedom from Religious Fundamentalism

Freedom from the kind of religious fundamentalism that limits scientific inquiry may turn out to be a twenty-first century advantage. The United States and Islamic countries are currently concentrating less on twenty-first century industry and innovation, and more it seems on demonstrating superior fealty to ancient beliefs. Although India is a religious country with its own history of religious conflict and China has its problems, they are comparatively free from religious limits on the future. While the Pope was warning in his Christmas 2005 message against the dangers of technological advance made in the absence of religious belief, it is more likely that fundamentalist strictures on science and technology will be the greater problem.

KEY ADVANTAGES OF CHINESE AND INDIAN DEVELOPMENT

If we accept that China and India now have economic advantages and are likely to grow to become dominant in the global economy, is this a threat? We will see constant efforts to paint this development as a threat, along with calls for protection, and, sadly, calls for an arms race. But the benefits from international trade and development flow from comparative advantage, not from absolute advantage. There is no zero-sum situation at all in most trade relationships. Logically, no country can produce comparative advantages over another country in all industries, no matter how often we may say that in theory China could produce every good and service for the whole world. This is not going to happen. Rather, in a global economy your competitors are those productive units with comparative advantage most similar to your own, while *your best trade partners* are the largest units, and those most distinct from you. China and India will be increased competition to the United States in the way that Europe has been for decades. But even Europe is *primarily a mutually beneficial trade partner*.

Thus, the benefits from Chinese and Indian development, even as they become larger economies than Japan and then the United States and the EU, will be greater than the competitive losses. This is not to say that the process will not be very disruptive, as we have discussed earlier. Nor is it to say that great emphasis ought not be placed on preserving jobs with better competitive strategies and policies. Continuous and effective pressure for fair practices regarding labor, environment, and currency issues ought to be standard practice. However, on the whole and in light of all the economic forces we have discussed, the fact that China is racing and India is gaining is a good thing for the future.

Beyond the general advantage of having two large and robust trading partners, two other benefits of Chinese and Indian development seem clear. One is the ability for these two cultures, each now standing with one foot in their agrarian past and the other in twenty-first century industry and education, to leapfrog into the future. That is, if development is done well, they could leap over the mistakes and lessons learned by 200 years of industrialization, into cleaner, more sustainable, and even more humane development. Of course current evidence for this being done is mixed at best, but the opportunity is there. The second additional benefit has simply to do with alleviating poverty. Being so vast in size and population, each country has its problems with poverty and if these two giants and only these two obtained economic leadership and a growing middle class, global poverty would be dealt a blow, though still with much to do.

CHALLENGES FOR CHINESE AND INDIAN DEVELOPMENT

If China and India are to get there, and if the mutual benefits are to accrue, then these two growing powers must face several significant challenges and succeed against them. Some are unique to each country, but many cross boundaries.

As Jin Lan (2005) put it, China sees three enduring challenges in its future: feeding the people, clothing the people, and enabling its people to live better. These are very simple and traditional goals. But to accomplish these things, China, and India too, must deal with environmental degradation, population growth and related policies, getting to the next energy era beyond fossil fuels, and finally with reconciling government policies with economic and innovative freedom.

Energy and the environment are on the minds of people in these countries. Describing his seminar with 25 Chinese mayors, Lan found that they were chiefly concerned with whether China was going to trash its environment and become simply the worker bees for the world, just to manufacture everything. This was not a future they preferred. Getting serious about green development, reducing pollution and carbon emissions, even as the economy grows rapidly is an area of increasing interest in China and India. In fact, contrary to common impressions of China as being unconcerned about the environment, the record shows that while China's GDP rose fourfold from 1980 to 2000, energy use only doubled. China emits 2.6 tons of carbon per 1,000 people, the United States 19 tons.

Still, China and India must come to grips with developing sustainable energy industries. Given their geographic locations and engineering abilities, if they move quickly they have the opportunity to emerge as the global leaders in the next energy era, while simultaneously adding to ecologically friendly prosperity in their own countries. As this plays out, China and India must resist the easy path to burning more and more coal, currently a primary means of generating electricity. One of the great races in the next decade or two will be to see who—China, India, the United States—or others like Brazil, Japan, and the EU will emerge as the leading innovators in transportation and energy. Millions of jobs will hang in the balance, as will the fate of the global climate.

On population policy, China faces two issues, soon. The one-child policy has succeeded in controlling population growth, as we have seen in the Chinese fertility rate. But China is now aging rapidly, and also approaching its tipping point into population decline. As these two forces converge, we can expect a relaxation of the one-child policy, even an overt policy for larger families. This will probably aim for a steady state, rather than actual growth. Meanwhile, India will need continued efforts to slow population growth and bring it into balance. As population growth slows around the world, a counterpressure will emerge to increase family size for economic and cultural reasons, but it will be important to resist these pressures.

Finally, China and India each face its own issues regarding government policies. In India large and continuing government deficits and public debt equaling 62 percent of GDP hamper the ability of government to improve infrastructure as fast as would be useful. Significant cuts in government subsidies and tax reform are needed. In China, leveling of the yuan in comparison to the dollar and euro is still in the future. The continuing evolution of economic freedom in the midst of a more open but still controlling government will be a challenge as well.

THE UNITED STATES LAGS

What should the United States do? We have mentioned the usual suspects. Return to saner fiscal policy by lowering the deficit and repealing some of the tax cuts. Vastly improve education, and invest more in basic science and technology again. Get serious about outsourcing, not so much with protections as with understanding the extent of the challenge. Make the preservation of high quality jobs a priority, and support research and innovation that produce new industries of the future. Revise the tax code to discourage rather than encourage offshoring. Institute policies that make U.S. companies more price competitive, national health insurance being one of these policies. Finance national health insurance in part with a national gas tax that provides market-based incentive for U.S. companies to seize leadership in the next energy and transportation era before it is too late and those industries are lost. Teach global entrepreneurship. As Michael Cox of the Dallas Federal Reserve says (Fishman 275), "There is no reason we can't have one of every four Americans working at home leveraging the work of ninety-five people elsewhere in the world." Matuszak (2005) advises us to "revel in the competition" and understand that when you do business in China, you will put your intellectual property at risk and the government may not help you. But set up business with China anyway. In particular, establish training programs in your business, so that the enterprise that emerges will share your business culture, and you can do business more easily in the future. Fishman (2005), required reading on China, summarizes this way:

> For America to stay productively employed, its skills, sophistication, and imaginative power must remain world-class, every day better than before. America itself must become a new place (282).

CHAPTER 4

How to Profit from the Next Energy Wave

The peaking of world oil production presents the United States and the world with an unprecedented risk management problem. As peaking is approached, liquid fuel prices and price volatility will increase dramatically, and, without timely mitigation, the economic, social, and political costs will be unprecedented. Viable mitigation options exist on both the supply and demand sides, but to have substantial impact, they must be initiated more than a decade in advance of peaking.

> —Peak Oil, a report for the U.S. Department
> of Defense by the Science Applications
> International Corporation, 2005

We're going to need everything we can get from biomass, everything we can get from solar, everything we can get from wind. And still the question is can we get enough?

> —Michael Pacheco, 2005

At the most, we have 50 years to make the world over again. But people change, adapt, and make crazy new stuff work.

> —Michael Parfit, 2005

THE END OF CHEAP OIL

The world is running out of oil. Just in time. When I fly into a major international airport, I never cease to be amazed as I look around while the plane taxies to the terminal. Very large airplanes burning jet fuel going in a variety of directions. The tarmac swarming with luggage tractors, fuel trucks, buses, service vehicles. Eventually I walk through the terminal, thousands of people from all over the world, milling and moving. Finally I get to the street or parking garage outside, where hundreds of cars and buses burning gas and diesel jockey for space, park, or drive away. And this has been going on, at this scale, for only about the past 50 years.

Conduct the following thought experiment. Un-invent computers and telephones. Un-invent nuclear energy and genetic engineering. Forget about nanotechnology, television, and radio. Let go of the electrical grid. Just invent cars and fast airplanes and put millions of people into them each day to travel somewhere else for business or pleasure. You will change the world, as indeed we did in the past half-century. How, I wonder in the airport, will we survive were this all to go away or to become prohibitively expensive? Some believe this is the future, as oil supplies go over the peak.

Should this happen, the changes will be big indeed. The twentieth century was the century of cheap oil, at least for those in developed industrialized nations. No more profound discovery has ever been exploited. A mature oil field is still amazing, costing only about $3 a barrel to retrieve the oil from the ground. What could be better? How could the impending end of the supply of conventional crude oil be good news? Because it comes just in time, almost as though earth, or Gaia, knows that it is time to bring this lucrative but wasteful era to an end.

Tossing tons of waste into the atmosphere is the first habit to break. "The greenhouse effect comes from digging up fossils . . . and setting fire to them. We humans have been doing this seriously for two hundred years. Setting fire to long-extinct life-forms is the human race's primary industrial enterprise. . . . This thriving business underwrites almost everything we do" (Sterling 2002, 279).

A second reason why declining oil supplies could be a good thing is the obvious one, turmoil in the Middle East. Some 75 percent of known future oil reserves belong to OPEC nations, mostly in the Middle Eastern countries of Saudi Arabia and Iraq. Saudi reserves are more precarious than is commonly believed, as we shall see. Iraq is very uncertain, in the short run because of the obvious mess that has been made there and in the long run because its actual reserves are unknown and will be subject to ongoing disputes into the foreseeable future. U.S. oil is now in permanent depletion, while non-OPEC discoveries have lagged for two decades. Non-OPEC supplies will peak no later than 2015 if they have not already. All reasonable assessments of future oil supplies assume that the United States will move from importing 60 percent of its oil from OPEC to importing 75 percent by the mid 2020s. Even veteran business leaders like Charles Shultz, a government official for presidents Richard Nixon and Ronald Reagan, respond to this likelihood as follows: "How many more times must we be hit on the head by a two-by-four before we do something decisive about this acute problem?" (Lovins 2005, xv). Chief among the problems created by overreliance on a single cartel for energy is the assumed need to protect these resources militarily.

Reducing reliance on OPEC oil might be a good thing for the United States and the world, but what about OPEC? The harsh reality is that oil has tended to be a mixed blessing for the countries that have it. It has led to tremendous wealth, to be sure, and having oil is better than not having it. At the same time it has contributed to tremendous inequality between rich and poor, has slowed rather than speeded up development of additional industry in affected areas, and it has contributed to high levels of corruption. A shift now to more diverse energy alternatives would enable a gradual rather than a sudden falloff in income for oil producers, a scenario that is more stable and hopeful than any other.

The end of cheap oil will also encourage U.S. communities to reconsider their design. A century of building communities that require one to get into a car and drive a few miles in order to buy a loaf of bread or pint of milk may have been fun while it lasted, but is counterproductive in so many demonstrable ways. Not the least of these is the now proven correlation between obesity and suburban living. Having a half-acre lawn is apparently less healthful than walking city streets, and this is about to change.

If the end of cheap oil could be good news, the great news is what is coming next, nothing less than a reinvention of our energy future. All signs point to this happening in the next quarter century or so. Taken together, the innovation and alternatives that will be needed will probably represent the largest business revenue opportunity ever.

WHAT THE PEAK IS AND WHY IT IS NEAR

To understand why the peak is near, we need a little history. In the 1950s oil geologist M. King Hubbard published a now famous forecast that U.S. oil production would peak in the early 1970s. He demonstrated that production from any given field increases fairly rapidly after initial discovery, slows down as you near the peak when half the oil has been pumped out, then declines at a faster and faster rate once the halfway point is reached. Makes perfect sense. And his mathematical calculations hit the mark when, indeed, production from U.S. oil fields peaked in 1971–1972.

He did not have the data to make a similar prediction for global oil supplies but pointed out that the same phenomenon was, quite naturally, inevitable. The only question is when. The evidence is increasing that the answer is sooner than later, perhaps very soon. This is controversial, we must acknowledge. The U.S. Department of Geological Services insists that reserves are sufficient to get us to nearly 2030 before the peak. In their annual energy outlook to 2025, the ever optimistic U.S. Energy Information Administration in 2004 forecast that by 2025 world demand for oil would increase from 80 million barrels a day in 2004 to 120 million, that in response OPEC would increase its oil production by 80 percent, and that prices would fall by $3 a barrel compared to 2010. Exactly how this is all supposed to happen is not clear, but obviously not everyone thinks oil is near its peak.

More and more experts and industry leaders believe it is, however, and are willing to say so publicly. As long ago as 1999, Mike Bowlin, then chairman and CEO of ARCO and chairman of the American Petroleum Institute said, "We've embarked on the beginning of the Last Days of the Age of Oil. Nations of the world that are striving to modernize will make choices different from the ones we have made. They will have to. And even today's industrial powers will shift energy use patterns. . . ." (Lovins, 2).

As the price per barrel of oil climbed to $50, then $60, and finally $70 in 2005 before retreating, attention to the question of whether the peak is near also reached a crescendo. As 2005 came to a close OPEC announced that oil was expected to stay at $50 a barrel in 2006, apparently the new floor for oil prices. Several books by leading researchers and oil market experts were sounding the warning that presumed oil reserves may be exaggerated, that what is left is far too concentrated in one volatile region of the world, that demand for oil would continue to increase as China, India, and other developing nations ramped up their energy use, and thus that the gap between supply and demand would inevitably widen. Most of these warnings are made in dire tones, as though the end is near. Some celebrate the impending end of the auto-centered suburban culture, while others wonder how we can survive.

Despite near record high prices in 2005, most oil companies are experiencing declines in production. ExxonMobil produced 4.7 percent less in Q3 2005 than they did in 2004. Shell's production fell 11 percent. These real production declines were masked by the record profits they made. Moreover, almost all oil companies are experiencing dramatic problems replacing the oil they sell with new reserves. In 2004 ConocoPhillips could replace only 65 percent of the oil it sold, while Shell replaced only 45 percent of its oil and gas.

Projections of dramatically increased oil demand and use in coming decades assume major new discoveries and slow depletion of current supplies. But discovery of new oil peaked in 1960 and has declined ever since. This is despite far more sophisticated technology and high price incentives. The idea that there are a number of Saudi Arabias just waiting to be discovered is not credible. The controversial Arctic National Wildlife Reserve oil field is projected to contain enough oil to satisfy a few months of global energy needs at best. And this is considered a major field.

Saudi Arabia has been reassuring but secretive about its oil reserves and the performance of its currently producing fields. However, energy investment banker Matthew Simmons blew the lid off Saudi secrecy when he revealed in his 2005 blockbuster, *Twilight in the Desert*, that Saudi reserves are far more uncertain than is acknowledged, and their record of new discoveries does not match expectations. In addition, Ghawar, the greatest oil field of all time, is nearer its peak than was generally believed. At the same time, massive use of twenty-first century drilling techniques and information technology are already in use, yet neither new discoveries nor production are increasing as promised.

So the consensus builds that a peak is near. Alan Greenspan, no wild-eyed radical, even got into the act in a 2005 speech to the Japan Business

Federation. "We will begin the transition to the next major sources of energy, perhaps before midcentury, as production from conventional oil reservoirs, according to central-tendency scenarios of the U.S. Department of Energy, is projected to peak. In fact, the development and application of new sources of energy, especially nonconventional sources of oil, is already in train."

True, Greenspan suggests the relevant time frame is 50 years. Others think the time is now. Retired U.K. energy geologist and energy expert Colin Campbell projects a global peak in 2007, while asserting that the most read-ily accessible oil already peaked in 2004. He says, rather ominously:

> The world is not about to run out of oil, but it does face the end of the First Half of the Age of Oil. . . . That [age] opened 150 years ago when wells were drilled for oil on the shores of the Caspian and in Pennsylvania. The cheap, convenient and abundant energy it sup-plied led to the growth of industry, transport, trade and agriculture, which in turn allowed the population to expand six-fold exactly in parallel with oil. . . . The Second Half of the Age of Oil will be char-acterized by a decline in the supply of oil, and all that depends upon it. . . . That speaks of a second Great Depression and the End of Economics as presently understood. (Fenderson 2005).

Who is correct? Has the peak already occurred, will it happen in 2010, or is 2027 a safer bet? Even if 2030 is the year we reach the halfway point, there is not much time to prepare. When the peak in supply is reached, demand will also be at a peak and rising. Whenever that is, we will have about a decade to replace half of what is currently done with oil. So we had better get started soon.

ALTERNATIVES ARE NOT ALTERNATIVE ANYMORE

So, we are going to run out of fuel? Despite the foregoing, the short an-swer is no. There are large, even gigantic supplies of unconventional fossil fuels such as oil that may be available in ultradeep offshore wells, oil con-tained in tar sands primarily in Alberta, Canada, oil contained in moun-tain shale deposits, particularly in Colorado, and what might be called digital oil, or oil that may be more effectively retrieved from current fields as the result of enhanced information and 3-D visualization techniques.

All together, these unconventional oil sources are estimated to be about 10 times the presumed supply of conventional or cheap oil. So what is the problem?

Nearly half the world's unconventional supplies are in tar sands. However, it takes a great deal of energy to recover it, which produces tremendous amounts of carbon dioxide even before it has been turned into useful fuel. Oil shale was considered a savior during the energy crisis of the 1970s, but the environmental degradation that comes with mining it made the boom short-lived. Now, Shell is investigating a means of cooking the shale in place. If the Shell approach is successful, it means that shale will be a viable source in the future.

So if we are thinking of the near future and possible revenue, there will be a great deal of investment in efforts to exploit these oil sources. At the same time, despite all the money that will be involved, events are likely to bypass unconventional supplies. As a Saudi oil minister once pointed out, just as the Stone Age ended before we ran out of rocks, the oil age will end before the oil is gone.

There are several energy alternatives involving gas. Reserves of natural gas, primarily methane, are estimated to be enough to last for 50 years. The challenge with gaseous methane is that it must generally be liquefied in order to be shipped, which is expensive. When methane trapped in ice crystals deep beneath the ocean or deep in permafrost, known as methane hydrates, is factored in, supplies are estimated as enough to last for thousands of years. The challenge is retrieving, liquefying, and shipping this gas, which has not been done with hydrates yet except experimentally. It is frozen and does not flow, so some means of melting it in place for recovery is necessary. Various methods are being tried. Technological feasibility, cost, and fears of massive climate change that the release of all this frozen gas might trigger will be factors in whether hydrates ever becomes feasible as a fuel source.

Coal is also in the energy mix. Used mostly to provide electricity, coal is historically dirty to burn as well as dangerous and environmentally costly to extract. Clean coal technology is touted these days, along with the possibility of liquefying coal to make synthetic gasoline, something done as long ago as the 1930s. Carbon emissions are very high when using coal however, and unless carbon can be economically sequestered by burying it, coal will not grow as an energy source much beyond its current use despite efforts to promote it. China is building coal-fired electricity plants today but has also established ambitious yet achievable goals for switching to renewable energy and its own large supplies of natural gas. Prospects that global warming will eventually lead to efforts to curb carbon mean that the day will come when coal faces a carbon tax as well as the cost of sequestration, making it more expensive than alternatives.

To summarize, unconventional and nonrenewable fossil fuel alternatives will likely be developed, but it will be costly and environmentally damaging. These sources may be cheaper than some of the sustainable energy alternatives in the short run. Their chief perceived advantage is that they challenge no current paradigms, in that the technologies for extraction, and especially for refinement and end use are known and for the most part familiar.

At the same time, it takes no crystal ball to see that sustainable energy alternatives are in position to grow substantially in the next several decades. Most renewable energy alternatives are already doubling every two to three years. These alternatives include both the production of energy and the saving of energy through conservation.

SUSTAINABLE ALTERNATIVES

Conservation

It has been true for decades that if you want to make money on energy, a good way is to save it. This is true even for individuals. After the first oil shock of the 1970s, per capita energy use in the United States declined from 1973 to 2000, after which it began rising. By 2005 the United States was using 47 percent less energy per dollar of economic output than it had 30 years earlier. More significantly, in the early 1970s oil was used for everything from heating homes to making electricity to driving cars. Now, the use of oil is pretty well confined to transportation and the petrochemical industries, massive though those are. In the United States the amount of electricity generated by oil has declined from one-fifth in 1973 to less than one one-hundredth today. Homes heated by oil have declined from one in 4 to one in 10.

It costs only $12 to save a barrel of oil, while its costs several times more to buy it. Simple engineering, not rocket science, is all it takes. The cost of energy efficient technology and design is falling rapidly. Compact fluorescent light bulbs have decreased in cost from $20 to $2 in two decades. Window coatings to insulate and reflect heat, on-demand water heaters, efficient electric motors, and energy saving appliances of all kinds have plummeted in price in recent years. It is not difficult to save energy, yet construction standards, government policies, and decades of habit still encourage energy waste rather than conservation.

Transportation remains a primary arena for conservation opportunity. Automobiles are notoriously inefficient when it comes to burning gasoline. About 1 percent of the energy contained in the fuel actually moves the passengers and 87 percent of the energy is simply lost to heat, friction, braking, and so on. This is incredibly inefficient when we know how to build lighter, safer, and smarter vehicles. Similar numbers apply to trucks and a revolution in trucking is near, as first more energy efficient fleets are built and eventually much greater information intelligence in the entire shipping enterprise leads to enhanced efficiency.

Biodiesel

Biodiesel is made from a variety of vegetable oils, animal fats, and even waste grease. It is a one-for-one replacement for regular diesel, meaning it can be used in current diesel vehicles with little or no modification. It is also carbon neutral, in that the plants that are mostly used to make it remove as much carbon from the air as that put into the air by burning the resulting fuel. It is biodegradable, nontoxic and obviously renewable so long as you can re-grow the plants. The best plants are soybeans and palms. The promise of biodiesel is such that former IT entrepreneurs such as Martin Tobias have gone into the business, creating Seattle Biodiesel. He points out that European refineries already produce a billion gallons of biodiesel from rapeseed, and wants to be a leader in a new U.S. industry.

Ethanol

A synthetic fuel made by distilling corn or sugar has been around for decades and is a major source of energy in some countries such as Brazil.

Used as an additive to gasoline rather than a pure transportation fuel, it can cut gasoline usage substantially. While so far it has not been economically competitive, at higher oil prices it is becoming so. Two new developments show promise. One is the use of less costly plant waste such as corn stalks as the source for obtaining ethanol, or using switch grass, a natural grass of the great plains. Such woody material produces twice as much ethanol per ton than corn. A Canadian refinery for turning cellulose into ethanol is being completed with a production cost of about $67 a barrel oil equivalent. Such development, if widespread, would boost not only the energy business but also agriculture. The other development, being driven by biotech pioneer Craig Venter among others, is the search for a genetically engineered bug that would convert cellulose to sugar much more cheaply. Venter is also, by the way, seeking a genetic solution to turn algae into a means for extracting hydrogen from water.

Solar Cells

Solar accounts for only .05 percent of the world's power generation. But solar installations are growing at double-digit rates, and they hold promise for bringing electricity to less developed parts of the world without the need to supply any fuel infrastructure. For the industrially advanced world, solar cells promise a clean and local source of electricity. Solar cell technology is still two to three times more expensive than fossil fuel generated electricity. But a possible future is emerging where solar leaps to the head of the line, certainly in terms of industry growth potential given a small beginning base. Current technology is allowing the manufacture of superthin films of silicon, bringing down the price to the point where, for example, at least 20,000 homes in the United States derive at least some of their electricity from solar cells as do 70,000 homes in Japan. The city of Shanghai announced in 2005 a goal to install photovoltaics on 100,000 buildings in that city alone. Where an electricity grid does not already exist, local solar power is already cheaper than building a grid.

Solar becomes even more feasible because of breakthroughs that are in development. Inexpensive "amorphous silicon" and semiconductor alloys are enabling the manufacture of cells 100 times thinner than conventional cells, and flexible enough to be applied as a coating on windows, roofing tiles, even skylights. Beyond these materials lies the promise of semiconducting pigments, nanoscale carbon fullerenes, and organic semiconductors capable of being sprayed onto a variety of surfaces with an ink-jet printer. These relatively fragile surfaces are then protected with a polymer coating.

A variety of companies are already selling flexible solar cells that are relatively efficient even in low light, and can be applied to virtually any surface from roofs to walls to cars and trains. Solatec sells flexible solar panels to incorporate into roofs of hybrid cars, feeding power straight to the car batteries and improving mileage by at least 10 percent. They also have a patent-pending design for a solar airplane ideal for unmanned vehicles. Konarka and ECD Ovonics have similar products. Italy unveiled the first solar train in 2005, with photovoltaic (PV) cells on the roof providing electricity for the train's various on-board systems. As one of the inventors of flexible, spray-on solar cells, Ted Sargent from the University of Toronto said, "If we could cover 0.1 percent of the Earth's surface with [very efficient] large-area solar cells, we could in principle replace all of our energy habits with a source of power which is clean and renewable" (Lovgren 2005).

Wind

An interesting threshold was passed in 2005 when wind generated electricity became cheaper than the alternatives for customers of some utilities in Oklahoma, Texas, and Washington. Customers who had opted to purchase "green power," even though it was more expensive at the time, suddenly were finding themselves paying less than other customers. Imagine that, wind is cheaper. Currently it costs about a million dollars per megawatt to install turbines and related equipment, but once installed the energy is available, forever, allowing for equipment maintenance.

The fact that wind is intermittent has been one conventionally cited reason that more wind energy has not been built to date, since it has been assumed that an equivalent amount of energy storage or substitute must be available when the wind is not blowing. But the wind is always blowing somewhere, and by adding intelligence to the energy grid this problem has been rendered unimportant. Even better is to build combination wind and solar farms; when the wind blows is it likely to be stormy, and when it does not blow it is likely to be sunny. The overall efficiency of the energy farm doubles and actually becomes more reliable than conventional power stations. More exotic are proposals to build flying rotors that hover permanently in the stratosphere, sucking up the jetstream and sending energy to the earth via cables or microwave. Want to leverage the future? Get into wind.

Ocean Power

In a year 2000 report the U.K. Marine Oversight Panel asserted that converting less than 0.1 percent of the ocean's energy into electricity would supply the total world demand five times over. More conservatively, the World Energy Council says that ocean waves could supply twice the current world consumption of electricity. Could this be part of the energy future? Wavegen, a Scotland-based company installed the first shore-based system to commercially produce electricity from wave action. At the same time, AquaEnergy Group is promoting an intriguing solution. In their system a network of floating buoys anchored a mile or two offshore would use pistons that rise and fall with the action of the ocean swells to generate power. Some of the electricity generated onsite could be used to run equipment separating hydrogen from seawater, thus supplying the fuel cell industry as well, a double benefit. A demonstration project producing a megawatt of electricity will be in place in 2006.

Smart Grid

Electricity generation is one thing. Distribution is another, and the current system of transmission lines was built on the assumption that all electricity would be generated at very large central plants, and then distributed via a hub and spoke system. The system is inefficient, not just because of the energy drain of sending electrons long distances, but because it is difficult for the system to adjust to changing demand patterns, much less to intelligently use energy for greatest efficiency. Progress has been made in this arena, but over the horizon is a vision in which a truly intelligent grid both accepts and feeds electricity to millions of local sites, local sites that generate electricity with solar or fuel cells for example, and use smart appliances. Imagine dishwashers, refrigerators, and air conditioners that can sense when the prices are best, when the grid is over- or under-used, and adjust their operation for the greatest benefit of the home owner and of the public grid at the same time. Intelligent distributed generation is another growth industry.

Hydrogen

The hydrogen economy has been heavily promoted and sharply criticized. Hydrogen is obviously abundant, but bound up with other elements, either oxygen in water or more complex molecules in natural gas, oil, and coal. Thus to be used as an energy carrier it must first be obtained, then stored and transported. These technical challenges, and the fact that some oil executives and people such as President George W. Bush have suggested that hydrogen is a long-term future option lead many alternative energy advocates to dismiss hydrogen as either a nonserious option, or too far in the future to matter. In a certain sense we entered the hydrogen economy when we switched from coal to oil and gas, because in doing so we went from burning mostly carbon atoms to burning one-third carbon and two-thirds climate-friendly hydrogen atoms. But an even more intensive hydrogen future has intriguing possibilities.

The first real commercial application breakthroughs are now coming in the use of hydrogen fuel cells. Not in transportation yet, but in local electricity generation. Quiet, clean, mechanically simple hydrogen-fueled power stations are beginning to compete with conventional local power stations such as gas turbines. UTC Fuel Cells is one company that has developed fuel cells sufficient to supply a medium-size office building. At this point such units are being used mostly as backup power sources, for example at data centers. Today fuel cell stacks cost more than natural gas turbines, but operate at greater efficiency while producing much less carbon dioxide. Warm water produced as a byproduct of fuel cell use can be used in heating systems. We can expect to see significant growth in installations of fuel cells for local power generation, particularly as fuel cells begin to use thin plastic membranes as the basic electrolyte structure, as well as finding ways to apply a platinum catalyst in ever-thinner coats, thus reducing costs. Eventually such fuel cells will migrate to homes as backup power generators, and then appliances themselves.

The holy grail in fuel cells remains the automobile. The market is enormous, the environmental advantage is obvious when you recall that most oil is now used in cars, and the possible benefits are systemic.

Consider this question. How many hours per day do you drive your car—one or two hours perhaps? What does your car do the rest of the time? Collect dust and evaporate a little gas. What could a fuel cell car do while it is not being driven? Generate electricity. Imagine a world in which you drive to the office and plug your electric car in, not to charge it up but to add to the power grid for the building. Drive home, and plug in to help power the home. Parking lots might charge a fee for conventional internal combustion cars but pay the fuel cell cars to park there, selling the electricity to the deregulated power grid.

If future vehicles are made of lightweight carbon or ultralight steel, as is proposed, then an SUV, weighing half of today's vehicle, would need only a 35-kilowatt fuel cell and one-third as much hydrogen as is commonly assumed. This means cheaper fuel cell manufacture and no need for breakthroughs in hydrogen storage technology. Somebody is going to produce such a vehicle. A million jobs hang in the balance.

In an ideal future world solar or wind or ocean energy farms would extract hydrogen from water, which would then be distributed to be used in fuel cells. If such an infrastructure could be built, a nearly pollution free energy system can be envisioned. Two immediate challenges are raised in response to this scenario, namely the storage of hydrogen and the cost of re-doing the gasoline distribution system. ECD Ovonics is but one company solving the storage problem with high pressure tanks, or with metal hydrides that soak up hydrogen, then release it with a slight increase in temperature. As for rebuilding the infrastructure this is a phony issue. Simple observation reveals that every gasoline station is replaced or completely rebuilt on about a 20-year cycle. The first hydrogen filling stations have already been built. If hydrogen became the transportation fuel of the future, the cost of rebuilding fueling stations would be not much greater than the annual cost of replacing them, anyway.

The use of fuel cells in transportation is tantalizing, both economically and environmentally. There is little doubt that automobile use will grow around the world. There is also no doubt that this increase will contribute greatly to greenhouse gases even with the substitutes for conventional oil that are most often mentioned. It is time to change this technology, and soon.

The hurdles between present reality and such a change are huge, however. The price of operating a gasoline or diesel engine is still many times cheaper than a fuel cell. And the durability of fuel cells is still a matter for research since replacing fuel cells too frequently would be cost prohibitive and an environmental problem. Safety is another fear, although researchers can demonstrate pretty conclusively that hydrogen storage, transport, and use can actually be as safe or safer than gasoline.

Nonhydrogen Fuel Cells

Research is also being done on fuel cell technologies that do not use hydrogen and require less expensive materials in the cells themselves. The direct methanol fuel cell is the primary contender. Although so far less efficient than hydrogen fuel cells they have one obvious advantage. Remember the discussion of the vast stores of methane assumed to exist. If methane is obtainable at costs and energy expenditures that are less than extracting hydrogen from water, coal, or natural gas, it will make more sense to go in this direction. Methane as a long-term solution depends entirely on whether technology can be developed to tap the frozen methane hydrates. It is a methane fuel cell that will come on the market to power laptop computers in 2006.

Batteries

Not really a renewable resource, batteries nevertheless are part of the future. Rechargeable batteries of the type being developed by the nanotechnology researchers, capable of virtually instant recharging, and used in plug-in hybrid cars are another alternative. A high efficiency electricity grid fed by decentralized and renewable power generation may make plug-in cars a more attractive option in the future.

Nuclear Energy

It is true that nuclear energy, construction of the plants aside, is climate friendly in that no greenhouse gases are emitted. But it is slow and very costly to build compared to decentralized and renewable alternatives, not to mention the still unresolved issues of waste. Thus, it is very unlikely that nuclear will be a major new energy source in coming decades, although a few reactors will be built.

Exotic Energy of the Future

Out there over the horizon may be a paradigm shift in energy. Concepts like zero-point energy, magnetics, gravitics, fusion energy using Helium-3 mined from the moon, and others are on the fringe, yet may lead to breakthroughs some day. These are usually considered the "home run" breakthroughs. That is, most experts assume quite logically that the next energy era will consist of many kinds of energy technologies combining to replace what now is done mostly by oil. A single breakthrough that changes everything is considered unlikely.

There may be one home run breakthrough that is more probable than all the others, however, a breakthrough that would revolutionize the energy industry overnight. As was pointed out by Mark Anderson in a 2005 speech to energy executives and reported in Strategic News Service, oil is nothing more than organic matter put under heat and pressure for millions of years. But so is diamond, which results simply from greater heat and pressure and longer periods of time. Apollo Diamond of Boston, among others, now can make diamonds in a week, diamonds that are indistinguishable from natural diamonds and that cost two-thirds less.

Given this development and what is happening in nanotechnology and biological research, it becomes increasingly probable that some discovery, accidental or deliberate, will result in a new way to produce energy.

THE BIGGEST BUSINESS OPPORTUNITY EVER

The convergence of the end of cheap oil and need for viable alternatives to be developed quickly combine to create perhaps unparalleled opportunity.

When we think of the transition to the next energy era, the temptation is to search for a single alternative, an energy source or discovery as dramatic as was oil two centuries ago. But this is unlikely. More realistically a combination of many alternatives must be developed and soon. Thus there are opportunities for many companies, large and small, to play a role in the coming era of new energy. Most of them will involve renewable energy, and many will involve decentralized or localized energy. And it will be lucrative, with many opportunities for innovation and exciting business possibilities.

Hydrogen generation, fuel cell development and manufacture (both methane and hydrogen fuel cells), solar cell development, solar manufacture and installation, wind turbine construction, and wind farm development are but a few of the business opportunities likely to flourish in coming years. This is in addition to all of the activity that will take place with traditional energy sources as the oil peak is reached and prices go higher and higher.

Beyond these opportunities will be tremendous enterprise in development and manufacture of lighter and more efficient vehicles, rethinking and retrofitting of community design for greater energy and transportation efficiency, green architecture design and construction, and the simple manufacture of more bicycles and motor bikes.

Energy is central to modern life and the future. The coming of a new energy era will either be an overwhelming challenge for an oil-based industrial world, or an amazing opportunity, probably some of both. In 2005 the world spent about $4 trillion on oil. Imagine the investment and growth potential if a portion of this spending is shifted to nano-solar rooftops, wind turbines, various fuel cell technologies, biomass fuels, hydrogen capture and storage, and so on. How will we acquire the energy to sustain seven to eight billion people on the planet at a reasonable living standard, while not so damaging the ecosystem as to make life too difficult or even impossible? The way that we answer this question has implications worldwide and for future generations.

PART II

HOW TO PREDICT THE FUTURE OF YOUR BUSINESS OR CAREER—AND PLAN FOR IT NOW

ASSUMPTIONS FOR THE FUTURE

We often think of the future as something that just happens to us. But we also know that the future is created by the choices we make. In fact there are only two things in life that you can't avoid. Death and choices. By choosing, you create one future. By not choosing you create another.

We also think of the future as quite unknowable. We invest lots of money and effort in attempts to know, but we usually fall back on the idea that the future is unpredictable. Yet there are aspects of the future that are knowable, and given our apparently innate ability to anticipate the future we ought to make an effort.

Something will happen in the next few years that will surprise everyone living today. It always does. Trend watchers learn early to beware the permanent trend. How do you respond to the unexpected, in your life or in your business? You respond according to the values that you hold. Thus, knowing your values, and clarifying them in your enterprise assists people as they adjust to an uncertain future.

Finally, the future creates the present, as we have already learned. Spending time developing a shared vision is a critical step in discovering a winning strategy. When you think of vision as simply a description of a preferred future state, and then work backward from that to what you ought to do next week, there is no concept that is more practical.

To summarize, four assumptions about the future stand out as critical if you wish to shape it.

1. The future is creatable, so you have choice.
2. The future is knowable, so you need to look.
3. The future is unpredictable, so you need values.
4. The future creates the present, so you need vision.

THREE-CONE MODEL FOR PREFERRED FUTURE PLANNING

If your goal is shaping the future you need more than basic assumptions. You also need mental models for creating the future. Three simple questions about the future form just such a model.

1. What is probable?
2. What is possible?
3. What is preferred?

These three questions drill down a level beneath the broad question of your image of the future. All future explorations and all planning activities are, in a sense, efforts to answer these three questions. The answers are shuffled and sorted and examined so that you can eventually identify what you need to be learning and doing right now, in the near-term.

The three questions were developed into a simple and elegant model for futuring when I was assisting a state as they developed a 50-year vision for transportation. The Three-Cone Model for Preferred Future Planning (Figure II.1) can be applied to any time horizon, long-term or short-term.

You begin in the present and look to the future. In the center is the cone of "probable futures," the realm of forecasters, planners, and predictors. Within this cone are two things. First are the events, trends, and developments that are likely to occur in your environment. These are the driving forces that you predict, get ready for, and leverage. In addition, within this cone is what your company will look like if you just keep doing what you do. Some of what you see there will be great, but some of what is probable if you just stay the course will not be great.

FIGURE II.1
Three-Cone Model for Preferred Future Planning

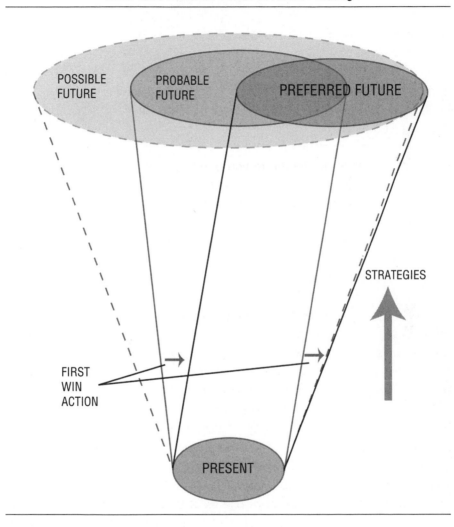

The largest cone is of "possible futures." It contains all future possibilities both in the external environment and in the company. What are developments that are not likely to happen but might? What are the things you might do, if you could? This cone has a dotted line for a boundary, because there will always be possibilities that we do not see, and cannot yet imagine. This cone is the realm of science fiction writers and inventors.

The third cone is that of the "preferred future." Inside this cone is your description of where you want to be at some point in the future. You might label it a vision, or you might use some other term to capture the idea. The preferred future cone might be placed anywhere on the Three-Cone map. But in my experience with hundreds of teams who have described a preferred future vision, it always lands right where you see it in Figure II.1. When people describe their preferred future, the resulting cone overlaps the probable and possible cones. That is, the vision is likely to include some things that will probably happen, along with some things you are already doing and wish to keep doing. The vision is also likely to include some things that are possible, but not probable. These parts of a preferred vision are not likely to happen, unless you do something different.

Look carefully at the preferred cone, and you will discover one other vital element. A bit of the preferred cone lies not just beyond what is probable, but *outside the possible future*. This is the part of your preferred future that others will say is impossible! It cannot be done. Great visions have at least some aspect that will be such a stretch that it appears impossible when the journey begins.

The elegance of the Three-Cone Model includes a simple way to capture strategies and actions. When the lines that create the cones are drawn back to the present, the real task of shaping the future becomes clear. You want to shift your trajectory from the probability cone to the preferred cone. If you just keep doing what you do, you will get what you always got, right down the middle of the probable future. If you want to head toward the preferred future, you have to make a shift, and that means you have to do something new.

A colleague, Bill Hainer, was the first to label these actions the "first wins." These are the initial actions, taken early, celebrated when successful, that have the effect of beginning to steer you in the direction of the preferred future. Hainer was a boater and often compared this notion to navigating. A boat captain takes a fix on a distant goal—an island, a beacon, a harbor—and heads toward it. At some point wind and current and obstacles will cause the boat to drift away from the desired trajectory, a new fix on the destination will be taken, and a mid-course correction will take place.

The Three-Cone Model illustrates a powerful notion about first wins and mid-course corrections. Small changes early in the journey lead to big differences as you approach the preferred future. Imagine a 10-year time line from the present to the preferred future. Notice that the longer you wait, the bigger the gap between the probable future cone and the preferred future. People in the organization often say they love the destination, but want to wait a while to get started, since everyone is so busy right now and time and resources are short. But the longer you wait the bigger the gap between the probable and the preferred may grow, and thus the more time and money and energy it will take to make the shift later.

The final feature of the Three-Cone Model is the concept of strategy. First wins get you started. But a journey to a preferred future takes a while, and that usually means the necessity of grouping some actions together into longer-term strategies. These are the sets of activities that must be coordinated and maintained over an extended time, usually at least a couple of years, in order to keep heading toward the preferred future.

If you simply make changes without a preferred future image, you will keep busy. You will get somewhere. But as the Cheshire cat in *Alice in Wonderland* pointed out, if you don't know where you're going you'll probably end up somewhere else. Successful action leads somewhere. Deciding on the somewhere is the province of strategic vision, which requires that you get into the future, the subject of Chapter 5.

CHAPTER 5

Plan for the Future—But Hedge Your Bets

Consciousness precedes reality, and not the other way around.
> —Vaclav Havel, president of the Czech Republic,
> speaking to the U.S. Congress, 1990

Nothing happens unless first a dream.
> —Carl Sandburg, n.d.

GETTING INTO THE FUTURE

In the late 1990s I was invited by the CEO of an organization to visit with his management team on their annual planning retreat. I asked what he hoped I would accomplish through my presentation and discussion. His answer was, "My management team keeps thinking that if we wait just a little while longer, things will 'get back to normal.' I want you to convince them that the rapid change we are living with is the new normal, and that there is no going back. Waiting just makes things worse." This CEO had a team standing in the present, and gazing longingly backward. As they did so, decisions on new initiatives were postponed, and the organization was living in the past.

Systems theorist Russell Ackoff (1999) described reactive, inactive, and pre-active perspectives for managing and planning. To be reactive is to focus on the past. Looking backward you can see the best practices that have worked in the past, you can remember when everything was simple and easy, you can recall your core values that have stood the test of time. You can recognize this perspective in your own organization when you hear people say things like, "That's not the way we do things around here," when a new idea is proposed. Or you might hear, "Why can't things work like they used to?" Or people might simply refuse to change, even when the need seems urgent. Understanding the history of an organization and retaining the best practices and values that will make sense in the future can be critical to sustaining a culture of success. The world is constantly changing, however, and companies have to be nimble. Looking backward is not the optimum perspective.

A second position is to stay focused on the present, the dominant position of most people in organizations. People say, "Look, the past was great and all that, and the future will be interesting, but I am too busy to look up just now. I have work to do, so leave me alone." People in this inactive perspective tend to be very busy. Not much of consequence would happen, in fact, if most of us were not in the present, focused on the present, most of the time. When this view is the dominant planning perspective in your organization, you will hear people saying things like, "The future is unpredictable anyway, so let's stay focused on what we can do" and "Why concern ourselves with ideas that won't be feasible anyway?" Ignoring the future to stay focused on the present will not suffice in the long run. Inertia and deep pockets might sustain you for a while, but not forever.

Any astute leader knows that one must look up and out and attempt to prepare for the future. You become pre-active when you define planning as making an accurate prediction of the future, and then preparing for that future better than anyone else.

When predicting is your only planning perspective, you struggle not only with the problem of making accurate predictions. There is an interesting second problem, which is the causal loop between our actions and the future that we end up with. This may not sound all that dangerous—reacting to our predictions is the whole point, isn't it—but the process may be one in which you never get where you want to go, because you don't ask the question of what that destination is. Finally, people typically make predictions by extrapolating current trends into the future, based on logical assumptions—more of this, less of that. Such simple extrapolation of the present into the future may help people see certain options, but more often than not it produces plans designed *to create a more efficient past rather than a truly new future.*

PREFERRED FUTURE PLANNING

With one simple step, a quantum leap if you will, you can discover something unique and potentially powerful, *preferred future planning*. In this perspective you leave the present behind, place yourself in the future, and look back at the present and the past (Figure 5.1).

Until a time machine is invented, you cannot do this in reality, so you time travel to the future as a mental exercise. This is actually something you do, all the time, for example when you daydream about being on a beach somewhere next month. You have time traveled to the future and taken a look at a preferred image. If that image is attractive enough, you might do something now to make it likely to become reality.

If you can place yourself figuratively in the future you can look around and take note of its features. Equally important, from this future you can look back at the present, whatever the time gap, and see things that you ought to do, back there, to end up here. This is called backward planning. It offers a powerful additional view from which to discover both strategies and first win actions and it will be explored in detail in Chapter 10. For now, we want to focus on what you see when you time travel to the future. It is that dangerous term, vision.

FIGURE 5.1
Preferred Future Planning Begins in the Future

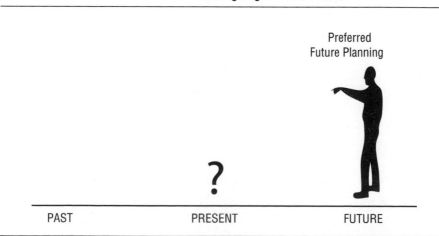

PAST · PRESENT · FUTURE

WHAT PREFERRED FUTURE VISION IS

Since you have control over what you see when you place yourself in the future—you are making it up after all—you might as well make it a future that you want, your preferred future. A vision is a compelling description of your preferred future. Such a vision is typically expressed in words, sometimes with pictures or other symbols. The level of detail may vary from a few words to the very complex.

Whole Foods describes its preferred future in this statement, which they post on the company web site and call their Declaration of Interdependence. Lengthy, detailed, it serves as a clear description of the preferred future state of the company. It concludes with these words:

> Our Vision Statement reflects the hopes and intentions of many people. We do not believe it always accurately portrays the way things currently are at Whole Foods Market so much as the way we would like things to be. . . . The future we will experience tomorrow is created one step at a time today.

A vision does not have to be long or complex. Disney, for example, still aims "To make people happy." Novo Nordisk says simply that they "strive to be the world's leading diabetes care company, and each of us takes this vision personally." Southwest Airlines adopted a famous vision in 1978, which has guided them ever since: "Provide safe and comfortable air transportation . . . at prices competitive with automobiles and buses . . . making the airline a fun, profitable, and quality experience for all."

Are these just so many words in the wind? Many people think so, dismissing vision as nice to have on the wall but not essential for success. However, in the early 1990s Jim Collins and Jerry Porras conducted a study, asking 170 business leaders to name the 20 most "visionary" companies. Collins and Porras then invested one figurative dollar in each of the 20 companies in the mid 1920s. Over the period observed the visionary companies outperformed the Wall Street average by a factor of 50 (Vision Thing 1991). Later, when they studied successful companies for their book, *Built to Last: Successful Habits of Visionary Companies* (1997) they concluded that the visionary companies had outperformed the market by a factor of 12.

Donald Povejsil, retired vice president for corporate planning at Westinghouse put it this way (1989, 42):

> My whole concept of what strategic management is all about has changed. Ten years ago I believed the key to strategy was tightly reasoned analysis of markets and competitors. . . . I have come to believe that the entrepreneurial vision, the visionary part of the process, is what's most important. Vision is the linchpin of strategic management; there's no other conclusion you can reach after a while.

Where enterprises have developed, affirmed, and used a compelling vision, there have been phenomenal results. One client of mine developed a 15-year vision and strategic plan, and after 2 years counted millions in additional revenue and a "quantum leap" in organizational openness to change. Another company had worked for three years on continuous quality improvement with some success. But once they stopped to develop and commit to a vision of what they wanted to accomplish through quality processes, they leaped from 40 percent on-time delivery of service to nearly 100 percent on-time delivery.

Magnetic

However expressed, a vision has to be magnetic. People in your company ought to feel drawn toward the vision. A vision about which people say, "Who cares," is not sufficiently attractive. If you are going to create and communicate a vision, you want something about which people say, "Wow, that makes a difference. I would like to work on that." Steve Jobs, known primarily as a brilliant product designer, described the vision of Apple in 1980 as "to make a contribution to the world by making tools for the mind that advance humankind." The language may have been a bit awkward, but the image was compelling and many creative people were drawn to it.

Transformative

A powerful vision ought to have reach, ought to represent a future in which things would be transformed for the better when the vision is accomplished. To reach for a vision is to leap beyond the routine of today. When McCaw Cellular Telephone helped launch the cell phone revolution and said their vision was, "Imagine no limits," they communicated an abstract vision with great reach, a vision that would be transformative if accomplished. This reach has to be long-term. Ten to thirty years for an audacious vision is not too long.

Flexible

A useful vision must be flexible. It ought to change as your company moves toward it, because the world will constantly change. In this sense a vision is not so much a statement written on stone. Instead it is a continuous conversation, in which people are constantly asking, "Where are we going, why do we want to go there, where are we now, and what are we doing next?"

Leverage Point for Change

As we have said previously, if you want to change your organization, change its image of the preferred future. Both folk wisdom and research affirm that we tend to move toward and become like that which we think about. If your company's image of the future is confused, you will probably behave in confused ways. If your image is clear, compelling, and flexible, you will be more likely to behave in clear, flexible, and strategic ways.

With You in the Present

The vision is of the future, but it is not really "out there." Instead, think of the vision as a holistic field of energy that surrounds you in the present. You have to see the vision happening, in the mind's eye, all the time.

Undergirded by Values

While a vision tells you where you want to go, behind it are values that tell you why you want to go toward the vision and how you want to behave as you proceed. Articulating these values clearly and overtly will greatly aid in the pursuit of a vision.

WHAT PREFERRED FUTURE VISION IS NOT

It is not unusual to confuse vision with other similar concepts.

Not Annual Problem Solving

Annual planning is known to virtually every U.S. organization. Such planning typically centers around comparisons to last year's goals, the identification of current problems, and the development of some new goals based on these two analyses. Such planning does not result in a vision.

Not Predictions

A very common error regarding vision is to assume that vision is somehow the prediction of the future. Predictions, explorations of the probable and possible futures, even deep analysis leading to foresight provide you with a sense of the future playing field. This is valuable information to have when deciding on a direction. But they are not the direction itself.

Not Mission

There is frequent confusion between the concepts of mission and vision. Vision is a description of the preferred future. Mission is a clear description of the organization's purpose or reason for being, today. Since mission is a more familiar concept, I have seen many companies use mission as a substitute for vision when they are best kept separate. As organizations try to be more future oriented, I have seen them rewrite their mission statement to reflect their ideal of what they would like to be rather than what their purpose is. When this happens they end up with a mission that neither describes the preferred future very well nor captures what the organization is about. People read it and say, "This is not really who we are." Only confusion results.

Not Wishful Thinking

Though a vision describes the preferred future, it ought not be just a list of wishes. To be a powerful, magnetic force the vision must communicate a refined, heartfelt sense of what people yearn for, tempered by an understanding of the forces shaping the future.

HOW TO CREATE THE PREFERRED FUTURE

Does vision come from a powerful individual, the company founder perhaps? Or does vision come from the collective of people who make up the organization? Either can work. What matters is whether the vision is shared, understood, and committed to. The process of creating vision, or "preferred futuring," involves a variety of activities that share these characteristics.

Explores the Probable, Possible, and Preferred Future

The process must at some point enable examination of and play with our three future questions: What is probable in the future? What is possible? What future do we prefer?

Done "in" the Future

To really experience the preferred future, and from that to articulate a vision, the process must enable you to step mentally out of the present and into the future. In other words, at some point you must somehow travel in time to the future and describe it in the present tense, as though you are actually seeing it.

Combines the Past and Future

If you don't go far enough back in memory and far enough ahead in hope, your present view will be limited. A complete effort to think through vision will include a look at your history, so that you can decide upon the best features to take with you into the future.

Provides "Look Back" Perspective

If you succeed in stepping into the future, from that perspective you can "look back" at today. By asking, "What did we do back there (the present) that enabled us to end up here (the preferred future)" you can acquire a powerful insight into strategy and action planning.

Creative Tension between Future and Present

An effective vision process, and vision statement, produces creative tension as people compare where they are now to where they want to be. The tension has to be just right—too much and people will get discouraged, too little and people won't care.

Process Is Critical

Ultimately the goal of a vision-based planning effort is not to create a wonderful plan. The vision is to serve as a star to steer by, not a map to be followed. Rather, the goal is to foster a daily stream of wise decisions, in the pursuit of strategic directions. The organization where this occurs will have vision as its linchpin.

ISN'T VISION THE PAST DECADE'S MANAGEMENT FAD?

Few management concepts last long, probably because of the need of both managers and management consultants to appear to have fresh ideas. So it is true that the word "vision" has often been replaced with substitutes in the past few years. Collins and Porras, who were writing about how to "build your company's vision" in 1996, transitioned to the concept of the BHAG—big, hairy, audacious goals—and conflated that with vision. Later, Collins (2001) addressed the secrets of moving from good to great, and focused particularly on the hedgehog principle, or discovering the one thing that you do best. Hamel and Prahalad (1989) moved from vision to a new term, "strategic intent," intended to communicate both a longer-range view and a sharper strategic focus. And the 1990s even saw "the vision thing" take on something of a ridiculous aura in the political arena. So the term is used with caution. Yet it is an everlasting concept. Without a vision, the people perish, says the Old Testament psalm.

PLANNING FAILS MOST OF THE TIME

We have argued here for visionary, preferred future planning. Yet readers know that planning fails more often than it succeeds, and some experts estimate that it fails to make a noticeable difference in organizations as much as 65 percent of the time. Very often it is a major waste of time. Why does planning fail? What are the pitfalls and how can they be overcome?

One critical reason for failure is misunderstanding what strategic planning is, and how it differs from the kind of foresight and futuring being presented here. Strategic planning is typically defined, in practice, as deciding what is feasible within the assumed resources of the organization. Literally, just as a team is getting into considering the future someone says, "Wait a minute. Why waste our time discussing things that are not feasible? Let's just make a list of problems and available resources, decide what is feasible to work on, and be done with it." And very quickly there is no future in the future plan, only limited problem solving.

Preferred future planning, on the other hand, can be understood as pursuing what is possible and preferred within the resourcefulness of the organization. The rush to feasibility is avoided for as long as possible. In the final analysis nothing will happen that is not feasible, so why worry about that at the beginning? Make a decision on a preferred future direction, and feasibility will take care of itself.

Earlier we noted that strategic planning is frequently confused with strategic decision making. Strategic planning is the making of plans to implement strategic decisions. Those decisions come best out of a futuring process that produces foresight, and then a decision on long-term direction reflected in a vision. The critical difference is between plans on the one hand and decisions about direction on the other. Mission, strategies, and first wins may be written down in a plan at some point but mindlessly producing long sequences of action steps on paper, without careful and fresh assessment of direction, gets you somewhere, but most likely not into the future.

There is evidence for why planning fails so often. John Kotter (1995) identifies eight major mistakes that lead to failure in organization transformation efforts. The mistakes are worth noting, particularly the top three.

1. *Not establishing a sense of urgency.* Change is more likely to happen when people feel they must change. That is why, as a futurist, I have most often been invited to consult when organizations believe they are facing more than routine change. Something big is afoot, it is feared, and so it is time to take a wide-angle and long-term view. Without a sense of urgency, even a magnetic vision may not be compelling enough to create change.

2. *Not creating a powerful enough guiding coalition.* Rarely can one or two people drive a vision and lead a change. Eventually a core team is necessary, and that team of committed people has to grow.

3. *Lack of a compelling vision.*

4. *Undercommunicating the vision.*

5. *Not removing obstacles to the vision.* Barriers 3 through 5, in one way or another, deal with the need for a clear and compelling vision that is created, understood, shared, and worked toward.

6. *Lack of small winning steps*, successfully completed and celebrated.

7. *Not consolidating improvements and making further change.*

8. *Failing to institutionalize new approaches.*

Barriers like these will undercut any vision and subvert any future oriented planning effort. But to Kotter's list we can add additional pitfalls. The most fascinating is the least expected.

• *Tendency of preferred future planning to increase uncertainty, when the opposite was expected*, particularly early in the process. Why do individuals and organizations attempt to plan for the future? Because the future seems uncertain, and it is believed that some effective planning will make the future more clear. What happens instead is quite simple. Explorations of probable and possible futures lead to discovering trends and developments, threats and opportunities that no one knew about. Options increase in number. Confusion reigns. I have noticed that planning teams, caught in this increasing confusion, often believe that if they research just a little longer everything will become clear, and, magically, a direction will be obvious and no one will actually have to decide anything. This is a vain hope. Clarity can be increased by analysis activities such as organizing uncertainty into plausible scenarios. But ultimately clarity depends on making a decision on a direction. The direction is clear, but the data leading to that decision may never be as clear as hoped for. Becoming comfortable with correct uncertainty rather than seeking incorrect certainty is simply a part of the process.

- *Early experience of IFD disease*, idealization followed by frustration followed by disillusionment. Early enthusiasm wanes as the daily grind continues, resources fall short, leadership changes, and all the other standard barriers to success get in the way. What seemed so alluring when the vision was agreed to now seems more distant than ever. When this happens the whole process can be experienced as disempowering rather than rewarding. The key to fighting this pitfall is in the regular accomplishment and celebration of small victories.

- *Misunderstanding what a "shared" vision means.* Sharing a vision does not mean creating it in isolation, and then selling it to everyone. Typically some persuasive communication is part of the picture, but a shared vision is one that people have some role creating and can see themselves in.

- *Seeing the vision as just another task to accomplish* rather than as the heart of the organization. The vision instead has to be lived fully and continuously. Staff meetings have to regularly ask the question, "What are we doing to accomplish the vision?"

- *Assuming that once people understand and share the vision they will automatically know what to do* to accomplish the vision. Instead, deliberate efforts are necessary to assist people in creating the small steps and adjusting their daily work to move toward the vision. Otherwise it becomes words on the wall that bear little relationship to what happens each day.

THE 15 PERCENT RULE FOR PREFERRED FUTURE VISION

One organization that I worked with established a 15-year vision. They were involved with natural resources, and thus a very long-term vision made sense. At the time they thought they were being quite bold. Two years later they made a qualitative and quantitative assessment of progress. How far had they come in the first two years? Their conclusion was more than halfway. What did this tell them? That they were making good progress, to be sure, but mostly that they had been too timid with their vision.

Some years ago when there existed a computer company named the Digital Equipment Corporation (DEC), a manager in the company decided that it would be a good idea to network all the computers. Personal computers were new. The whole concept was that each person would have one and that each would be independent. This particular manager could see an advantage if they all could communicate and set out to convince people that it was a good idea. After months of trying, he received the go-ahead to attempt a network, and at its height DEC had more than 60,000 computers networked, in the days before the public Internet. Recalling that experience the manager made a wonderful observation. "When we started," he said, "we knew at most about 15 percent of what we needed to know to accomplish the vision. We just believed it would be important to try."

From that story I composed the "15 percent rule for a compelling vision": *If you know more than about 15 percent of what you need to know about how to accomplish your vision, your vision is too timid.* Working on a project called Atlanta Vision 2020 I cited this rule in an op-ed piece. A consultant friend traveling through Atlanta read the piece and called me up. "How do you know it is 15 percent," he asked. Suppose the number is wrong. Suppose that if you know 50 percent of what you need to know, then your vision is too timid. Perhaps it is 75 percent. What seems certain is that if you know 100 percent of what you need to accomplish your vision, there is little doubt that you are overcautious. Yet planning teams, focused on feasibility and on not looking foolish, pull back on the vision again and again until it is so bland they are sure it can be accomplished. But no one cares whether it is or not.

There is a wonderful story about the power of vision that occurred almost six centuries ago. It is a true story, and one can travel to Spain to see the evidence for it. In the year 1401, on July 7, a group of people gathered in a place called the Court of the Elms. They were a religious order, the Order of Seville. There in the courtyard they made a solemn vow together: "Let us build a church so great that those who come after us will think us mad for having attempted it."

And so the cathedral of Seville was built. It took more than 150 years, which those taking the vow knew would be the case. Would you be willing to embark on a vision that you knew would take several generations to accomplish, was much larger than yourself, and that your neighbors would think you crazy for trying?

CHAPTER 6

Be Your Own Futurist
and Focus Your Organization on the Future

Skate to where the puck is going, not where it's been.
—Wayne Gretzky, 1990

Exceptional leaders cultivate the Merlin-like habit of acting in the present moment as ambassadors of a radically different future, in order to imbue their organizations with a breakthrough vision of what it is possible to achieve.
—Charles Smith, 2005

A friend of mine, now a business consultant, was once employed by IBM. Attending a sales meeting in Nashville, Tennessee, he used some spare time to drive out into the countryside, to see what rural Tennessee was like. As he drove, he came to a railroad crossing. This crossing had no flashing lights or dropping cross arms, just a simple railroad sign on a wooden post next to the road. On the post beneath the sign, however, someone had tacked a hand-painted warning. "The train takes exactly 21 seconds to pass this crossing—whether you're on the tracks or not."

This sign captures four alternative responses to the future.

1. Get on the tracks, locate the train that is barreling down at us, and try to stop the future. In the early 1990s, as I was hired by a health care association to assist them in long-range planning, I asked the CEO what the members were looking for. She replied that many of them were hoping to find a way to get on the tracks and stop health

111

care reform from happening. As the record from the era shows, they and their colleagues in health care, both providers and insurers, basically succeeded in stopping the train. In another sense, however, they merely succeeded in postponing the future and making the changes to come more difficult. If stopping the future is your only response, all the time, the odds are against you.

2. Get on the train, take a seat in the passenger car, and adjust to wherever the train goes. Adapting to the future is, naturally, the response that occupies most of our time. This response, while useful and necessary, does not do much to shape the future.

3. Get on the train and take the same seat in the passenger compartment. This time however, we'll hire an expert to predict where the train is going, so that we will be prepared for the destination before anyone else is. This is the predict and prepare response. We are smarter passengers, to be sure, but still we sit and wait for the train to arrive wherever it is going.

4. Shape the future. This involves getting on the train, moving up to the engineer's compartment, and playing a role in steering or controlling the train. Imagine an array of tracks before you, and the ability to decide which track to follow and at what speed. This is creating the future.

You might object that in real life we have little control over the train. But that all depends. In your career, your family life, your neighborhood, or local community you almost certainly have more control than you imagine. Which track should you take? How fast should you go? These are personal decisions. In larger, more complex systems, like your company or your nation, your influence may be more diffuse and shared with many others. Yet the choice between adapting, predicting, or shaping is still relevant. History is full of stories of individuals who made a simple choice that turned a large system down a new track. Rosa Parks comes to mind, someone who by simply refusing to move from a seat in the front of the bus to the back turned an entire nation down a new road.

Are you a leader capable of focusing your organization on the future, and taking it down a track toward fundamental, transformative change? To shape the future you must become a futurist yourself.

Four ingredients stand out as critical to focusing your organization on the future, and leading transformative change. These characteristics are:

1. Being future oriented.
2. Being vision driven.
3. Being collaborative.
4. Being strategic.

These ingredients represent characteristics and behaviors of leadership that go beyond management. They are skills and perspectives that you can learn and apply in order to lead an enterprise in transforming its nature, its function, its condition. Introducing a profile of 50 leaders *U.S. News & World Report* concluded that "Their leadership styles are as varied as the organizations they manage. . . . But what they *all share is a clearly articulated vision, measurable results, and in the words of one management guru, Big Hairy Audacious Goals*" (2005, 19, italics added). In other words, these are necessary components of shaping the future.

BE FUTURE ORIENTED

Anyone who has led an organization, or merely worked in one, knows that the urgent always seems to crowd out the important. The same is true for organizations as a whole, often full of people who can see the train coming, but who are simply too busy to do anything about it. The transformational leader has to work deliberately to overcome this inertia, by being future oriented.

We are capable of remembering the past and anticipating the future, while we live in the present. As Ed Lindaman once said, "If you don't go far enough back in memory, or far enough ahead in hope, your present will be impoverished." To be future oriented is to make a conscious effort to live in the past, present, and future simultaneously. This sounds impossible, but what it suggests is making an effort to expand and inform your perspective. Effective and future oriented leaders work to see further and with a wider angle than do leaders who merely adjust to whatever happens.

Being future oriented means asking the three core questions about the future in a continuous conversation to sharpen your understanding of the future and to expand your vision. One of the key leadership tasks in making the organization more future oriented is to create opportunities for this conversation to happen. One leader, for example, required that new managerial hires meet with him regularly for their first year, with the assignment to bring to each meeting an entrepreneurial idea taking advantage of a future trend or development. In this way he was attempting to train them to be futurists themselves.

At the same time, future oriented leadership is not an effort to discover what to do "out there, in the future." Instead, the focus is on understanding the future in a way that makes it more obvious what you ought to do here and now. In other words, the ultimate focus is on strategic decisions in the immediate future, informed by an enhanced view of the longer-term future. Thus, to be truly future oriented is also to be action oriented.

Finally, being future oriented does not mean ignoring the past. What worked before? What has changed? What have we lost that we would like to regain? What lessons have we learned or forgotten? In our daily hurry we often don't take time to remember, and to be future oriented is to remember as well as to look ahead.

BE VISION DRIVEN

Komatsu is a Japanese manufacturer of construction equipment, established in 1921. It produced its first bulldozer in 1947. In the 1970s, languishing in sales and market share, the leaders of Komatsu proposed a new vision, captured in two simple words, "Encircle Caterpillar." Perhaps no better two word vision has ever been written.

With this clear and simple vision driving both strategy and daily work, in the ensuing 20 years Komatsu succeeded in taking on Caterpillar. Although they never surpassed Caterpillar in global sales of construction equipment, they became the leader in Japan and second in the world. Vision was the key.

The vision that creates such movement is not boring, not a mere extrapolation of the present into the future. It is not simply saying that next year we will sell 10 percent more than we did this year.

When leadership teams and companies sit down to consider a corporate vision, they almost always err on the side of creating a vision that is too modest, rather than one that is too bold. The fear when developing a preferred future vision is being seen as crazy. This is despite the fact that for years business literature has been full of stories and exhortations to set stretch goals, or to find the one thing that can drive the company to be great.

In the late 1980s I was invited to speak to 100 high school students attending a two-week summer leadership program. Managing the school that year was an old classmate of a young entrepreneur, whom he had also invited to speak. The entrepreneur's name was Bill Gates and his company was called Microsoft. The two of us, Bill and I, spent three hours one evening perched on stools in front of the hundred kids, exploring the future and what the world might be like in the early twenty-first century.

Years later, when speaking on the topic of business vision I would sometimes have people say that the idea of vision was all well and good when the world moved slowly, but just look at Microsoft, they would say. Microsoft has no vision, they just follow the inventors, pick off the best ideas, and outperform and outcompete everyone else in delivering the idea.

Hearing that, I would recall what Gates had told the kids that evening in the late 1980s. Technology development cycles were such, he said, that it was difficult to say precisely what technology would be available beyond about 36 months. So, he said, he was only imagining the world of 2001 when he guessed that the following might be possible. Paraphrasing the story as I remember it, "I get up in the morning," Gates said, "and my first thought is, 'Today I would like DaVinci.' I turn to the wall and ask for DaVinci, and all the pictures in the house turn into DaVinci. With some time before I have to go to work, (yes, we will still be going to work) I decide to have some recreation. I sit down in my virtual surround display, where I take a short simulated walk in the Grand Canyon, accompanied by two celebrities. Being celebrities, their personalities have been turned into software, and I can carry on a simulated real time conversation with them, as though they were really there. Perhaps my virtual surround unit will also enable me to experience other senses than sight and sound, such as smell or even touch. Now," Gates continued, "I don't know for sure that computing technology will develop fast enough for all of that to be possible, but that is the kind of computing world I imagine."

So I always smile when people tell me vision is nice, but Microsoft survives without it. Not that many years later Gates built a house where the pictures can do just what he imagined. The virtual surround entertainment center is not here yet. And Microsoft more or less missed the impact of the Internet for longer than they should have, so fixed were they on the vision of a computer on every desk, with independent, boxed software for each computer.

Today Gates suggests in speeches that all great visions meet the laugh test. That is, people initially laugh at great visions, and if no one laughs, your vision is not pushing the boundary far enough.

The vision-driven, transformational leader works, then, to counter the tendency to be too timid or to focus on feasibility instead of possibility, by challenging people to step up to their wildest dreams. The goal is to create the right amount of dynamic, creative tension between where we are and where we wish to be. When they created Google, founders Larry Page and Sergey Brin thought big from the beginning. "They could organize not only the Web, itself a massive undertaking, but all the world's information. And they could make it available to everyone. . . . While still at Stanford, 'we thought we should actually digitize the libraries'" (LaGesse 2005, 26).

It is important to understand as well that the vision is not so much a point in time or a fixed destination but a conversation. Ask people how what they are working on is taking the enterprise toward the vision. Ask them what needs to be reconsidered or stretched further. Howard Shultz, CEO of Starbucks coffee is one of the great visionary leaders of our day. "You don't start out by saying, 'I'm going to create the world's largest coffee company.' You start with a sensibility that says, 'I'm going to create a different kind of company'" (Meyers 2005, 50). In this pursuit Starbucks has continually expanded and updated its vision, adding for example music sales, and becoming involved in efforts to support environmentally sound ways of growing coffee, and supporting clean water worldwide. Shultz is famous for his open conversations one-on-one with Starbucks associates and in employee meetings, seeing ideas and feedback and commitment.

Ultimately it is vital to recognize that shared vision is the linchpin of leadership. With a powerful and shared vision, actions take on a purpose and direction. Without vision, actions just keep you busy.

BE COLLABORATIVE

Both world and business history is replete with stories of effective, visionary leaders who were not particularly collaborative. But this lone eagle style of leadership is diminishingly effective in our hypercomplex, interconnected world. There are few enterprises today where noncollaborative leadership will suffice. This is recognized even in corporate advertising, as when Chevron produces an ad featuring a letter from David O'Reilly, chairman and CEO discussing the upcoming transition in energy, in which he says, "At Chevron, we believe that innovation, collaboration and conservation are the cornerstones on which to build this new world. We cannot do this alone" (*The Economist* 2005, 7).

When leadership is non-collaborative, effective leadership may be seen as a matter of communicating the leader's ideas and directives to employees, so that they know what to do. In a collaborative leadership paradigm, leaders work to enable alignment in thinking and acting at all levels of an organization.

A variety of skills are necessary to be collaborative. These include dealing with complexity and uncertainty in an honest way, learning to network, and learning to negotiate interests in order to help resolve differences.

A rare skill among senior leaders is the ability to facilitate group interaction in order to mobilize action. This was demonstrated most effectively by Alan Lewis, president and CEO of Grand Circle Travel, on a management team strategic retreat that I addressed in the summer of 2005. Grand Circle is a company whose vision is to be "the world leader in international travel, adventure and discovery for American travelers—providing impactful, inter-cultural experiences that significantly improve the quality of their lives."

During the retreat I watched as Alan used collaborative skills to empower and motivate the leadership team. Facing his team, who were seated around small tables in groups, Alan laid out a key component of the company vision, and then noted that it was time to take the next huge step. "Propose five things we can do next year that will get us there," said Alan. "You have 15 minutes." The groups worked quickly and within 15 minutes had proposals to make. What happened next was genius.

The first group to report provided their summary. When they had finished, Alan asked the entire gathering, "On a scale of 1 to 5, how bold is their plan, 1 = not bold enough, 5 = very bold? Everyone hold up one to five fingers. Okay, about a 3, okay but not as bold as we need to be. We need to push it further!"

Using this simple, collaborative methodology Alan was teaching his team two critical lessons, first that they had a role to play in the future of the company, and second that it was vital to the company to be bold, if it is to maintain its market leadership and achieve its vision. A little more of what they had always done was not good enough.

Such collaborative skills are often seen, in management and leadership research, as strengths of women as leaders but not of men. This is not a trivial difference. Introducing a special report in *Fortune* (2005, 144), writer Janet Guyon noted, "The difference is not merely one of personal quirks. After 25 years of interviewing CEOs, I can say definitively: Men love to lecture, women like to listen." A growing body of literature suggests that women "collaborate, listen, and try to build teams. Men are more apt to direct, blame others, and use the vertical pronoun" (144).

Is this a difference that makes a difference? Apparently so, as the collaborative, team oriented approach seems correlated with an enhanced ability to see the big picture. Leaders with this style see crises coming before their counterparts. Thus, man or woman, it is advantageous to be collaborative, if your goal is to focus your organization on the future. Note, however, that being collaborative does not equate to being indecisive.

Meg Whitman, CEO of eBay, is frequently cited as among the most powerful of women in business, extremely future oriented, and the epitome of collaborative leadership. Despite that, when describing the 2005 acquisition of Skype by eBay, Whitman described the process in the following way: "When we evaluate acquisitions, we always ask three questions. Are there synergies? . . . Second, do we like it as a standalone business? And finally, what's the cultural fit? I went to London three times to talk with Skype's management, and I decided that these are very direct people who view the world the way we do. I decided to go ahead. We bought it in October" (*Fortune*, 146). Note Whitman's combination of collaboration, initiative, and clear responsibility for the final decision.

When used as a means of avoiding decisions, collaboration can be a nightmare. Writing in the *Wall Street Journal* Jared Sandberg tells the story of a technical writer's boss: ". . . his boss made so few decisions that no one ever knew what she wanted. Yet she had to be involved in every decision that she never made" (2005, B1).

Whether collaboration is more naturally the domain of women or men as leaders is immaterial. All organizations are rich resources of ideas for creating the future. Collaborative futuring skills tap these resources most effectively. The two most important collaboration skills are asking questions and listening. Organizational consultant Peter Senge (1994) points out that the most effective way for a leader to create shared vision is not, as you might expect, to persuasively communicate or sell the leader's vision. Instead, the most effective tactic is to ask people what their vision is, both for the organization and themselves, and to talk about how the two connect and how they compare to the leader's vision and the company vision. A genuine act of asking and listening can be more powerful than the most persuasive speech.

BE STRATEGIC

Finally, to be your own futurist you must be strategic. There are several important aspects to being strategic, but the first focuses on the word "be" rather than the word "strategic." That is, to be a futurist as a leader means seeing strategy as a way of being rather than as a task to be accomplished. How often have you participated in a "strategic planning" session that concluded with a set of key actions and assigned responsibilities? Everyone returns to work, and after some period of time has it occurred to you that the "strategic action" that was agreed to is languishing, everyone being so busy? So a meeting is called and everyone recommits to follow-through. This time, a few things are done and some progress is made, before key people become distracted by the urgencies of the day. Perhaps a second reminder meeting is called somewhere down the line. This sequence is an all too typical experience.

What is happening is that people are viewing the strategic work as an interruption of their actual work. People understand and agree that the strategic plan is important, but there are pressing matters that have to be dealt with before the additional work in the plan can be taken on.

To be strategic is to move to integrate daily work with strategic work, so that over time they become one and the same. If one is "being" strategic, then virtually all work activity can be seen and is interpreted for how it contributes to the agreed upon strategic directions. Rather than the strategic work being seen as an interruption of daily activity, daily work that is not strategic is seen as the interruption. This is a complete reversal of common experience.

If you are being strategic you will find yourself doing things like envisioning a web of actions that can be constantly updated and refined, as you respond to changing conditions. You will continually anticipate future happenings to be in a position to seize them as opportunities. Attempting to see the whole picture, you may try to think through unintended and second-order consequences of strategic actions.

Robert Austin, co-author of *The Broadband Explosion* (2005) pointed to the value of anticipating second-order consequences: "A second insight: A lot of the benefits from the broadband explosion will probably arise from non-obvious, second-order effects—things we can't see clearly right now. The human tendency in trying to predict what will happen in the future is to extrapolate in a straight line from today. So we imagine doing more of what we do with communication today when we have more bandwidth. But that's a mistake . . ." (Grant 2005).

When the success stories of Komatsu or Canon or Honda are told, it is often noted that they take the long view, in comparison to their global and in particular U.S. competitors. This is a matter of *being* strategic, not of composing 20-year strategic plans. They succeed at being future oriented. They are driven by a long-term vision, whatever language is used to capture that idea. They are collaborative in finding ways to involve everyone deeply in pursuing the vision.

In fact, for an enterprise to succeed in the twenty-first century, it must pursue 10 strategic directions simultaneously, and it is to these 10 vital characteristics that we turn in the next chapter.

CHAPTER 7

Ten Key Practices
of Future Oriented Enterprise

The good-to-great companies understood that doing what you are good at will only make you good; focusing solely on what you can potentially do better than any other organization is the only path to greatness.

—James Collins, 2001

In November 2005 an internal e-mail from Bill Gates and a memo from Chief Technology Officer Ray Ozzie, then being circulated within Microsoft, were revealed, announcing that it was time once again for that great company to reinvent itself. In the beginning, Microsoft had played a key role in reinventing computing with the idea of a computer on every desk, each with its own independent software. The model was fabulously successful as we all know, but in 1995 Bill Gates broadcast to his employees a famous message that the World Wide Web was the new key to success and that all Microsoft products and services needed to reorient themselves to be web-friendly. Criticized for coming a little late to this realization, Gates was nevertheless applauded for turning a now giant company on a dime, and it was not long before the company dominated the critical Web browser market by integrating it into its basic products.

Still, standalone software on now web-connected computers remained the cash cow, and while products operated ever more seamlessly with the Web, the basic model did not change as much as it might have. Now, however, the threat and opportunity appeared more serious yet. Software was, the 2005 memos said, shifting to the Internet, and it was time for

121

Microsoft to make another revolution in its business, this time to build strategies around Internet services.

Microsoft was going to pivot in a new direction once again. Peter Drucker argued that if you are not rethinking your business about every 36 months in today's rapidly changing world, you don't understand the times you are living in. Some business advisors recommend even shorter cycles for small businesses. "The one advantage that a small business has over a very large company is that it can reinvent itself and move very, very quickly," says Jeff Hyman. . . . it's very important for a small business to leverage that one advantage by reinventing itself, and I think every year or two is not too frequent" (Virtual Advisor, 2004).

But what kind of enterprise can do that? What would be necessary characteristics of a flourishing enterprise as we enter deeper into the twenty-first century? There are 10 such characteristics.

MAKING STRATEGY A WAY OF LIFE, NOT A TASK

With few exceptions in most enterprises, as we have noted earlier, the urgency of daily activity tends to crowd out longer-term strategic thinking. It takes strong and effective leadership, and continual reinforcement to turn the daily work in a new strategic direction. Over time, the goal needs to be to merge the two streams of work, the strategic and the daily, into an integrated whole, so that most tasks each day can be explained and experienced in terms of how they are moving the enterprise in a strategic direction.

LEVERAGING RAPID CHANGE

The game is *not* managing or coping with change, but leveraging the rapid change all around us so that we move in preferred directions. When faced with rapid change, our tempting reaction is to circle the wagons, in the hope that at some point things will settle down and either return to an earlier state of affairs or become more clear in terms of what the future is demanding. The automobile business is a good example. Producing hybrid vehicles at a tepid pace while claiming there was not that much demand for them meant that when gasoline prices doubled in 2005, there was inadequate hybrid inventory compared to possible demand for most fuel efficient vehicles. The leading hybrid maker Toyota reported lengthy waiting lists.

Attempting to leverage the rapidly changing energy environment, Ford announced an initiative to redesign and retool in order to produce 250,000 hybrids a year by 2010 and to offer hybrid models for half its fleet. We can be sure that powerful voices within Ford were making a counter argument, that if Ford just waited a while, gas prices would come down, as they always have, and the market would return to normal. But Ford leadership was doing more than simply positioning the company for a more expensive world of fuel. Ford was also leveraging rapid change in order to move in the direction of their well publicized and apparently sincere vision of becoming the greenest of the car companies. We will know by 2010 whether Ford has made the right bet.

RESTRUCTURING FOR THE LONG RANGE

Imaging the longer-term is the starting point. Intel has a 10-year vision to put hundreds of cores on a single processor, enabling it to put dozens of arrays on a single chip devoted to individual functions, such as graphics, voice, or video. Long-term intentions like these and additional ones such as "humanizing" computing are expressed in white papers that describe the world of 2015.

After years of experience with community vision, Kenneth Hirsch of Hirsch Architects concluded in a keynote to the American Institute for Architects (2005):

> The expression of a vision for 200 years is becoming commonplace. It's not about what it will be; it's about what you want it to be. Expressing what you want for the future influences the choices you make today. . . . Future leaders will be skilled facilitators empowering others to express their vision of the future. I challenge all architects to express what they want for the future and to have that vision prominently placed as a daily reminder of where they are headed. The larger the vision, the more powerfully it pulls you into the future.

Neil Golightly, the aptly named director of Sustainable Business Strategies for Ford, captured the essence of restructuring for the long range in an interview, saying, "As Bill [Ford] put it in our newest sustainability report . . . we're a 100-year-old company that wants to reach 200" (Elkington and Lee 2005).

Restructuring for the long term does not mean waiting or doing things slowly and deliberately. Just the opposite. The key strategy is to become agile and quick. Agility means adapting swiftly to take advantage of emerging opportunities and to rapid changes in the business environment. This kind of agility has become "the sine qua non of organizational fitness." In fact, in giving its CIO 100 Awards in 2004, *CIO Magazine* noted that "agility" was named as a specific core strategy of 85 percent of the winners, who came from 18 different sectors of industry, nonprofits, and government agencies. "'Agility is in our governance, our project management, our vendor management and in the ways we set up funding,' says Marilyn Delmont, CIO of the city of Chandler, Arizona, . . ." one of three municipalities honored (Prewitt 2004).

Agility means cultivating in people a desire to embrace change rather than avoid it, using techniques to observe triggers of change in the external environment, and structuring internal systems and processes to be able to adapt swiftly. Specific tactics will vary by industry and may include flexible manufacturing systems, continuous training, more participative management, and rapid information gathering cycles with customers.

GETTING BEYOND CONTINUOUS QUALITY TO SUSTAINED INNOVATION

Meeting global standards for quality and making continuous improvements in quality have become givens in the competitive global environment. They represent the entry fee to play the game. In the twenty-first century it is sustained innovation that will provide an edge. This innovation must come in three domains according to Gary Hamel (Sparks 2005), who has established the new Management Innovation Lab at the London School of Business. These three are "institutional innovation, which includes the legal and institutional framework for business; technological innovation, which creates the possibility of new products, services, and production methods; and management innovation, that changes the way organizations are structured and administered." It is management innovation which has historically produced the greatest improvements in business productivity, according to Hamel. Golightly (2005) at Ford summarized their view: "We're focusing on innovation because meeting twenty-first century needs in innovative ways is the surest way to business success."

RE-LEARNING FOR KNOWLEDGE-BASED WORK

Continuous learning has become a given. An increasing percentage of U.S. jobs may require scientific, technical, and/or advanced thinking skills. All jobs require the learning of new knowledge, continuously. We undertrain our work force today.

The future will see a day when people are paid as much to learn as they are to work. The learning we refer to is particularly that designed to add deep knowledge value to employees, to products, and to systems. Such learning goes beyond simple training, which is also necessary, to enabling people to become more flexible and independent. To be continuous is to offer any time anywhere access to learning through online classes, web casts, learning communities, online forums, and more.

MANAGING INTERCONNECTEDNESS

If there is anything that has increased in the past 50 years it is complexity. More stakeholders must be included in more decisions and old boundaries have dissolved. In fact, the continual dissolving of boundaries is a useful image for understanding today's trends. This puts a premium on skills of collaboration and communication, which may not be primary strengths of key people, but can be learned.

TAKING SERIOUSLY A MULTICULTURAL SOCIETY

Leaders must step up to the challenge of creating a common culture of opportunity and success for all sectors of the society. This requires innovation but above all commitment. First generation immigrants currently make up nearly 12 percent of the U.S. population, the highest level since the immigration wave of the first decade of the twentieth century. More than 50 percent of post 1970 immigrants to the United States come from Spanish speaking Latin America, more than half of those from Mexico. These numbers are large but still mask the impact on the work force. In the 1990s, half of new wage earners were immigrants who had migrated in that decade. Even more dramatic, 8 of 10 men entering the labor force in that decade were new immigrants. Since U.S. immigration, legal and illegal, has only increased in the first years of this century, we can assume these numbers are holding steady in terms of new workers.

Interestingly this challenge now extends to many other regions as global migration has brought multiculturalism to Europe, Australia, and now Asia. Australia, though accustomed to a high percentage of immigrants in its population, now sees increasing diversity in its immigrant population, as does Europe. Ease of travel, economic disparities, the ability to stay connected via modern communications, local labor shortages, and family dynamics combine to encourage migration. Barring draconian anti-immigration policies, global migrations will only increase, and thus the challenges of multicultural societies will intensify.

TAPPING EXPENSIVE MATURE WORKERS

We explored earlier the dramatic, even discontinuous aging of societies and work forces around the world, particularly in the mature industrial nations. Current practices in human resources are based on the assumption that older workers will and ought to be moved out of the work force. But the time is coming very soon when the game will change and the challenge will be seen as keeping these workers on the job. Innovation in flexible work arrangements along with flexible pay and benefit packages will be needed to accomplish this. Initially seen as expensive, it may in the long run be less expensive to employ the untapped 20–25 percent of the population in their elder years within the next two decades, rather than allowing this resource to lie fallow. The net gain is potentially greater when one considers the tiny retirement savings and fragile retirement benefits supporting this large group. Work will also enable them to participate in the consumer economy. Beyond these basic needs is the possibility of life extension, which will change the profile of the employed even more.

USING GREEN POWER

Twenty-first century enterprises that succeed for the long term on something other than inertia will almost certainly be those that have made it a strategic priority to be "green." Future markets are going to demand "innovation around fossil-fuel efficiency, lower greenhouse-gas emissions, a decreased ecological footprint, greater safety, lower congestion, less noise, more equitable access to mobility . . . and that's just a partial list" (Elkington and Lee 2005). Going green will thus meet market demands, and lead to greater efficiency in the process.

Enterprises of all kinds are moving on the issue of sustainability and in particular reducing their emissions of greenhouse gases and reducing their overall environmental footprint. Harvard University, for example, has begun a university-wide Green Campus Initiative (2005) to reduce emissions and footprint, and has invited other universities to join them. They targeted building design, construction, renovation, procurement, landscape, energy, water, waste, emissions, transportation, human health, and productivity as factors for improvement. A single university project may sound rather inconsequential, but taken together the environmental footprint of U.S. universities alone surpasses that of many small nations. The initiative established six sustainability principles worth noting:

1. Demonstrating institutional practices that promote sustainability.
2. Promoting health, productivity, and safety.
3. Enhancing the health of campus ecosystems.
4. Developing planning tools.
5. Encouraging environmental inquiry.
6. Establishing indicators for sustainability.

It has been long established that economic success and caring for the environment go hand-in-hand and make good business besides.

MAINTAINING AND PROMOTING BALANCE

Seeking balance in personal and organizational life is of increasing concern. *Fortune* magazine even featured the issue in a 2005 cover story, "Get A Life: The 24/7 grind hurts—but corporations are helping executives escape it" (Miller and Miller 2005). Noting the astonishing trend in the United States to 60- and even 80-hour work weeks for executives, they concluded that balance is "a lesson that corporate America needs to learn before an entire generation of senior talent melts down or decides to stay home."

Achieving balance, or integrity, is a discipline for learning organizations. Balance begins with the simple balancing of work itself. When the final industrial revolution enabled people to move off the farms and into factory life, better and more secure pay was one enticement. But another was that work had a beginning and end. It may have been 12 hours a day, but still the whistle blew in the morning and again in the evening, after which the worker was "off." Now, with 24/7 telecommunications, the hyperspeed of work life and the hyperconnectivity of a global marketplace, workers are perhaps even more likely to find themselves working continuously than was true on the farm. There is an upper limit to our capacity for this, and promoting balance will be an increasingly valued activity.

Balance is a concept that goes well beyond balancing time between work and personal life, or achieving some physical exercise in a sedentary world. More deeply, it means balancing the energy that one is putting out with the energy that is coming in, so that one can achieve what they hope for mentally, physically, emotionally, and spiritually (T. Hiemstra 2001). Issues such as these have not been the historical domains of the workplace, but twenty-first century companies will treat work–life balance as a competitive advantage and institute policies that make such balance possible.

Fortune advises business leaders to take some simple steps. First, quit defining balance as a "women's issue." Second, echoing the research, start to look at bringing balance to senior positions as a competitive advantage. Third, assume that progress can be made and fourth, create an environment where balance is an appropriate topic for conversation.

MAINTAINING HOPE AND VISION IN THE MIDST OF TURMOIL

The twenty-first century is not likely to slow down and become simple. Instead, turbulence, flux, and change are likely to be the norms. Calling attention to the possible and the preferred and increasing our capacity are vital to maintaining hope and vision. Positioning your enterprise and yourself by engaging the 10 key characteristics outlined here will, it is likely, increase your chances to flourish.

PART III

PREFERRED FUTURE PLANNING EXERCISES, TOOLS, AND ACTIVITIES

In Part II we explored a set of perspectives for futuring, for becoming your own futurist, and for the twenty-first century enterprise. We presented the Three-Cone Model for Preferred Future Planning, organized around the three critical future questions—what is probable, possible, and preferred. In Part III we offer perspectives, tools, and activities designed to assist you in shaping the future. The basic approach is summarized with an outline of questions organized around the components of the Three-Cone Model.

PREFERRED FUTURE PLANNING OUTLINE

1. Honest Assessment of the Present.
   - What is our situation—specifically, how do we compare to the world best?
   - Who are our customers—what do we know and not know?
   - What do we do better than or worse than our key competitors?
   - Which of our current assumptions and paradigms are obsolete?
   - If we could stop doing one thing, what is it and why?
2. Exploration of the Probable.
   - What are the critical events, trends, and developments (ETDs) shaping the future environment, looking out at least two decades?
   - What is probable in our industry and stakeholder environment?
   - Where are we: on-trend, or off-trend?

- What opportunities are appearing on the horizon?
- If we don't change, what do we look like in the future? What are the risks and benefits?

3. Exploration of the Possible.
   - What is impossible for us today, which, if we made it possible, would change things fundamentally for the better?
   - If we sat down with our customers and stakeholders, and designed the best possible system, product, or service, what is it like?
   - How did it happen that we renewed ourselves and ended up on the cover of _____ as a benchmark or great organization?

4. Exploration of the Preferred.
   - What is my or our preferred future, and how can I or we describe it?
       Physically—products, structures, technology, and so on.
       Intellectually—systems, management theory and practice, processes used, and so on.
       Emotionally—workplace climate, organization culture, feeling, community, satisfaction, and so on.
       Spiritually—our higher purpose, ultimate aim, achieving personal mastery, and so on.
   - What would we look like and be doing if we had no limitations and knew we could not fail?
   - How does our preferred future align with my personal vision, and any larger vision?
   - Which aspects of my or our preferred future stand out, are the most magnetic and compelling?
   - What, in appropriate level of detail, is my or our refined vision?

5. Achieving the Preferred Future.
   - Does my vision fit the 15 percent rule?
   - What do I or we need to do first to move toward the vision—what is our first win?
   - What vision critical strategies must we pursue over time?
   - What is a quick, simple, and regular cycle for checking progress that we can establish to make certain we follow through?
   - What barriers must we remove to progress toward the vision?

If you work through these questions systematically and in order, and do nothing else, you will conduct a simple yet incisive exploration into the present, into the future, and into strategic decision making. The following chapter introduces some methods for gaining foresight through the exploration of the present and the probable future. Then, we learn methods for deciding on strategic direction through the exploration of possible futures and making decisions about preferred futures. Next, we look at techniques for turning your decisions into action. Finally, you will have the chance to apply lessons learned to your own career.

CHAPTER 8

Forecasting the Future: Activities for You and Your Enterprise

Everything should be made as simple as possible, but not simpler.

—Albert Einstein, n.d.

Originality is simply a fresh pair of eyes.

—Thomas Wentworth Higginson, 1871

Planning can be complicated, or it can be simple. My bias is toward the simple. Planning is about making decisions, rather than about finding an answer. Planning teams whom I have worked with over the years typically believe that out there, somewhere, is *the answer*. In reality, out there you find endless information, and an ultimate need to make judgments.

I discovered early in my futuring career that endless research and exploration and discussion and writing of missions and goals and objectives and strategies and tactics and debating what these things actually mean and whether a goal has numbers or not and designating responsibilities and debating budgets and what is feasible and setting time lines and debating again whether we are talking about a strategy or a tactic or maybe it is actually a goal and we should put it there and when is the next meeting, all are designed to keep anything from happening, while giving the appearance of action. Be careful of this.

Quantitative tools for forecasting and planning are being developed all the time, particularly if you are interested in the very short term. For example, "prediction markets" are among the hottest of new things in the forecasting business. Tech Buzz is an example, an online auction site in which players "buy" fictitious stock in a variety of current technologies, from mobile phones to HDTV formats. The assumption is that the "stocks" that go up indicate which technologies are most popular and will therefore win in the marketplace. There is evidence that the wisdom of swarms, captured in activities like these, can be quite predictive, especially for the immediate and near term. A similar auction site, NewsFutures attempts to provide short-range predictions for news events. Like an odds maker might treat a horse race, the site will sell shares, for example, in whether public approval ratings of the president will go up or down in the following month, and, based on what is selling, will make a prediction about those ratings.

We are interested in something simpler, strategic, and longer-term in perspective. We want foresight. This word, a combination of forecast and insight, describes the most valuable of all business information. With proper effort, technique, and probably some luck, events, trends, and developments on the horizon can be better understood and thus leveraged or avoided.

Foresight assumes that the future is knowable, not just in the short to medium term, the realm of predictions, but also in the medium to longer term, the realm of forecasts. For example, we know a great deal about the future shape and nature of the European population, both in the short and long term. It is a simple matter to anticipate the size of the population or its age profile in a given time period, though it is much harder to predict where people will live and how future immigration policies may change things.

Technology and business developments can be anticipated as well, though this is more difficult. Mark Anderson of the Strategic News Service (SNS) predicts the short- to medium-term technology future, with respectable results and in fact can demonstrate that about 90 percent of SNS predictions are accurate. In the technology domain, it is often said that if you can learn what is in the research labs or gain personal contact with industry leaders as inside sources you can predict what will be in the market in 18 to 36 months. Instead, according to Anderson, making accurate technology business predictions depends on (1) knowing what is in the marketplace today, (2) knowing larger social and global trends, (3) knowing something about basic science and advances being made at that level, and (4) most critically, developing a logic of what is needed and thus likely in the market in the near- to mid-term future.

Predictions and foresight are not quite the same thing. Predictions are shorter term, aimed at reducing uncertainty by being correct, focused on probabilities, and usually quantifiable. In contrast, the time horizon of foresight is usually longer, and it aims not so much to reduce uncertainty as to explore uncertainty. The focus is on trends and countertrends, on discontinuities and surprises at least as much as probabilities. Quality insight is the desired outcome, rather than measurable accuracy, and tools can include environmental scanning, scenario building, consensus, and intuition.

METHODS TO GAIN FORESIGHT

Foresight begins in the present, not in the future. A fundamental challenge facing organizations and individuals is taking time to clearly understand their current situation. Referring to the Three-Cone Model introduced earlier, a planning team member once asked, "What if you think you are here, but you are actually over there? Then your whole future view and plan will be off."

Begin with a profile of the business or organization. This means making a careful and detailed inventory of the organization, looking for strengths and weaknesses and comparing organization domains against standards for best in industry. Domains to assess will vary by industry and organization but generally may include:

- Products.
- Services.
- Customers and stakeholders.
- Human resources.
- Technology.
- Systems.
- Supply chain and supply chain relationships.
- Facilities or plant and equipment.
- Continuous quality and innovation.
- Evaluation, performance assessment.
- Decision making and governance.
- Finance.

As you conduct this assessment or with the basic assessment in hand, you will want to ask questions such as the following, from the Preferred Future Planning Outline presented earlier in the overview of Part III:

- What is our situation—specifically, how do we compare to the world best?
- Who are our customers—what do we know and not know?
- What do we do better than or worse than our key competitors?

This assessment can be gathered into a table such as in Table 8.1. Each domain in your list should be compared with measures from similar organizations and industry standards. It is particularly useful to compare your organization to the best in the field, in order to benchmark your per-

TABLE 8.1
Assessing the Present Situation

CATEGORY	PRESENT CONDITION	INDUSTRY BENCHMARK
Products		
Services		
Customers, Stakeholders		
Human Resources		
Technology		
Systems		
Supply Chain Relationships		
Facilities, Plant, Equipment		
Innovation, Quality		
Evaluation, Assessment		
Governance, Decisions		
Finance		

formance against industry leaders. The objective is to provide an accurate, honest picture of the organization. Honesty is very hard to find in most organizations. It is not that individuals are dishonest, though that is certainly a problem. It is that organizations are institutionally dishonest, when the truth is difficult to bear or to look at. When we do not compare with the world best, it is simple human and organizational nature to want to avoid looking at that fact, because the implications are that things will have to change. If you can achieve an honest view of the present, and thus know your actual starting point on the Three-Cone Model, then you can begin to ask questions such as:

- Which of our current assumptions and paradigms are obsolete?
- If we could stop doing one thing, what is it and why?

Some answers may be obvious by now. But it is more likely that the answers will appear with greater insight after you look to the future by using tools for forecasting.

ENVIRONMENTAL SCANNING

Environmental scanning involves an effort to identify events, trends, and developments, or drivers shaping the future. These ETDs are usually evidenced in published material but may also be explored through interviews, focus groups, or other means of involving subject matter experts. Scanning focuses on the volume of attention being paid to issues as a way of indicating a dominant issue. Scanning also focuses on leading edge or unique developments for which there might only be a marginal amount of current attention. Scanning especially involves an effort to understand which issues might take your enterprise outside or beyond your current paradigms, or way of doing things.

Scanning needs to be conducted on a regular basis, to be able to track issues as they move from being "beyond the horizon" to "on the horizon" to today's issues that are "on the agenda." Regular scanning can also help identify anomalous issues. Scanning is similar to the academic literature review but the issues noted tend to be more focused on the enterprise and more news item driven. Both breadth and depth are important, as is relevance to the organization in terms of potential impacts.

WHAT A SCAN DOES AND DOES NOT DO

For leaders, an environmental scan report offers both value and pitfalls. A good scan will suggest the nature of the world in which the organization will be deciding what future it wants. Second, a good scan brings a wider angle and longer-range view of the future into the organization. In doing so the scan stretches both strategic and creative thinking beyond normal boundaries, while suggesting new possibilities to be considered.

Pitfalls include making misleading or incorrect assumptions about the future, and the fact that local conditions may not be reflected in a general scan. In addition, it is often mistakenly believed that if we search hard and long enough, get the scan just right, then the strategic decisions will be so obvious that they will make themselves. Scanning becomes an end in itself, but it never ends because the answers never appear. Finally, future predictions associated with scanning are generally made by extrapolating past and current trends into the future, based on various assumptions. As mentioned earlier, this can lead to blind spots and the creation of plans to create an efficient past rather than a better future.

Typical objectives of an environmental scan include the following:

- Provide a comprehensive overview of a variety of trends, including social, scientific and technological, economic, political/governmental, and professional.
- Provide analysis of implications of these trends for society, the relevant industry, and the marketplace.
- Provide preliminary analysis of implications for the enterprise itself.
- Provide rich and current information that can be updated regularly.

The scan itself can be outsourced, or assigned to an internal team. Such a team can be from either a strategic planning group, or it may be created as a task force from a cross section of the enterprise. When an internal team is formed to conduct a scan, the following process is recommended.

1. Form a scanning team from a cross section of the enterprise. An ideal size is about a dozen people.
2. Designate a team member as the coordinator of the effort.
3. Hire an expert with experience in scanning and futuring to help the team achieve its goals through a consensus building process.
4. Assign members of the team to various domain arenas to collect data over a period of time.
5. Convene the scanning team after a time to compare notes and make suggestions to one another on additional avenues for research. After an initial face-to-face meeting, following meetings can be virtual if necessary, and probably will be if the team is dispersed geographically.
6. Hold an intensive retreat at which the team compiles their information, using an Environmental Scan Table (see Table 8.2), filling in the various areas of the table as relevant issues emerge.
7. Communicate the basic scan within the enterprise in a way that allows for feedback.
8. Repeat the process annually with rotating team membership.
9. Periodically involve external stakeholders and outside experts by conducting a national survey, using focus groups, or in a retreat setting.

There are many variations on the process just described. The actual practice that you use will depend heavily on the amount of time you have and wish to devote to this activity. This process assumes that you are willing to devote a year to conducting a scan, and then to annual follow-up. Of course, in practice, organizations these days tend to be in a hurry, and if that is the case for you, the entire process can be telescoped into a few months or even a few weeks.

An excellent tool for telescoping time is to conduct a think tank in which a form of environmental scanning takes place. Recent Futurist.com think tanks have brought together internal teams, stakeholders, and several external experts, including in some cases science fiction writers.

TABLE 8.2
Environmental Scanning

GENERAL FUTURE DOMAINS	SOURCES	PRESENT CONDITIONS	PROBABLE FUTURE ETDS	URGENCY: EVENT HORIZON & IMPLICATIONS
Demographics				
Economic Conditions				
Science & Technology				
Cultural Trends				
Environmental Trends				
Political and Government Trends				
Global Trends				
Industry Domains • • •				
Enterprise Domains • • •				

Working together for a couple of days, these think tanks produce a version of an environmental scan that can be sufficient for the planning purposes of the enterprise in question. While not as thorough or detailed as a full-on process, the results can be both creative and satisfactory.

USING THE ENVIRONMENTAL SCAN TEMPLATE

Scanning takes place across three broad subject domains:

1. General Future Domains: Provide a broad view of the future in the areas of population demographics, science and technology, politics and government, economics, the environment, and cultural and global trends.
2. Industry Domains: Provide a view of the future regarding the business the enterprise is in, whether that be product or service.
3. Enterprise Domains: Provide a view of the future regarding how the enterprise works, such as personnel, finance, facilities, technology, community and customer service, ethics, vision and values, and information management.

As research and exploration within these three broad domains and their subheadings occur, you will be looking for events, trends, and developments (ETDs) that fit, roughly, into three time horizons. In the near term, the next two or three years are the issues that are "on the agenda." These are the developments that require decisions or are being actively pursued or developed in the market. In the mid term, about four to six years out, are ETDs that are "on the horizon." These are issues that are being noticed, but no actions have yet been taken. If you can identify issues in this zone, you can either begin to learn about them, or to develop or respond to them ahead of competitors. Finally, in the long term, beyond seven years to as much as a couple of decades, are the ETDs that are "over the horizon." Such issues are far enough in the future and of a nature that only specialists tend to be aware of the possible developments, but otherwise no one is yet paying attention. Despite the difficulties of such long-term scanning, one can immediately see the potential competitive advantage of discerning such developments when others are not looking for them.

When the scanning information is compiled and analyzed, within each domain area the following information can be reported, using the format presented in Table 8.2:

- *Sources:* Specific sources for particular items and example sources for further investigation.
- *Present Conditions:* Brief summary of the present situation with regard to the domain being addressed. This will already have been completed with regard to the enterprise management domains, if the review of your present situation, discussed earlier, has been done.
- *Probable Future Events, Trends, Developments:* Overview of both general and specific future developments.
- *Urgency and Implications:* A judgment about the urgency of the development and implications for the enterprise. Urgency is reported by noting whether the development being discussed fits within one of the three relevant time horizons:
    Over the Horizon: Long Term, 7 years or more.
    On the Horizon: Medium Term, 4–6 years.
    On the Agenda: Short Term, 0–3 years.

Each report cycle should include a brief listing or summary of key trends, along with the full report.

SCENARIO DEVELOPMENT

During the past decade, scenario planning gained a great deal of traction as a planning tool in organizations, both the corporate and public sector. The technique is an excellent way to explore probable and possible futures and to gain foresight from such exploration.

Developed and refined during the 1970s and 1980s, the purpose of this approach to planning is to anticipate possible futures and imagine alternative strategic responses to these futures. Future scenario development is not designed to determine a "most likely" scenario, nor is it designed to develop a "range" of scenarios such as "high-low-medium growth scenarios." The classic objective is to develop several plausible stories that describe how the world may in fact develop, given certain future events, trends, and developments and then to note triggers that will indicate whether a particular scenario seems to be emerging. Then, the task is to discern strategic responses to these plausible futures. As such, this process recognizes the uncertain and often surprising nature of the future as it actually unfolds. It is this recognition of uncertainty that makes scenario development attractive as a tool, as it seems to match the nature of the real world. It is also typically a tool for taking a longer-range look at the future than usual. We have found it to be an outstanding tool for gaining long-range foresight, and since the late 1990s Futurist.com has been asked to assist enterprises in the creation of scenarios as often as any other process for exploring the future.

There are three alternative ways to create scenarios: (1) Contracting out to a research firm is one method, frequently used. The ideal is for an internal team to work for an extended time, developing deep insight. (2) As practiced at Shell, a pioneer with the technique, the preference is for an ongoing team with fixed leadership, working over many months to create scenarios. However few companies are willing to devote that kind of time with their own people. (3) A third option, when time is short, is to have a team create scenarios in a single concentrated event, or short series of events.

Scenario creation begins with the development of a set of assumptions about the probable future, often called the "predetermined elements." These are the driving forces that are considered quite likely to happen within the time span in question, and applicable to all possible scenarios. Examples of typical predetermined elements for the next couple of decades may be that the population will grow older, and computing technology will become faster and cheaper. Each development, while not guaranteed, is so likely as to be considered predetermined. Such driving forces may be identified early in the scenario process or could be pulled from a recent environmental scan.

The second step is to assign different scenarios a unique set of possible futures, often called "critical uncertainties." These are events, trends, and developments that are not likely to happen, or which could go one way or another. But whatever happens the uncertainty will have a major impact within the time period in question. For example, for a long time it was uncertain that evidence of global warming caused by humans would become over-whelming. Recent evidence suggests that this development is moving from the uncertain to the predetermined column, though some will yet debate. Another example is the possible development of a cheap and nonpolluting means of harnessing ocean energy. This may occur in the next two decades, or not, and for some scenarios whichever happens could be critical. There are a great many uncertainties about the future, and only the most critical are selected for use in a given scenario. Usually, two or more unique and crit-ical uncertainties are assigned to a given scenario, uncertainties that have a certain logic to them. Using the preceding examples, if evidence of human causation of global warming becomes a given, it would be logical that greater efforts in alternative energy would contribute to quicker develop-ment of ocean energy. Creating a scenario in which the uncertainties break in this direction would make sense.

With a common set of predetermined elements and a unique set of critical uncertainties as a starting point, the third step with a particular scenario is to outline and eventually develop a written history of the fu-ture. As the story takes place, the predetermined elements and the critical uncertainties play out according to the scenario builders in ways that are plausible. The goal in fact is a plausible story, one that makes sense.

Good scenarios are difficult, because they resemble creative story telling, not a natural skill for many people. Literal plot development techniques are often recommended to scenario teams as an aid to imagining the future. The key point is that good scenario development makes use of writing and story tools, rather than being merely a list of developments over time.

These processes create the classic or probable future scenario. Typi-cally, an organization will want to produce three to five future scenarios, each plausible in its own right. Each scenario will have within it clues as to which events, trends, and developments are likely triggers of the scenario moving from story to reality. Suppose you had a scenario in which cheap oil is assumed but a key uncertainty is a shift to expensive oil. In this case a development such as war in Saudi Arabia, or simply a price that goes over $100 a barrel may be appropriate triggers. The users of the scenarios will know, with the triggers in hand, that if oil reaches a certain sustained price, then a given scenario is more plausible. And should oil fall to the floor once again, a different scenario may come to the fore.

Reading other examples of good scenarios is highly recommended before you attempt your own, and the References offer several possibilities. Chief among these are Shell scenarios, available in public form on the Web.

DEEPENING YOUR INSIGHT

At this point, you will have a set of data about the probable future and an assessment of your present, based on the earlier activities. But you still have to turn this data and information into foresight. Several simple analysis tools are available. All are designed to enable you to get at one or more of the key questions raised in the Preferred Future Planning Outline about the probable future:

- What are the critical events, trends, and developments (ETDs) shaping the future environment, looking out at least two decades?
- What is probable in our industry and stakeholder environment?
- Where are we on-trend, or off-trend?
- What opportunities are appearing on the horizon?
- If we don't change, what do we look like in the future? What are the risks and benefits?

STATUS QUO SCENARIO

There is a unique scenario for exploring some of the key questions about the present and the probable future. With the present assessment in hand, and with a solid sense of the future environment based on environmental scanning or scenarios, you can explore the "status quo scenario." This simple scenario assumes that every enterprise changes over time, even when it is trying not to change. Yet at the same time, when an enterprise is not making any *fundamental change* in the face of turbulent developments in the external environment, the enterprise is living out the status quo scenario.

To conduct the activity, form a team to create the scenario. Ask the following question: "Ten years from now, what do we look like, assuming that the external environment changes in the ways that we have forecast and imagined, while internally we make no fundamental changes? What if we just keep doing what we do now? Describe our enterprise at a future date if we maintain the status quo."

When the brainstormed list is complete, the team can step back, and ask, "What does this mean? What are the risks and the benefits of maintaining the status quo while the external environment evolves?" If the status quo scenario matches what the organization desires in its preferred future, you are all set. But this will not be the case, as organizations dare not stand still.

PARADIGM SHIFTS

Exploring obsolete paradigms and paradigm shifts is another simple but powerful analysis tool. When a review of the future reveals that paradigms in the external world are changing, then it is probably the case that paradigms within an enterprise must change as well. While paradigm has a scientific and a popular definition (Barker 1992), the best definition for the purposes of this activity is that a *paradigm* means "the way we do things around here." This may be the way that products are designed, or the way you manage supplier relationships, or the way that customer returns are handled. Organizations have ways of things that are usually both known and relatively fixed.

When the world changes the standard paradigms start running into problems. To assess what these problems may be, create a from-to chart (Table 8.3), and then ask, "Of the ways that we do things around

TABLE 8.3
Paradigms—The Way We Do Things around Here

Paradigms—The Way We Do Things around Here	
From . . .	To . . .

here, which are already obsolete or are going to become obsolete in the next few years? What will we be moving from, and what will we be moving to?"

DIALOGUE ON DISCONTINUITIES AND SURPRISES

Recall that foresight was contrasted to prediction in part by the idea that predictions focus on reducing uncertainty, while foresight explores uncertainty and discontinuous change. Foresight looks for surprises as well as dominant trends, and then attempts to figure out what they mean for the organization in the future. It is fundamentally important to get beyond the superficial to a deeper level of understanding the future. Joseph Voros (2005) suggests a final model for achieving foresight, with the following steps:

1. Input: Look and see what is happening.
2. Analysis: Ask, "What seems to be happening?"
3. Interpretation: Ask, "What is really happening?"
4. Prospection: Ask, "What might happen?"
5. Output: Ask, "What might we need to do?"

In his discussion of this technique for analysis, Voros adds a final step involving deciding what to do and how to do it. With the foresight gained from examining the present, and exploring probable and possible futures, one can shift time perspective and move into the future itself. It is in the future that strategic direction is decided, the subject of the next chapter.

CHAPTER 9

Choosing a Direction:
Activities for You and Your Enterprise

If human kind could spend just a fraction of the countless millions of hours and millions of dollars we spend trying to predict the future, instead on imaging preferred options together, we'd be living in a different world."
—Edward B. Lindaman, 1982

As we see our future, so we act. As we act, so we become.
—Barbara Marx Hubbard, 1984

At the end of the day, preferred future planning comes down to this. What direction do you want to go? You might label that direction with a variety of terms—a vision, a goal, a strategic direction, a strategic intent, a hunch, a dream, a single focus, a decision. Whatever term you use, you are trying to say, as simply as possible: Today I am here, tomorrow I would like to be there.

In this chapter we explore some ways of creating vision and clarifying values. Both are important to establishing strategic direction. A vision is nothing more than a description of a preferred future, the answer to the question, Where do I want to go? Values are the answer to two questions: Why do I want to go there, and how shall I behave on the journey?

Vision begins, in a most important sense, in the future, whether it be a possible or a preferred future. That is, in order to see the preferred future some means of leaving the present behind and placing yourself in the future is required. Once there, you can look around, notice both possibilities and the best features, and recall them when you arrive back in the present. How can you do this?

The great science fiction writer Ray Bradbury (1988) once wrote a short story called "The Toynbee Convector." In the story the lead character, dissatisfied with the direction in which the world is headed, convinces the public that he has built a real time machine. He announces that on a given day, he will enter the time machine and travel 100 years into the future, and at a fixed time after that, he will return. He invites the press to attend and, using an elaborate hoax, appears to have vanished. At the appointed time, he returns using the same hoax. Upon his arrival back in the present, he describes the future. It is grand. He has impressive film and recordings from all over the world, and reams of documentation of a planet in which pollution has been cleaned up, war has ceased, poverty is a thing of the past, and people live healthily into old age. He has spent several previous years creating the detailed and fictitious evidence that he now presents. In Bradbury's story, humanity is thrilled and relieved that everything is going to work out after all, despite all the conflict, fears, and angst that plagues the present day. And so humanity gets busy making sure that the future so documented and now clearly guaranteed will, in fact, come to pass.

We don't have time machines, but we do have the ability to create our own fictitious images of the future, which, if truly preferred and committed to, have the potential to inspire present-day strategic actions.

THE POSSIBLE FUTURE

We can begin with the questions from the Preferred Future Planning Outline. Even with no particular processes, just working your way through these questions will get you to a useful vision. The first step is to explore several *possible* futures from which you will choose your *preferred* future. The goal is to create a set of "future images" that can be refined. As you create these images, you might explore questions such as these:

Exploration of the Possible

- What is impossible for us today, which, if we made it possible, would change things fundamentally for the better?

- If we sat down with our customers and stakeholders and designed the best possible system, product or service, what is it like?
- How did it happen that we renewed ourselves and ended up on the cover of _____ as a benchmark or great organization?

Ideas generated in discussions like these can be raw material for envisioning the preferred future.

THE PREFERRED FUTURE

Once you have possible images available, you can push them further by creating images of the preferred future. In the same way as with the previous questions, just working with the following list can enable you to explore and make decisions about a vision. The preferred future questions include the following.

Exploration of the Preferred

- What is my or our preferred future, and how can I or we describe it?
  Physically: Products, structures, technology, and so on.
  Intellectually: Systems, management theory and practice, processes used, and so on.
  Emotionally: Workplace climate, organization culture, feeling, community, satisfaction, and so on.
  Spiritually: Our higher purpose, ultimate aim, achieving personal mastery, and so on.
- What would we look like and be doing if we had no limitations and knew we could not fail?
- How does our preferred future align with my personal vision and any larger vision?
- Which aspects of my or our preferred future stand out, are the most magnetic and compelling?
- What, in appropriate level of detail, is my or our refined vision?

The possible and preferred future questions can be explored in sequence, or a selected set of questions might be focused on, or even a single question might be used. In general, the first step is for individuals to create their own images of the future. The next task is for small groups to compare and combine their responses into a set of preferred future images. As a final step the relevant decision-making team combines the various images and refines them into a vision.

Notice how the questions are designed to encourage a "whole system" vision, one that accounts for all aspects of an enterprise, including both the concrete reality and the more abstract concepts that motivate and inspire and bind people together. As we do the preferred future creation activities, we constantly remind ourselves to look at the whole, to image the structures, technology, physical products, the systems and processes, the culture, climate, and community, and finally the ultimate purpose of doing what you do. In this set of questions you can also see how your personal vision begins to fit in, as well as what is referred to as a "larger vision." To understand a larger vision, think of Henry Ford. At one level his vision was to build cars really cheap and really quickly. But the reason he had that goal was his larger vision, which was, literally, "to bring mobility to the masses." It was this larger vision that caused Ford to make the strategic decision to pay his people enough that they, themselves, could eventually afford the cars. He could see how the whole system fit together. Narrowly focused visions miss these larger connections.

TOOLS FOR PREFERRED FUTURE VISION

There are many ways to get to the preferred images. Simple dialogue is powerful. Margaret Wheatley (2002, 9) notes that ". . . human beings have always sat in circles and councils to do their best thinking, and to develop strong and trusting relationships." Whether the dialogue is around a fire or in a windowless corporate meeting room, she concludes that ". . . as we slow down the conversation to a pace that encourages thinking, we become wise and courageous actors in our world."

Brainstorming (or nominal group technique), visualization, and preferred future scenarios are three additional tools that have worked well in my experience with many kinds of organizations, from Fortune 100 companies to small, rural communities attempting to create a community dream. Each process is completely low tech, requiring only a team of people, a room, some chart paper, and perhaps some pads of sticky notes. I have used electronic polling with handheld keypads, networked laptop computers, and other technologically enhanced processes as well, and they can help. Obviously, how you apply the tools will be adjusted according to who you are and what works in your setting. The way I often describe it, for example when training facilitators for a particular project, is to say, "Grasp the purpose of this process, the outcome we are trying to produce. Then, adjust the process as needed to get that result."

Brainstorming is a quick way to create a list of preferred future images that you will then discuss, prioritize, and refine. From this initial list of preferred future images you are trying to get to a refined vision, usually a small set of ideas that are most potent, most attractive, and most critical to your successful future. Building consensus, using various voting procedures, and simply engaging in dialogue and debate until the best ideas become obvious will all get you to your most preferred images. With these in hand, you have the basic ingredients for a vision, the basic requirements for deciding on your strategic direction.

Visualization of preferred futures is still, in my experience, potentially the most powerful tool for discovering a vision. It is important that such a process be skillfully led. I do not use it all the time because some groups find it too soft or simply too outside their normal business practice to be willing to try it. But when groups make a serious run at visualizing, they can discover ideas that they never knew were in their consciousness.

Visualization is simply tapping your active imagination, and then describing what you see. Seeing a preferred product or system through customer-stakeholder eyes, asking how you ended up as a benchmark award winner, or describing the whole system at some point in the future all work very well with visualization. The process can be elaborate, or pretty simple. One Fortune 100 company that I worked with actually had, for a time, a visualization room, where executives and product teams could come to work. Full of white boards and chart pads, pillows and chairs, and the capacity for dimming the lights and playing music, the room was used to visualize the future, or perhaps to answer a business problem, then to record the ideas, and finally to debate and discuss and come to conclusions. On the other hand, visualizing can be done without a special setting at all.

However accomplished, visualization must involve some means of freeing the mind from the present, and time traveling to the future, and then, while there, capturing in the mind what is seen. If you have never done such a thing deliberately, you will be amazed at both the rational and the intuitive insights that can emerge. The visualizing process can be accomplished in a single meeting or event, although with a large group or multiple groups it can take a great deal of time to report, discuss, and combine the ideas that result. It is important to allow sufficient time for the final refinement step, where the images are refined into a final vision. Doing this over several sessions, with time in between for reflection, is valuable. The final step, in which you work to ratchet the vision up to be more bold is vital. Here you remember the 15 percent Rule for Preferred Future Vision, and stretch the ideas further. Both concern about feasibility and the natural inclination of group processes to push toward lower common denominators encourages teams to settle for a vision that is less than the best. This must be resisted.

Preferred scenario building is an effective alternative, more contemplative than either visioning or brainstorming. Visioning processes, despite their effectiveness, can seem too intuitive or even mystical to some. Basic or classic scenario development is not designed to a single vision. The classic objective, rather, is to develop several plausible scenarios.

When hybridized with preferred visioning, the task is expanded to discern preferred strategic responses within each plausible future. The ultimate task becomes one of developing a single preferred strategic direction or vision. This unique process, when used for planning, recognizes the uncertain and often surprising nature of the future as it actually unfolds, while at the same time calling on people to identify their preferred vision. This, it should be noted, is not a generally accepted move by those who teach pure scenario building. But for the purposes of developing strategic direction it can be very effective.

The process follows the same steps as explained in the previous chapter for researching predetermined elements, identifying critical uncertainties, and composing alternative future scenarios. The hybrid is created by adding additional steps. First the alternative scenarios of possible futures are redeveloped into scenarios of preferred futures. This is done by maintaining the external factors in each scenario as they are, but examining the organization's responses within the scenario, adding preferred elements, and removing nonpreferred elements regarding the organization itself. That is, each scenario now reads as though the world develops as before, but the organization's preferred future within that world is now part of the scenario.

The preferred scenarios are then compared and common preferred organization elements across scenarios are highlighted. Each separate preferred scenario is then reconsidered and a preferred vision for the organization is summarized. These alternative preferred visions are compared, common themes noted, and a composite vision is created that expresses a preferred future for the enterprise, in any given future world.

The final step is to work backward from the preferred vision, and to develop the critical strategic implications and design elements for the organization that the preferred scenario suggests. These strategic implications and design elements may then become the "things we must do regardless of which way the future actually goes." As with classic scenario development, the results are communicated and used in the organization, and revisited periodically.

CRITERIA FOR A VISION

At the end of a visioning process, you will want a product of some kind, typically a written statement. The vision statement can consist of words, bullet points, paragraphs, stories, and visual images. In my experience people fret more than necessary over this statement. It is not possible to make it perfect, and at some point I usually tell people that a valuable criterion that tells you that you are finished with the vision is that you are simply tired of working on it. Changing a few more words here or there is unlikely to make it better, so it is wiser simply to declare victory and get on to asking how to make the vision reality.

There are some useful criteria for a winning vision besides fatigue, however, and the following have proven very effective.

- Vision must describe the preferred future. This usually works best if the language is in the present tense, as though you are there, in the future, describing what has taken place. But it can also be written in other tenses and still work, so long as it is describing the future. Compare "Encircle Caterpillar," "We will encircle Caterpillar," and "In 2020 we have encircled Caterpillar." Each can work, each describes the preferred future.

- Vision must be compelling, magnetic. People overestimate the importance of language for this criterion. All other things being equal, zesty, exciting, enticing words are better than bland ones. And surprisingly difficult to find. However, this criterion has much more to do with reach than with words. The Collins and Porras (2000) term BHAG, for big, hairy, audacious goals, gets at the same issue. For a vision to be compelling, it must capture the right amount of "stretch" between the present and the future, so that people feel it will make a difference and thus be empowered and excited to go for it. You want people to say, "That sounds hard, but it is critical that we make the effort." Too little stretch and people will say, "Who cares?" A vision that is obviously impossible will only discourage people, the opposite of what is desired. "Encircle Caterpillar," again, was compelling not because of exciting language but because it expressed the right amount of reach to magnetically pull people toward it.

- Vision must account for real world data. If a vision seems to pay no attention to the real world, nor any attention to future trends as we understand them, it will not work. It ought to be obvious to people that the vision takes into account what is really going on, as best we understand it, rather than ignoring both present and future reality.

- Vision must be expressed in sufficient detail to provide direction, yet be as simple as possible. This criterion hangs people up frequently. Some want a very short, pithy vision. Others want lots of detail. There is no hard-and-fast rule, except to use the right level of detail for those who will work with the vision. Experience seems to favor shorter visions however, as teams who do a vision process several times over a few years invariably find themselves writing shorter visions each time, discovering that simplicity works. They also find themselves writing fewer and fewer strategies, and perhaps no plan at all, as they have discovered that all the work that went into elaborate planning had been for naught when the world changed. Better to decide on the strategic direction and commit to it, and then get to work, than to hash out elaborate plans that will never be implemented.

- Vision must express not just the best ideas, but the heart's desire. We commit to things we care about, and this means tapping into the heart as well as the head. Compelling vision tugs at the heart, the conscience, the soul. It aligns with your values.

SHARING THE VISION

Visions come, visions go, and most business visions are little noticed. But some visions make a difference. These are the ones that have become a shared, mutual commitment to a strategic direction. How is a vision shared? There are three basic methodologies. One is for a leader to create and communicate a vision so compelling that everyone wants to be a part of it. This is possible, but rare. A second method is to invite extensive, bottom-up participation in creating the vision of the preferred future. If the process is good, participation will create a sense of shared destiny, and solid commitment results. This method is difficult in larger organizations simply because of the numbers involved, and thus is also rare. The Futures Search conference for all employees is one way of attempting to involve everyone in moderately sized organizations (Weisbord 2000).

The most practical method for creating shared vision is to provide everyone an opportunity to provide feedback to a vision statement that is in process, and in doing that to answer the question, "What is your vision?" Asking the question genuinely, and to mean it, makes it possible to demonstrate how individual visions, the executive's vision, and the company vision line up. When people feel they are striving for something they also want personally and have a chance to comment on, commitment is more likely. Peter Senge summarizes the concept of shared vision this way (1990, 206–209):

At its simplest level, a shared vision is the answer to the question, what do we want to create? . . . Shared vision is vital for the learning organization because it provides the focus and energy for learning. . . . A vision, uplifts people's aspirations . . . [is] exhilarating . . . changes people's relationships . . . creates a common identity. . . . compels courage. . . . [and] fosters risk taking and experimentation. . . . You cannot have a learning organization without shared vision. Without a pull toward some goal which people truly want to achieve, the forces in support of the status quo can be overwhelming.

CLARIFYING VALUES

Values underlie the vision. Values are why you want to accomplish the vision. Values capture how you want to behave as you seek the vision. No better example exists than the 2005 debate in the United States about whether to ban torture or not. For decades and more, it was considered a given in the world that while other countries might torture, U.S. values meant that it would not engage in torture. Then the conflicts of 2001–2005 changed all of that and it was revealed that torture had become officially though secretly sanctioned. The U.S. Congress set out to rein this policy in, with a bill to establish that torture was out of bounds. The vice president argued that torture ought to be kept in the arsenal. Senators argued the opposite, with this telling point that illustrates what a value is. To ban torture, they argued, was to make a statement about U.S. values, not about terrorists. That is, not torturing was to be the way that the United States was to behave as it sought its vision of winning the war on terror.

Clarifying a set of values can be a valuable tool in reinforcing both a vision and a company culture. Typically this involves naming a few core values in a simple statement. Here is an example, from an entrepreneurial non-profit, which went from $8 million in annual revenue to $32 million after engaging in a futuring project.

Values and Beliefs
- *Change* is essential to human development. Every individual has the potential for a more productive and satisfying life.
- *Responsibility for change* is an individual decision and commitment.
- *Action* characterizes our daily work.
- *Ethical behavior* is fundamental to life and work.

- *Respect, understanding, and compassion* for individuals and their differences are the foundation upon which our organization is built.
- *Teamwork* is the power that drives us toward organizational efficiency and effectiveness.
- *Excellence and quality* must be relentlessly pursued in our services and products.
- *Creativity and humor* are imperative in developing a supportive and productive work environment.
- *Sound financial performance and enterprise* are the cornerstones of a self-sufficient and growing organization.

This statement, and others like it, are usually the result of hours of hard work by a team of people. They may use surveys and other methods of gathering input within the organization, but mostly they hash out what the core values of the organization are and ought to be by reviewing history, looking at the vision of the company, and aligning organization values with individual values. Gathering and comparing others' values statements can also be very helpful in discovering language that works.

It is true that if you compare organization values statements you will be struck by the similarity. This is not surprising, given that they come from a set of common human values. The key is whether the enterprise really means to live by what they claim are the values.

Some experts on processes for vision and values suggest that it is desirable to define values before moving on to vision, on the grounds that a vision ought to spring from core values. There is a certain logic in this approach. Others work the opposite way around. My experience is that either sequence can work, but in general it is preferable to develop the preferred future images and draft vision first. This allows for imaginative thinking with fewer constraints. And, while values change slowly, a new insight about vision might lead to the discovery of a new or changed value. With a description of where you want to go in hand—a draft vision—you can explore values, asking Why do we want to go there, and how do we want to behave? If you do this after you have drafted a vision, but before you have finalized and signed off on it, you will have the benefit of maximum creativity, with the opportunity for revision based on values before you finish.

USING THE VISION AND VALUES

If a vision and values are going to make a difference, people must be committed to them. As we have noted, participation and listening are fundamental requirements to achieving a shared vision. But there are two pitfalls to watch out for. One is a lack of executive commitment, and the other is false consensus.

I was once invited, early in my futurist consulting career, to assist a division of a Fortune 100 company in creating a vision and plan for implementing a particular new program. The division head explained to me that he wanted a team of 30 people to create this vision and plan, in a highly participative way. So we developed a powerful three-day event in which the team created the vision, concluding their exercise with great enthusiasm and excitement. Immediately upon finishing the final day, I walked down a long hallway with the boss, on the way back to his office. He said, "Glen, that was terrific, it exceeded my expectations. There is one problem, however. The plan they settled on is not what I want. If we implement that plan, this whole place will change and I won't fit this job anymore. So, while I appreciate the work you just did, you need to know that the plan will never be implemented, not as long as I am here."

I was stunned. But a powerful lesson had just been taught to me, one that a colleague named John Scherer had warned me about as I began my consulting career but that I had not experienced until now. Executive leaders often believe that they would like to have their organization create a new vision, until the moment they realize that things might actually change fundamentally as a result. At that time, they pull back or even sabotage the whole enterprise. And now I had seen this in action.

Executive commitment to the future vision is essential. Without it, there is little reason to engage in efforts to create vision. The most effective projects that I have seen have been ones in which the chief executive plays an active role in shaping the vision. It is not their vision alone, but they lead in such a way that people know what they want, what their dream is, and the final vision for the organization reflects that fully. The executive who invites people to dream a new future and stays quiet during the process, perhaps out of a desire not to dominate, actually undercuts the process because everyone knows nothing will happen unless the executive is on board.

Another pitfall that I have seen is false consensus. People get together in a retreat or series of meetings to develop a vision and strategies. A few people are skeptical, having gone through this unsuccessfully before. But mostly they work hard and are excited. Then they get tired. Final decisions are looming, and not everyone is satisfied. But the leader or facilitator is skilled at moving things along, the clock is ticking, and everyone wants to reach a conclusion and call the project a success. So heads begin to nod, objections cease being discussed even though they are felt, and soon everyone is raising their hand to indicate approval. When the project is complete, people walk away feeling that they have created a new vision, that consensus was achieved. But once outside the meeting rooms, perhaps immediately or perhaps weeks later, objections come up, commitment wanes, doubts appear, and the whole thing goes off track.

What happened is false consensus. People in such meetings believe that consensus has been achieved, suppressing their doubts. A desire for a successful outcome overcomes a desire to get it right, or to dream big. It is false consensus in particular that causes participants in a vision project to ratchet their ambition back, because agreement becomes prized over boldness. So on paper the whole thing looks okay, a vision has been written down, and everyone has voted for it. But too many people are not really on board, and only appeared to go along. This does not work.

Overcoming the executive commitment pitfall is simple but not easy. Organization leaders have to be in the game. Preferably they have to lead the game and not assign this task to subordinates. If they are not actively leading a vision project, they have to express their own views and make sure at every step in a futuring process that the directions that are emerging are their directions as well by providing both input and feedback to the outcomes. This is contrary to the leadership style of many executives, who prefer to be presented with alternatives, and then to choose option A or B. But strategic direction in the form of vision is too central to future success to be decided in this manner. This is a time for participatory, collaborative leadership.

Avoiding false consensus is not simple, and not easy. The first thing to do is to inoculate against it, by warning futuring or vision teams of it at the beginning of any project. Carefully defining both consensus and levels of commitment are useful tools that can act as a hedge and increase the likelihood of both real consensus and bold thinking.

Defining Consensus

For the purposes of collaborative work on vision, or on scenario building or strategy development or planning itself, for that matter, the following definition of consensus works. It is not the only nor the most accepted definition of consensus, but it works.

Three Criteria for Consensus

1. I am in substantial agreement with the decision, direction, or outcome. Not perfect agreement, which is unlikely or impossible, but substantial agreement.
2. I see no fatal flaws. A fatal flaw is one that, if allowed to go forward, will sabotage the effort. Every outcome will have some flaws, but the flaws that exist are not fatal.
3. I can commit to implementing this decision, direction, or outcome.

Literally, when attempting to overcome false consensus, it can be important to go around the room and ask each person to respond to these three criteria, out loud, and in public. At the end of the day, it is still possible that someone will nod and smile without meaning it, but false consensus is less likely if you have taken this step.

Levels of Commitment

The second definition tool has to do with commitment itself. There is little reason to work on a vision if people are not going to commit to it. So, as a decision is made, first describing and then testing levels of commitment is done. There are five possible levels of commitment to a vision or direction.

1. Level −1: Today I will smile and nod, but later I will sabotage behind the scenes.
2. Level 0: I don't really care about this whole vision one way or the other. Whatever.

3. Level + 1: An acceptable idea. It will be interesting to watch the rest of you work on it.
4. Level + 2: This is an excellent idea. I will help out whenever I can.
5. Level + 3: This is a critical idea. Our future depends on achieving this vision. I will devote my time and energy to seeing this through.

Appropriate use of vision involves fundamentally understanding that the vision is to be the star to steer by, not a map to be followed. Those who advocate for organization flexibility or resilience as opposed to planning are right as far as they go, but they tend to miss the importance of vision, conflating it with a plan, which is different. The vision is a guide, a magnetic force, a rallying point. How you pursue the vision may change day by day as the world shifts, but the vision pulls you forward.

And the vision is not a fixed point in space, but rather a conversation about where you want to go and why. If it does not change as you move toward it, you are not paying attention to the world. A vision needs to be updated consistently.

Used most effectively, the vision and the values are made evident in the enterprise. When I see vision statements and values statements on the wall in a company, I don't cringe but rather applaud—if the vision is a living thing. If it is living, for example, management meetings are not just problem-solving sessions but also a regular opportunity to report what is being done to pursue the vision and whether the enterprise is on track. When difficult issues are on the table, a quick review of company values can ground people, not tell them what to do specifically but remind them of how they want to judge themselves.

Communicating vision and values can be done in many ways. The most powerful is executive reinforcement. The CEO of Grand Circle Travel, whom I have mentioned before, constantly reminds people of specific elements of the company vision and asks key people to account for what they are doing to pursue it. Another CEO I worked with some time ago also took every opportunity with his management team to call attention to the very bold and agreed upon vision and values, and asked people to describe how their daily activities were seeking the vision and living out the values. He asked them to set ambitious quantitative goals and to meet them, in pursuit of the vision. In another company the vision and values were imprinted on the backs of business cards, printed on mugs and onto plaques, and people were asked to report on progress. Way back at the time of the *Apollo* program, my mentor Ed Lindaman, the director of planning, set up a program in which he would make a weekly televised report to the farflung work force, all of whom were pulling together to accomplish the crazy vision of men on the moon. Each week he would personally visit a part of the program with a TV crew, and assist the workers in explaining how their piece of the project, no matter how small, was vital to mission success. The live broadcast, seen by everyone on the program for a few minutes, would thus draw everyone into a shared vision.

Such focus and communication is easy to maintain but tends to fade as the rigor of daily crisis takes its toll. So periodic celebrations of success and at least biannual updates to the vision are vital. Senior leaders are critical. If they stay engaged and reinforcing, the vision will stay alive. If they wander off into other interests, the vision will fade quickly into oblivion.

PERSONAL VISION AND VALUES

Let's turn now to the subject of personal vision and values. Senge has argued that developing a shared vision within the company should involve a process in which employees have the chance to compare their own visions, for themselves, with the enterprise vision, so that they can discover self-reinforcing overlaps. This would require knowledge of a personal vision. Beyond this purpose, you may simply want to think through your vision for your own career or life.

When working at the individual level, you are once again confronted with the chicken and egg question, which comes first, the vision or the values. Tracie Ryder (1989) suggests that at the deeply personal level it is values that come first because they drive your behavior. A variety of tools are available for clarifying personal values, which are "principles, standards, or qualities considered worthwhile or desirable, things that are important in your life" (41). The process of valuing is one in which you consciously examine and choose your values, updating them from time to time.

For example, you might value certain end states of being, such as wisdom, freedom, wealth, or peace of mind. And you might value certain ways of behaving, such as honesty, creativity, and fun. If you engage in any of a number of valuing exercises, you can identify a short list of the values that are core to you. With these in hand, you can move to creating or re-thinking your vision.

At the personal level a vision is the same as at the enterprise level—a description of your preferred future. Similar exercises work at the personal level for vision as well. Close your eyes and imagine yourself time traveling to the future and note what really looks good to you. Then open your eyes and jot some notes. Or brainstorm a list of preferred images for some point in the future—your family life, your career, your recreation, your state of health. Or engage in free writing, a process in which you take pen to paper or fingers to keyboard, give yourself a time limit of a few minutes, and when you say the word *go*, write without stopping or picking the pen up from the paper as you describe your ideal future. In all of these vision processes, as with the enterprise, do not worry about feasibility at first but account for the real world. For example, saying that in five years I see myself living on Mars is fun, but pointless. Saying that in five years I see myself working in the space tourism industry as it gets underway is both bold and grounded in a probable future reality.

Vision and values are operative at many levels, personal, enterprise, and community. Choosing a direction requires that you state your vision and values out loud, which can be challenging and even threatening, because once you have done so, you are on the spot to do something.

FINAL POINT—THE MYSTICAL POWER

We have emphasized the need for shared vision and for continually searching for ways to keep the vision alive and in focus. It is very important to realize that the vision comes to you as much as you go to it. Michael Jordan captures this best (2005, 97):

I couldn't have imagined everything that has happened. But dreams are like that. That's what makes the journey so interesting. Put all the work in, and then let the future emerge. It's what I did on the basketball court. I let the game come to me before I imposed my will. That's a lot different than forcing the issue because you are worried about an outcome that hasn't been determined yet. Anything can happen if you are willing to put in the work and remain open to the possibility. Dreams are realized by effort, determination, passion and staying connected to that sense of who you are.

Many times I have been told the following story by former clients, both private sector and public. The story always involves having created a vision using appropriately inclusive and participatory processes, and then later discovering the difficulty of keeping it on the front burner, so much so that it would seem the whole vision effort had been lost. In my favorite case, my client, the city manager of a medium-sized city, had put the vision in a desk drawer and had taken it out to re-read from time to time. Several years later, when he re-read the vision again, he realized it had mostly been accomplished, even though deliberate planning and implementation efforts had begun years before and then seemed to have faded. Yet as he looked around the vision was either completed or in process. This is the magnetic power of vision in action, of choosing a direction.

CHAPTER 10

Planning Activities
for You and Your Enterprise

In preparing for battle I have always found that plans are useless, but planning is indispensable.
— Dwight D. Eisenhower, n.d.

TO PLAN OR NOT TO PLAN

Strategic planning is the effort to turn foresight and vision into action via strategies and small wins. In recent years two schools of thought on planning have emerged. One says don't bother. The other says it is more vital than ever.

The "don't bother" view says that planning has become a waste of time, or even counterproductive. This view is expressed by Karl Weick and Kathleen Sutcliff (2001, 79): "Plans, in short, can do just the opposite of what is intended, creating mindlessness instead of mindful anticipation of the unexpected." They argue that planning tends to create assumptions and beliefs that blind you. Other critics of planning insist that the world is simply changing too fast and thus any plan is obsolete before you finish the conversation, so the conversation itself is pointless. If you have ever been part of a situation where the practice seemed to be "make more plans, take no action," then a perspective that skips planning altogether may be attractive. Avoiding plans and concentrating on flexibility and quickness is fine, but only if your mission is unchanging and the dominant vision is maintenance of the status quo.

The alternative perspective suggests that strategy matters, perhaps now more than ever. Best exemplified by Michael Porter in his classic *Competitive Strategy* (1980, 1998), the thinking is that if you focus only on flexibility or on core competencies you are likely to become too inward, too random, and insufficiently capable of surviving in the highly competitive business climate of today. Business managers agree. Weick and Sutcliff (2) cite a study of pressing problems identified by managers who found "thinking and planning strategically" to be the second most pressing problem they face.

The best approach to "thinking and planning strategically" is to put a great deal of effort into the thinking part, as we have suggested in previous chapters, and then just the right amount of effort into the planning part. Recall that strategic planning has been defined here as the making of plans to implement strategic decisions. Strategic planning can be better understood if we refer back to Figure II.1, the Three-Cone Model for Preferred Future Planning. Having made a decision on a preferred direction, your task is to shift your trajectory from the probable cone to the preferred, so that you are aiming correctly. If the vision is more than a few months in the future, then figuring out all that must happen between here and there is, on its face, not possible. That map cannot be drawn. So it is pointless to try.

But it is not pointless to figure out two fundamental things. First is a limited set of strategies. Second are the first wins or initial activities that get you started. We will deal with each separately.

DEVELOPING STRATEGIES

Strategies are actions, or sets of actions that must be pursued over some period of time to move toward the vision. The most important strategies to identify are the "vision critical" strategies. When, in the Three-Cone Model, the lines are drawn from the preferred future back to the present it is clear, conceptually, that in order to shift trajectory from the probable to the preferred you must do some things differently. The search for strategy is to figure out what these things are.

Tools for Developing Strategy

The simplest tool for developing strategy is brainstorming and conversation. Place yourself mentally within the preferred future previously defined, and from that perspective look back at the present. Ask, "What did we do that enabled us to end up here?" Alternatively, from the perspective of the present look to the future vision and ask, "What are the things we must do to get from here to there?" Using either a backward planning or forward looking perspective, make a list.

Typically this simple activity will result in a rather long list of things that could be done. I have seen such lists begin with as many as 40 or 50 items. Even after you spend time combining the ideas into broader strategies, the list can be very long. And you know two things when you look at the long list. First, there are all kinds of things not on the list that you must continue doing. Second, you will never have the resources or time to do all the new things on the list. So some filtering mechanism is needed.

Here is where the concept of "vision critical strategies" comes into play. Reviewing all the possible strategies, ask, "Which of these possible strategies is really 'vision critical'? That is, of all of these strategies, which ones must we do to make progress toward the vision? Alternatively, if we do not do this, we will not make progress toward the vision." When you use this simple filter, three to eight strategies will tend to emerge as the ones that are obviously vision critical. This is a manageable number, which recognizes that people within organizations can take on only so much at one time.

When organizations have narrowed their possible strategies to a few that are vision critical, the results might include strategies like these:

- A hospital decided to "build an awareness of the business of health-care throughout the organization."
- An aircraft manufacturer listed Total Productive Maintenance as vision critical (this is a method of preventing equipment breakdowns).
- An association decided to "develop nondues-based revenue streams."

- A school district decided to "develop a preferred profile of the district graduate in the year 2010."
- A health care company decided to "change the roles of staff and management toward self-direction and responsibility."

Additional tools for developing strategies include the use of scenario planning. Particularly if the preferred future scenario methodology has been used, once a vision is in place you can return to the preferred scenarios and either discover possible strategies within them, or re-think them so that possible strategies emerge from the analysis. Once the possible strategies are on the table, you can again run them through the vision critical filter to make priority choices.

On the subject of priorities the question will come up whether the vision critical strategies ought to be rank ordered in some way. This is an option, particularly if the strategies have an obvious time sequence, in that one needs to be complete or underway before another begins. But if you have narrowed the strategies to just a few that will be worked on simultaneously, further prioritizing is not necessary. In fact efforts at additional prioritization may be a delaying tactic to keep anything from actually changing, the old paralysis by analysis ruse.

In their work on "strategic intent" Hamel and Prahalad (1989) outlined four broad categories for strategy, and it can be useful to use a scheme such as this to assist you in conceptualizing possible strategies. Specifically, they suggested four approaches to competitive innovation, and it is possible to examine each for strategy ideas that will aim you toward your vision.

1. "Building layers of advantage" can be done by improving quality, improving reliability, building channels, strengthening brands, going global, and similar strategic moves.
2. "Searching for loose bricks" involves finding an element of surprise by going after underdefended products and services, which are perhaps just outside the area of concentration of key competitors. It takes careful analysis of competitors to identify loose bricks.

3. "Changing the terms of engagement" means redefining the industry and the standard business practices that are common within it. Open source and web-based software is a twenty-first century example of this, which recently caused Microsoft to have to react in a big way.

4. Finally, and most interestingly, is collaboration with competitors, exemplified these days by a variety of Chinese companies. Collaboration enables one to learn the business, gauge competitor strengths and weaknesses, and observe loose bricks. It sounds a bit ruthless, but it is one of the most common of all forms of competitive strategy.

By using this four-part formulation or other models to help stimulate thinking about strategy, you can discover alternatives that would otherwise be hidden. The goal, again, is to decide upon a limited set of vision critical strategies that you intend to pursue for the next few years. Five years for a strategy is a big stretch, and two years is more realistic. Within that time frame you will be coming back to strategies and assessing what is complete, what is still in play, what is not working and ought to be dropped, and what new strategies have emerged, given how the world has evolved.

TAKING THE FIRST WINNING STEPS

With vision, values, and critical strategies in hand, you have just about all the plan that you need, if you are committed to what you have. But you still have to get started. Refer once again to Figure II.1, the Three-Cone Model. Note the arrows at the bottom, nudging you from the probable cone to the preferred. These are the "first winning steps," the small, affordable, feasible actions that can be accomplished in the first six weeks to six months that get you started, that point you in the right direction. We call these "winning steps" rather than the "action plans" or the "tactics," to indicate that these small steps serve as victories that are worth celebrating, just as a team might celebrate winning a game. And in fact, John Kotter (1995) identified a lack of "short term wins" as a critical ingredient in the failure of planned change efforts.

Tools for Developing First Wins

As with strategy, the simplest and best tool for developing first wins is brainstorming and conversation. First wins operate at two levels, the organizational and the personal. At the organizational level the challenge is to take a look at each critical strategy and ask for each one, "What is the first win that will get us started on this strategy?" To qualify as a first win, three simple criteria must be met:

1. Can be fully completed within six weeks to six months.
2. Is clear and specific—who does what by when is spelled out and understood.
3. Will be seen and celebrated as a victory.

If you have a strategy, and designate a first win on the organizational level, you can begin. It should be obvious that before too long you will need to ask what is the next win, and the win after that, to fully implement the strategy. But you do not need to know all of this at the start, and in many ways it is better if you do not try. If you map out a sequence of steps, it can be a reference point, but it needs to be flexible and open to change, lest it blind you rather than guide you.

A Fortune 100 company with whom I worked once gathered 150 managers and line employees for a day, to ask them specifically to name small steps, or first wins, that would move their particular division within the company closer to its vision. Working together in small brainstorming teams, the participants had no trouble naming dozens of small initiatives. The line employees were especially excited to be asked, though skeptical that anything would actually be implemented. One of them, in that session, suggested changing incandescent light bulbs to the new fluorescent bulbs, at a time when few had even heard of such a possibility. Other organizations have designated first wins like the following:

- An association collected 10 examples of nondues income generating endeavors from other associations.
- In a rural school district, educators wanted to participate in a new, onsite master's program but were unsure about the cost. The

superintendent went to the local banker and arranged a loan for educators in the program. As a result of this first winning step, nearly 25 percent of the district's staff went on to obtain the advanced degree.

- A hospital began development of a new short report form to educate staff on the financial and resource situation at the hospital.

First wins also operate at the personal level. Suppose you have created a personal vision that in two years you would like to be taking a year off and sailing around the world on a sailboat. Now, suppose that you don't own a boat and have only limited experience on them. What would be a logical and valuable first win? It might be investigating the cost of boats. It might be locating and interviewing three people who have sailed around the world in a year. Or it might be contacting a local yacht club and signing on to help crew a boat in some upcoming events, so that you can discover whether you actually like it that much.

Within an organization, personal first wins can be equally important. One way to elicit personal wins is to engage everyone in the company to spend a few days reviewing their work over the next few days. The charge is to identify some aspect of their work that would be different if the shared vision was a reality and the strategy(s) were in play. Each individual can then ask, "What aspect of my work can I change, now, to move us closer to the shared vision?"

This will not involve immediate major transformations or complex activities. Rather each person focuses on one or two simple things that can be done in a couple of weeks that will contribute to the strategies and vision. Ideally there is a means for recording these ideas, noting their anticipated outcomes, then checking on the actual result in a few weeks, and finally sharing stories about progress or lack of it in an open atmosphere. If this is repeated, the vision really does become a continuous conversation about where we are, where we are going, and what we are doing next to get there.

TRACKING PROGRESS AND MANAGING CHANGE

Peter Drucker once observed that it is a myth that people hate change, but on the other hand people hate being changed. At this point in preferred future planning you are ready to embark on a journey but face two obstacles, how to manage change and how to keep track of progress.

The Concerns Based Adoption Model (Hord 1987), well-known in educational circles but little known within business, is an effective tool for understanding how to manage change. Based on research into numerous efforts to introduce innovation into organizations, the model posits that when confronted with change people go through a regular and predictable cycle of reaction. This cycle is developmental, in that it involves four stages of concern that people move through in sequence.

When a new idea is introduced, people at first may have no interest at all. They reach the informational level when they begin to ask what this change is all about. Once they have this level of awareness, and are satisfied that they understand the change to some degree, people move to stage two, the level of personal concerns. Here people want to know how the change will affect them personally. Will I have a job? Will I have to come in earlier?

Once personal concerns have been addressed, people can move to level three, management and implementation concerns. Here people wonder how to best manage the change, how to incorporate it into their work, how to collaborate with others. At this stage concerns are all about "How do I do this?" Finally, when people get comfortable at stage three they are ready to move to the fourth and final level of concern, refocusing or improving the change. Here people look for ways to enhance and modify the change so that it is more effective.

People working with a preferred future plan will confront each of these levels of concern, in themselves and in everyone else in the workplace. A key task, then, is to assist people in moving from the initial concern level to the advanced level, by providing ways for people to answer the questions they have. Only when people are satisfied at one level will they move to the next. Simply listening to the questions that people ask as they deal with a change will give you clues about the level they are on and thus what needs to be addressed.

We have previously discussed how common it is for people engaged in any kind of planning activity to experience that activity as an interruption of their work, rather than as the work. When the futuring and planning tasks are finished, people are relieved because now, finally, they can "get back to work." Once there, the vision and strategies begin quickly to fade. Now and then a meeting will be held to address a new strategy, and then it is "back to work." A second tool for managing change and in this case encouraging progress is the use of a model, Figure 10.1, as a think piece designed to combat this common experience.

The objective illustrated in the model is, over time, to merge routine work and strategic work. Rather than finding work on a particular strategy to be an interruption, the routine work of the day is increasingly experienced as strategic, and the strategic work as routine. They become the same thing.

The CEO of a financial services company of about 250 people implemented a project to make his company "vision driven." After a presentation that I attended he was asked, "Now that your company is vision driven, how often do you revisit the vision? Do you meet every other year, once a year, more often?"

The CEO answered, "The vision is what we do now. Every time the

FIGURE 10.1
Routine and Strategic Work

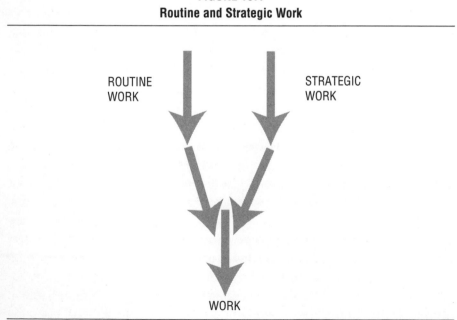

ROUTINE
WORK

STRATEGIC
WORK

WORK

management team meets what we talk about is the vision and how we are doing in achieving it." This is someone who understands the value of merging the strategic and the routine.

Tracking Progress

A simple process for keeping track of progress is desirable. One such sequence that will enable progress toward a vision is as follows.

1. Choose a strategic direction—a vision.
2. Designate the critical strategies.
3. Select a first winning step to shift the trajectory toward the vision.
4. Keep track of the impact that the step has on progress.
5. Determine whether the winning step is in fact a win—has it moved the enterprise closer or further away from the shared vision?
6. If progress is positive, reinforce the action and create the next win.
7. If progress is negative, determine a new action.
8. Review the new present conditions in the enterprise and repeat the process again, and again, and again.

Students of continuous quality in its various forms will recognize this list for what it is, a version of the P-D-C-A cycle, or plan-do-check-act. There is no great mystery to tracking progress. Repeating this cycle over and over enables you to keep track of changing conditions in the environment, respond to surprises and unexpected events, and keep the vision and strategies flexible and in process.

Using a process like this recognizes the reality of moving toward a vision, which I often express in the following way. When you are on the planning team, perhaps on a retreat in an attractive resort, the world looks a lot like the clean and tidy Three-Cone Model for preferred future planning. But when you get back to work, the world looks more like the one in Figure 10.2.

Rather than simple lines of progress from the present to the future, unexpected events, trends, and developments begin quickly to interfere, push you off course, perhaps even obscure your direction altogether. Making progress and managing change becomes a process of continuous adjustment, as you reassess where you are, and develop new actions and revised strategies to get you back on track.

FIGURE 10.2
Preferred Future Planning in Reality

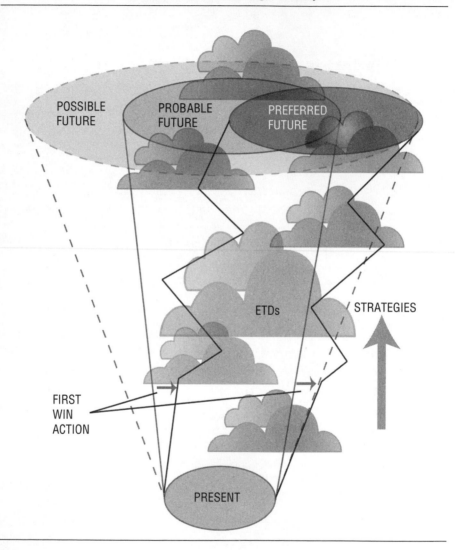

CHAPTER 11

Tailoring Your Career to the Future

Ten years ago, I turned my face for a moment, and it became my life.

—David Whyte, 1994

THE CHANGING NATURE OF WORK

The traditional 9 to 5 job began in the twentieth century. People have always worked of course, and even have largely defined themselves by the work they did. But they did not have jobs. In order to say that, we have to define jobs in twentieth and twenty-first century terms. To have a job means that you go to work for someone else at a specific time each day and do work you are largely instructed to do. In exchange, you are provided security, which comes in the form of wages and benefits, namely health insurance and retirement benefits.

Using this definition, in 1900 it's estimated that only 13 percent of the available work force in the United States had a job, and the numbers would have been similar or even smaller around the world. The majority of human beings were self-employed, as farmers, ranchers, peddlers, craftspeople, and so on. Then the final industrial revolution took place, assembly-line factories and office towers appeared, wages increased, benefits were invented, unions formed, and working conditions improved. People left the farms, which themselves were mechanized to be more efficient, and the twentieth century became the century of jobs. In fact, by 1990, again in the United States some 87 percent of the available work force had a job, and full employment had become a standard political cause. At the present time we can see a similar pattern playing out in China, India, and other developing nations.

But this is changing. Though work is not disappearing, jobs are. This has profound implications for your own career. Jobs cannot be disappearing you might argue, since in times of decent economic growth there are hundreds of thousands of new jobs created each month in the United States, and when we look globally, jobs are being created by the millions.

"Jobs" no longer fit the twentieth century definition. Wages are meandering toward the middle, between the cheap rates of developing nations and the expensive rates of developed nations. Even more dramatically, jobs today are less and less likely to have health care and retirement benefits attached to them. An entire social-political compact is in doubt. The assumption that everyone who wants a job will have one and every job will take care of health care and retirement is disappearing. So far there is no substitute, as witnessed by the annual increases in the number of uninsured Americans and the declining percentage of people covered by employer pensions. No real solution for dwindling benefits has emerged.

As important as these issues are, they are not the most fundamental difference in work that will affect your career. Not only did twentieth century jobs come with wages and benefits, they also tended to come with longevity. A stable career, often with a single employer was a reasonable, if not universal, expectation.

In today's world, jobs are being replaced by stints, at a rapid clip. A stint is a short-term assignment that comes with wages but not necessarily benefits, and by definition without any promise of longevity. You are a stint-based worker when you go to work for a company that is bought-out two years later and downsized, and then you take an assignment on an 18-month project with another company after which it is known that the stint will end although new projects might also appear, and when a project does not appear you set up shop in your home as a consultant and you get some work, but after two years the income is not enough plus the isolation gets to you and you get an opportunity to join a start-up but it goes under after three years and then you take a job with a company that has been around for decades and you breathe a sigh of relief, but after only 14 months your division is outsourced to Indonesia and you despair until you finally get a secure job with a large corporation but the work is stultifying and there are rumors of outsourcing here, too, and you are not sure you are going to stay beyond three years. You are, in other words, a stint-based worker. The number of people working in this way is not clear, but Peter Drucker expected that more than half of all workers would be living the stint-based lifestyle before 2020.

For three decades a favorite futurist forecast was "seven careers in a lifetime." This never made sense, because even dedicated stint-based workers tend to do similar jobs in different settings, rather than actually changing careers. Two or three career changes might become normal, along with many stints, but the situation is not quite so chaotic as seven careers would suggest. This is an important clue when you consider how to tailor your career to the future. You are, in a very fundamental sense, a business of one, equipped with a portfolio of skills and experience, and you are very likely to carry that portfolio from stint to stint for a lifetime. Stable skills will be applied in unstable settings.

We will come back to your portfolio of skills in a moment, but there is one other, deeper shift that may be occurring with work. It is entirely realistic to imagine scenarios in which, in the next two or three decades, a combination of intelligent machines and low-wage labor in developing countries becomes capable of producing virtually all the goods and services needed by the global population. It is possible, in other words, to imagine a future in which work by everyone is simply not necessary. If it was no longer necessary to work, what would this mean, both in terms of how you pay to put food on the table, and how you define your identity? This may sound farfetched. One could have taken Thomas Jefferson aside in 1800 and whispered into his ear that the day would come when only 3 percent of the population would be farmers, not 97 percent, and he would probably have despaired in wonder at what everyone would do. What we did was build cars and skyscrapers and web sites. One must be exceedingly careful in suggesting that in the future it may not be necessary to work, because surely new jobs will appear. Perhaps we will be building magnetic levitation automobiles and space elevators and downloading brains. Except such things are more likely to be done by really smart machines with minimal human intervention and supervision. It is merely an article of faith that millions of new and as yet uninvented jobs will appear in coming decades. We must acknowledge the possibility that new jobs will not be necessary and will not appear, and thus that in the next several decades humans—you and I—will confront a profound question: "What is it that we are all supposed to do, if it is not to produce the basic goods and services that we need? If it is no longer necessary for all humans to be doing this, what is our purpose for being here?"

OPPORTUNITIES WAITING TO BE TAKEN

Most incomes will come from three broad arenas in the next couple of decades. These include developing and implementing the next technologies, responding to changing demographics, and helping institutions and cultures adapt to change (Knoke 1996).

We have explored a variety of current and relatively near-term next technologies, and each represents opportunities for growth. These include in particular the big three, information technology, biotechnology, and nanotechnology. Within these categories there will be a need for scientists and designers, but also for the range of skills required to build and run companies that exploit the technologies, from human resources to marketing and sales. There will likely be a great deal of activity in the next energy era, both in diminishing traditional energy resources and in developing the next ones. Much of the activity will be entrepreneurial and high risk. New energy technologies will not be as geographically fixed as have traditional supplies, as bio-fuels, wind, solar, ocean, and other options can be exploited or developed almost anywhere.

Responding to changing population dynamics will be an obvious growth industry. Opportunities will range from dealing with elder populations to developing unique travel and recreation experiences, to coping with the global migrations that are coming as people respond to the global economic forces and to environmental challenges.

If anything characterizes the coming two decades it will be change— rapid and massive. Thus, assisting individuals, organizations, and whole societies to deal with change is a growth industry. From therapists to personal coaches, to human resource and organization development specialists, to educators and reeducators, and to international negotiators there will be a growing list of needs.

One can also find, with a little research on the Web, clever lists of jobs that are going to disappear and those that may emerge. Much of this information is mere entertainment, but it sparks your imagination. When you see forecasts of new work for gene-pharmers, Turing testers, VR actors, space tourism agents, multimedia correspondents, and data miners, it is possible that new vistas will open. I have suggested that there may be future jobs such as robot personalizers that will work to make robots friendly, vehicle inventors who will make a paradigm shift in personal travel, and aging advocates who will work as agents for individual elders helping them navigate complex systems of support. As you study such a list you can see that inventing and using new technologies, responding to population dynamics, and helping individuals, organizations, and societies adjust to change are indeed the dominant categories. You may see one additional factor at play. What are all the things that machines are unlikely to do, even extremely intelligent machines? Whatever they cannot do is what humans will do.

Though traditional jobs will remain in place, more and more work will become both technical and personal, requiring high technology skills and strong interpersonal skills. Barriers to entry in all kinds of fields are smaller than ever, because access to knowledge, capital, and global networks is simply greater than ever. Thus, I recently suggested to a governor's task force on employment training in a Western state that they stop thinking of how to train employees and start thinking of how to train employers.

WHAT YOU CAN DO WITHOUT CHANGING YOUR CAREER

Ask yourself the following two questions. Could the work that I do be done more cheaply elsewhere in the world? Could the work that I do someday be done by smart machines? In category after category the answer is yes, and, if it is, you will probably change jobs if not careers at some point. Even if your answer is no, ask yourself a third question. Suppose that I stay healthy, anticipated health care breakthroughs come to pass, and I am simply lucky. You might live to be one hundred, and not retire, if you retire at all, until age eighty. Do you want to do the same thing for 60 years? As you consider whether to change or not, clarifying your personal vision and particularly your values becomes vital.

Three tactics stand out if you want to flourish in your current career. First, become more technologically competent. If you are a digital immigrant (over age twenty-five) then occasionally recruit a younger person to teach you how to better use your digital devices. Learn new software. Play with multimedia. Scan technology forecasts. Know what is coming.

Second, improve your communication skills. There is no simpler or more powerful path to success. Opportunities for learning how to make better presentations, conduct better interviews, write better material, communicate interpersonally at a higher level abound. Take them.

Finally, complexify yourself. Observe the world with a wider angle, longer-range lens. Travel abroad once a year. Read at least one science fiction book a year. Read at least one leading edge management book a year. Subscribe to a science and technology journal and an international business and economics journal. Identify a few blogs of interest and read them. In other words, join the future world.

INCREASE YOUR OWN KNOWLEDGE VALUE

Whether you hope to stay in one place or change careers several times, you face the challenge of keeping current. This is both easier and more difficult than ever. There was a time a couple of centuries ago when to be an educated person meant that you would read a canon of a few hundred books. No more. If you define intelligence as the percent of the world's knowledge that you possess in your brain, you are getting dumber by the minute and there is no avoiding it. At the same time, you have easy access to information and knowledge at the tap of a computer key that our ancestors would never have imagined. We have talked for decades about lifelong learning, and it is rather a pain to have to do it. But learn we must, and that is the simple answer to what you need to do to increase your knowledge value. Ask yourself what you have learned in the past six months, and how. Then ask what you plan to learn in the next six months and follow through. Get on a learning curve and stay on it.

PART IV

WHERE AMERICA IS FAILING THE FUTURE

Whether we are in a small village or a giant corporation, in any country and in any type of work, we are being asked to work faster, more competitively, more selfishly—and to focus only on the short term. These values cannot lead to anything healthy and sustainable, and they are alarmingly destructive. . . . I believe we must learn quickly now how to work and live together in ways that bring us back to life.
—Margaret Wheatley, 2002

I am sitting next to an alpine lake high in Washington's Cascade Mountains. My eldest daughter, age twenty-four, and I have hiked here on a beautiful sunny day in the summer of 2004. Sitting at the highest lake on this hike, however, our view is obscured by smoke from a forest fire, pouring over the crest of the mountains from the east. As we sit on a rock and look at the lake through the smoky haze, I tell my daughter about a science fiction book I am reading, the name of which escapes me these years later. The book is set in a postglobal warming world. As it opens parts of the world are so hot that they are simply on fire much of the time, as vast forest and range fires sweep the planet. Intending simply to make conversation, I am surprised when I glance at my daughter and see that she is crying quietly. Seeing my glance, she says, "It just seems so unfair, that my generation will have to live with the mess that yours and those before you have made of the planet."

We are failing the future. Deny this we may try, but there is little doubt about it. The entire world joins in this failing, but rich and powerful nations like mine, the United States, bear a special responsibility and is the focus of this final section. Here in this nation we can not only see what is happening, we have the means to do something about it. But we watch and wait and do not act, not to the extent that would serve future generations as well as we serve ourselves.

Ironically, in failing the future, we may also miss out on the most compelling business opportunities of our generation. It is true that timing is everything in business, and moving too soon on a business opportunity will lead to likely failure, as the technology or the market is not ready. But when the fate not of a business but of the planet hangs in the balance, waiting is not the best option. This final section of the book examines some ways in which we are failing and points to opportunities currently being missed but potentially still available.

We examine two domains in particular, first environmental issues and especially global climate change. Business opportunities that accompany these challenges are actually well-known and already being leveraged, but not yet at the scale that will be needed and soon. The second domain I call the "great divides," the core issues that divide humanity within and between nations. These divides are less amenable to business solutions, yet must be addressed successfully if we are to endow the future with success rather than failure.

Confronting these twenty-first century challenges is a pathway to prosperity and to sustainability as well. Who will invent the next energy, the next transportation, the systems for sustaining an urbanizing human population, food production, manufacturing systems, the systems for managing international finance, the methodologies for making peace instead of war, the conceptual breakthroughs that bring down religious walls without the need for one religion to win, the means for keeping an elder population healthy, the financial tools for relieving debt, the systems for rationalizing labor, and the policies and technologies for combating global warming and sustaining the future environment? These are the tasks for twenty-first century humanity and for twenty-first century business as well.

CHAPTER 12

Environmental Imperatives

People have been talking about the greenhouse effect for more than a hundred years. The trend now is very clear. If the twenty-first century cannot find some better way to power itself, it means ruin.

—Bruce Sterling, 2002

Dr. Roger Payne is a scientist known for his co-discovery of the songs of the humpback whale, for his stirring public television series on whales, and on the voyages of the research vessel the *R.V. Odyssey*. We met in late 2004 when I facilitated the first World Ocean Forum. Roger brought the meeting to stunned silence when he described the biggest public health problem the world has ever faced, the buildup of toxins in the oceans, the vast dumping ground into which everything flows. He has collected evidence from sperm whales, showing concentrations of organohalogens (an organic molecule with extremely poisonous bromine or chlorine attached) *ten million* times greater than the original concentration released into the water by human activity and considered perfectly safe at the release level.

What else is in the ocean? All of the "cides"—insecticides, herbicides, fungicides. If the name of the substance ends in "cide" you know it is designed to kill something. There are also DDT, DDE, myrex, aldrin, endrin, dieldren, dioxins of 75 varieties, furans, PBBs, PBBEs (fire retardant), and 60,000 more chemicals produced at this time.

One of the most toxic substances is PCBs. According to the U.S. Environmental Protection Agency, PCBs cause cancer and have additional adverse health effects that impact the immune system, reproductive system, nervous system, and endocrine system. PCBs are so toxic that if you find a vial with a concentration of 50 parts per million of PCB, you have to dispose of it in a toxic-waste site. Because of the accumulating effect of the food chain, Payne found 400 parts per million in orca whales in the ocean, 3,200 parts per million in beluga whales in the Gulf of St. Lawrence, 6,800 parts per million in dolphins living offshore of major U.S. cities.

This matters to humans, because we eat fish. In fact, 70 percent of humanity, more than 4 billion people, relies on fish as their primary source of animal protein. The fish we eat are mostly predators, living near the top of the food chain—tuna, swordfish, shark, striped bass. All of which are highly polluted. They are, literally, poison, particularly if they are large and old. Animals that nurse their young, like whales and humans, pass the toxic concentration they carry on to their offspring, accelerating the accumulation.

We are failing the future environment. I say this knowing full well the many success stories of the past 30 years, cleaning up rivers, reducing air pollution, increasing energy efficiency, greatly reducing point-source pollution from factories in developed countries, and all the rest. Kudos to us.

But we are still failing. Our failure comes particularly with slow environmental crises, those that involve millions of actions producing minute amounts of damage over many, many decades, until the damage accumulates into something serious. We don't see it because each act, each release, is so small, and because the damage is not apparent for perhaps an entire lifetime. We often go out of our way even to deny there is any impact at all, because we cannot see it, not yet, particularly regarding the ocean, global warming, and clean, drinkable water.

For a water covered planet, Earth has surprisingly little drinkable water. Only one percent of water is safe and drinkable, not much for six billion people, eventually eight billion. Lack of basic sanitation combined with contamination of groundwater means that the amount of clean, safe, drinkable water is declining. One and two-tenths billion people lack access to clean water, and two and six-tenths billion do not have adequate sanitation, leading to the mixing of sewage and drinking water. More than two million died in 2004 from waterborne disease, 90 percent children under age five. Half the hospital beds in developing countries are occupied by persons there because of water-related illness. These numbers will double in the coming two decades if action is not taken to preserve clean water, increase access, and improve sanitation. The shift of population to mega cities, previously discussed, adds to the pressure on water and sanitation systems.

As an environmental imperative, water does not seem a problem to those who have easy access to it. Even in advanced countries, water is not safe from contamination, with similar effects as when toxins reach the ocean. In one study, the tap water of every one of 29 U.S. cities was found to have trace amounts of at least one weed killer. It is in the developing world where the problem is acute. Water is the most fundamental of human needs and the UN Water for Life goal of a 50 percent reduction in the proportion of people without access to clean water and sanitation by 2015 is an important goal.

GLOBAL WARMING IS REAL

Three things threaten human survival on a large scale. Terrorism is *not* one of the three. They are instead, a massive asteroid or comet strike, a global pandemic, and runaway global warming. With asteroids there are some efforts, such as a sky survey, to account for the potential threat. On pandemics, few things garner more attention in the news or urgent action to take preventive steps. With global warming, despite 25 years of warnings and innumerable conferences and treaties, we mostly, it seems, do not yet care. A 2004 Gallup poll found that nearly half of Americans worry "not at all" or "very little" about global warming. An ABC News poll in July 2005 found 66 percent of Americans saying that global warming will not affect their lives.

These blasé attitudes came home to me in the fall of 2004. I was leading a session on long-range trends for the board of directors and senior management of a national insurance company. Gathered in a meeting room at a waterfall-side resort in the foothills of the Cascade Mountains, we talked about the future as outside a rainfall of historic proportions sent the river and falls well over flood stage. At one point, I raised the issue of environmental imperatives and global warming in particular. "Have you noticed," I asked, "how hard it is raining?" Confused stares. "Well, it is

November in the Pacific Northwest, of course it's raining," came a response. I persisted. "But have you taken note of how many 100-year floods and torrential downpours we have now, in just the past decade, even while the region is often in an overall draught?" Response? "Let's talk about interest rates next quarter."

I knew, as apparently these insurance executives either did not know or more likely chose to ignore, that for 25 years climate scientists had forecast that among the signs of global warming would be anomalous weather patterns, wild weather. Like most other business executives I meet, this group took comfort in counterclaims to global warming that suggested either that the data was insufficient yet to make any claims, or that any measurable warming was a natural pattern about which we could do nothing or that would shortly return to normal.

Scientists by 10,000 to 1 believe the evidence points to real warming, and that this warming is fundamentally caused by human activity, namely the release of greenhouse gases into the atmosphere in the past 200 years. The Intergovernmental Panel on Climate Change (IPCC) released a report in 2001 concluding that "Most of the observed warming over the last 50 years is likely to have been due to the increase in greenhouse gas concentrations" (McCarthy 2001). More recently a survey was done of all 998 studies of climate change published in refereed scientific journals from 1993 to 2003. All the peer-reviewed research agreed that warming is real. All. Not a single peer-reviewed article offered counterevidence. None.

The year 2005 came in as the hottest on record since such information was recorded in 1880, continuing a trend that finds the 10 hottest years in history all recorded since 1990. The increase is being felt most in northern latitudes, in particular the Arctic, which is warming twice as fast as the rest of the planet. There, an annual survey of sea ice in September of each year, a simple satellite photo, shows 20 percent less sea ice now than in 1979, leading scientists to forecast that the Arctic could be ice free in summer months by 2050 to 2070. Think of that. Let it bounce around your mind awhile. In your mind's eye see all those photos of intrepid explorers making their way across the vast frozen ice flows on dog sleds, and then observe as all of that ice turns into open sea.

Greenland is another melting story. On this mini-continent rests 10 percent of the world's freshwater ice, the remainder located mostly in the Antarctic. Average temperatures in Greenland have risen five degrees Fahrenheit (three degrees Celsius) in the past decade. The thickness of the glaciers covering more than 80 percent of Greenland is declining a meter per year. And the glaciers are on the move. One of the largest, the Helheim, is flowing into the sea at 110 feet a day compared to 70 feet in 2001. Scientists now fear that a tipping point has been reached and that this melting will accelerate. While conventional global warming forecasts have assumed that melting in Greenland would raise sea levels from 4 inches to 36 inches in the twenty-first century, newer models that take into account this recent acceleration suggest that another three degree increase in average temperature will cause melting that could raise sea level 20 feet. Goodbye, much of Florida and Manhattan.

But there is more, something I first learned about from climate scientists in 2000 at a conference on the next 1,000 years. The Gulf Stream is an ocean current that brings warm water up from the equatorial Atlantic to the north, a conveyor belt of warmth that keeps the United Kingdom, Ireland, and northern Europe temperate in climate. As Greenland melts it not only raises sea level. More importantly, it pours huge amounts of fresh water into the northern end of the Gulf Stream. As the volume of melt increases, scientists anticipate that the Gulf Stream could *shut down*. They know this is possible, because it happened 12,700 years ago. When it collapsed, Britain, which is actually at the same latitude as Siberia, was covered in permafrost for 1,300 years. For the United Kingdom, global warming will not mean Bermuda shorts and tropical drinks. It will mean ice hotels. This is a paradox of global warming that skeptics use to discount it. Hah, they retort, global warming scientists cannot even decide if the world will get hotter or colder. The point is, it will do both.

TIME IS NOT ON OUR SIDE

One need only read the last few paragraphs or better yet the extensive and detailed documentation on global warming (see the references) to understand why, well, we just don't want to think about this, much less do anything. But time is not on our side.

In July of 2005 while leading a think tank on the 50-year future for transportation, we listened to a speaker, Karen Henry, from a U.S. Army Corps of Engineers lab that specializes in cold-weather infrastructure. She explained how the Arctic is melting, showing photos of roads breaking up as the permafrost melts. Then she made a startling statement. The first human migrations in response to global warming are underway. It turns out that in Alaska, the Canadian arctic, in the Southwest Pacific islands of Vanuatu, and in New Guinea, villages are being moved inland, to escape decline of pack ice, rising sea levels, and erosion. In the case of the Carteret atolls of New Guinea, the expectation is that they will be underwater by 2015. But that was not all that Henry suggested. As she concluded she offered an eerie speculation. "I have a feeling," Henry said, "that the day will come when people in Florida and on the Gulf Coast begin to move away, as they say, "I just can't live through another one.' (Henry 2005).

And then came Katrina and Rita, and the worst hurricane season in history. Government spokespersons dutifully went before the microphones to solemnly intone, "There is no evidence that any particular storm is caused by or related to global warming." But we can see the obvious, as we read the data on the Arctic and the hotter than ever ocean temperatures that spawn hurricanes.

One more illustration of global warming and then we can look for answers. The example comes from Bruce Sterling, one of the great writers of this generation. Carbon dioxide (CO_2), the primary outgas released into the atmosphere from burning fossil fuels, has been skyrocketing in the age of coal and oil. In 1950, atmospheric concentrations were 310 parts per million. In 2002 when Bruce wrote *Tomorrow Now*, it was up to 360 parts (as this book is written, concentrations are now at 380 parts per million). When combined with other greenhouse gases, this is enough to trap sufficient heat to equal two and a half watts of energy per square meter of the planet. Two and a half watts is equivalent to a birthday candle. So, cover the earth with one meter square tables, on each table place a cupcake, and in the cupcake light a birthday candle. That is how much heat is being added at this time.

Ten or fifty years from now we might hope that it was all a mirage, that the earth did not warm, and that our millennia of easy living has continued. But it is more likely that future generations will say, in the words of Sterling, "You thought *that* was the greenhouse effect. Ha! (2002, 285)."

GREEN BUSINESS IS THE KEY TO YOUR SURVIVAL

Each of these three critical environmental issues has solutions that are partly a matter of public policy and political will, and partly a matter of business entrepreneurship. Political progress has been modest, ranging from successes such as the protocol to reduce chlorofluorocarbons (CFCs) to the failure of the Kyoto Accord to reduce CO_2 and other greenhouse gases. When the United States ostentatiously walked out of the most recent round of talks in Montreal aimed at reducing greenhouse emissions, it was just another blow against efforts to rein in global warming. To date China, India, and the United States refuse to join in the goal oriented approach, preferring to rely on the market and private initiative. So far this is not working, as the U.S. Department of Energy reported a 2 percent increase in gas emissions in 2004 over 2003, with the total now 16 percent higher than in 1990, the Kyoto target. Eighty percent of U.S. emissions are CO_2, from fossil fuels burned for electricity, transportation, manufacturing, and industrial processes.

If this is going to change, business is going to have to go green, quickly. The good news is that it can, and those who lead will become wealthy. The energy transformation, as we have said, will be the greatest revenue opportunity of this century. Each month that passes increases the stakes.

Cutting greenhouse gases is great for the bottom line. DuPont, winner of the 2005 *BusinessWeek* Green Company award, for example, has decreased its emissions of greenhouse gases 65 percent since 1990, a reduction of 11 million metric tons, and has saved more than $2 billion by cutting its energy use 7 percent below 1990 levels. Ford Motor Company shares similar goals, and reduced CO_2 emissions from its facilities by 15 percent from 1995 to 2000. More recently, as we have noted previously, Ford has announced the most ambitious U.S. effort to produce hybrid cars, though they still trail the Japanese by an order of magnitude in this regard.

The U.S. EPA announced its One Million Solar Roofs initiative in the late 1990s, and it is now beginning to show results in many states. In 2004 the governor of California announced the California Hydrogen Highway initiative, a vision to make hydrogen available to every California driver on major highways in the state by 2015. We previously reviewed the promise and problems with hydrogen, but it will take visions this bold to head off the extreme effects of global warming. The Green Entrepreneurs network of Europe offers a variety of tools to get into green business, or to achieve savings via green practices in existing businesses. GreenBiz.com and Sustainablebusiness.com in the United States are but two of many networks promoting green business opportunities.

On December 13, 2005 the California Utilities Commission announced a preliminary decision to create the California Solar Initiative, a $3.2 billion 10-year program to develop 3,000 megawatts of solar energy for the state. Two months earlier the same commission had announced that going forward California would no longer buy electricity from coal-fired power plants, unless these plants had economical programs in place to sequester carbon dioxide so that greenhouse emissions did not exceed comparable natural gas plants. In November of 2005, Sterling Energy Systems, Inc., of Phoenix, Arizona, announced ambitious plans to build a four mile square energy farm of mirrors and sterling engines in the California desert 80 miles from Los Angeles. This farm when completed could generate 500 megawatts of electricity, enough for 300,000 homes. A similar energy farm 100 miles square somewhere in the American Desert could provide all the 2005 electricity needs of the country, although the amount of aluminum, steel, and other materials required would dwarf typical domestic production of such products.

Where are the opportunities in the coming decade? Where will the future be turned into revenue? Wind power, flexible solar voltaics, sterling engines, nanosolar, biomass, biotech to produce hydrogen, redesign and retrofitting of cities away from exurbia and to the center, green architecture, energy efficiency, LED lighting systems to replace both incandescent and vapor lamps, on-demand hot water, insulation, carbon sequestration, carbon nanotube heat pumps, hybrid cars, super-lightweight carbon composite and lightweight steel cars running on hybrid or even small fuel cells, mass transit, sidewalk construction, bicycles, power assisted bicycles, plug-in hybrid vehicles, better batteries, nano batteries, software for energy management, distributed power generation of all kinds, intelligent HVAC, software for selling power back to the grid, replacing the old electricity grid with an intelligent grid, smart appliances, co-generation, onsite hydrogen fuel cells, and ocean energy systems are only a few of the opportunities that are available, and desperately needed.

Here is a hint at where you can make some money. Microsoft, a mature business, is now growing 8 percent a year. Solar is growing at 20 percent a year, wind energy at 24 percent a year. Both are expected to improve in the high oil cost era we are now in. Riskier but potentially huge.

Climate change is not the only arena for green business, just the largest and most urgent on a massive scale. As for clean water and sanitation, there are many opportunities. A 2005 product of the year in many lists is the LifeStraw, a simple water filter in a large plastic straw from Vestergaard Frandsen in Switzerland. Costing only $3, it can literally be dipped into any water source, sucked on, and the filters make the water safe for drinking. Vost Water Systems, one of many companies working on solutions, produces a sanitation system that recycles waste in 90 percent less land area and with substantially less energy than conventional systems. A simple technology using a vertical shaft instead of a vast field, it appears highly desirable for both developed and developing nations alike. The energy savings alone would be significant contributors to reducing greenhouse emissions.

Finally, the issue of toxins in the ocean, with which we began this chapter, is also available for business opportunity, even small business. The basic task is to stop the entry of the harmful substances into the ocean. In many cases the disposal is actually fairly easy—you oxidize it or you reduce it some way chemically, into harmless molecules. We just don't bother much of the time. This is no longer acceptable. On the larger scale we are talking about major international protocols and industrial scale pollution prevention programs and products.

Other environmental imperatives aside, when we look back I believe we will see that 2005 marked the tipping point on global warming, the point at which the evidence became, unfortunately, irrefutable, and the public became convinced that global warming was real. The only questions now are What we are going to do, and is there time to do it?

CHAPTER 13

The Great Divides

*New and creative approaches are needed to convert poverty
into an opportunity for all concerned. That is the challenge.*
—C. K. Prahalad, 2005

Today there is much that divides us, including income, education, access to technology, and religion. Such divides threaten the future. Division is deep in human history, but not inevitable. "The other" is often imagined as over the horizon, around the bend, waiting to destroy. Politicians are quite fond of warning about "the enemy" who "lurks." Technological capabilities of the future may close or expand these divides. Small groups of angry, disgruntled people can cause great damage. The fundamental divides are a brake on our collaborative journey to the future, holding us back from prosperity and from our true potential as humanity. These divides confront business with responsibilities, but more than that with opportunity.

There are also divides related to race and gender, access to health care, and exposure to diseases like AIDS and malaria. There are divides in degree of political power and of freedom. Though difference is often our greatest source of strength, divisions are failings or areas where we still need to evolve.

WEALTH DIVIDE

Bucky Fuller, it was pointed out earlier, believed that by the late 1980s humanity had acquired the requisite connectivity, technology, and knowledge to enable billions of "millionaires" to live together on this planet, were we only to devote our intelligence to "livingry" rather than "weaponry" as he used to say, and to apply our intelligence to working smarter. But we have not done this.

Of six billion people on the planet, some three billion live on less than $2 a day. This is surprising, if you examine history. Until about 1820 the most common experience in the world was poverty. Then what we now refer to as the developed world began an economic takeoff. Fed by geographical advantages, coal and then oil, access to technology, relative political and economic freedom, and later by global empire, the income difference between rich countries and poor countries went from a ratio of 3 to 1 in 1820, to more than 90 to 1 today. One percent of the global population owns more than fifty percent of global wealth, and a few hundred people at the top now own more wealth than the bottom 2.5 billion people on the planet.

In the United States an income gap is growing as we seemingly attempt to re-create the Gilded Age of the late nineteenth century. We live in a time when a small percentage at the top of the income pyramid are amassing mega fortunes, multiple estate homes, and expensive yachts. The tax system has been re-wired to enable the superrich to amass more and more while shifting the main tax burden onto wage earners. The 2003 federal tax cut, for example, returned $93,000 to each millionaire, and $217 to each middle income wage earner.

Wages have stagnated by most measures since the early 1970s, in real terms. Families have compensated in the meantime by shifting first to two wage earners, and more recently to multiple jobs. From 2000 to 2005 wages for the bottom 20 percent fell 7.8 percent, from $11,141 to $10,264. For the next 20 percent, average income fell 5.7 percent, from $27,818 to $26,241. Meanwhile the gap between the top and bottom increased. People in the top 20 percent now earn 15 times the average income as the bottom 20 percent, compared to a difference of 12 times average earnings in 2000.

Poverty is growing in the United States. The poverty rate is officially set in dollar terms at $19,000 a year for a single person, $29,000 for a family of four. By this measure, 37 million Americans live in poverty, 5.4 million more than in 2000. The poverty rate in the United States exceeds that of the other nations in the Organization for Economic Cooperation and

Development (OECD). "Income inequality is high and rising in the US compared to the rest of the OECD. At the bottom of the income scale, US poverty rates are higher and living standards are lower than for those at the bottom of comparable economies. Moreover, income mobility appears to be *lower* in the US than in other OECD countries" (Mishel 2005). While U.S.-style poverty may not compare to Latin American or African poverty, it is still real and debilitating. This is particularly true for children, 21 percent of whom live in poverty in the United States. Moreover, poverty is becoming more long-lasting, even self-perpetuating as nearly 15 percent of the population lives in "permanent poverty."

The bottom line is simple. We can sugarcoat economic statistics, point to skyrocketing housing values, crow about GDP growth figures that mean little to average wage earners, and the reality is that the wealth divide is growing at the present time, and in the long run this is deeply problematic. It would be less so if all boats were rising but they are not, as evidenced in the numbers from this century.

EDUCATION DIVIDE

Everything works together, of course. In the United States today, if your family earns more than $75,000, you have a 69 percent chance of getting a college degree, from $25,000 to $75,000 the chances fall to 49 percent, and if your family falls below the poverty level of about $25,000 your chances of completing a four-year college degree are no better than 17 percent. A longitudinal study by the U.S. Department of Education from 1998 to 2005 found that family income was a much better indicator than test scores of whether a student would complete college. High income students with low test scores are still more likely to complete college than low income students with high test scores.

How are we responding to this disparity? By increasing the cost of college education while simultaneously cutting funds available to low income students, particularly grant funds. Contrast this to the years after World War II. How is it that the United States in the 30 years after that war built the largest and most financially successful middle class the world has known? The answer can be found primarily in the GI Bill. Returning soldiers were promised, and provided, a four-year college education, regardless of their income. No policy in history has done more to create an egalitarian, upwardly mobile society than that, and when it faded the middle class began to fade with it.

Education divides are reflected in the U.S. literacy rate. An estimated 37 million Americans, 1 in 10, are functionally illiterate, according to the 2005 report of the U.S. Department of Education. The United States ranks fifteenth of 30 countries in reading literacy, and these gaps cost $158 billion a year according to one estimate.

Globally access to education can be deeply disparate, particularly with regard to women. The UN estimates that two-thirds of those still illiterate in the world are women, some as the result of national or cultural limits that deny education to women. At the same time there have been great international strides in education since the 1990s. Only half of age relevant children worldwide were enrolled in secondary education in 1990, but by 2002 this had risen to 65 percent. This drops to 50 percent if the focus is only on upper secondary education (equivalent of grades 10–12) but still is much improved. The lowest rates are in Africa, where in some places participation falls below 40 percent. This is in contrast to China where rates are 97 percent, while they are more than 90 percent in Malaysia.

A global gap widens when it comes to tertiary or postsecondary education. In Europe and North America the average is three years, but in Asia and South America the average falls to one year. This is despite the rapid growth to an average of two years of postsecondary education in China. In Africa, tertiary education has no impact, as the average years in school number only 7.8. Postsecondary education exceeds a year only in South Africa and Tunisia. In India the average is less than a half-year. The top 10 countries provide 30 times the average postsecondary education as do the bottom 10. This divide must be addressed.

DIGITAL DIVIDE—ACCESS TO INFORMATION AND TECHNOLOGY

Interestingly the divide that has received perhaps the most attention in the past 10 years is the digital divide. When computers were few and very expensive, concerns were raised about whether they would become tools that only the elite could have, while the poor would fall further behind.

The divide has been real enough and obviously connected to poverty, literacy, and geography. Access is improving as costs come down. In the United States, computer ownership ranges from 63 percent for families with incomes under $20,000 to 93 percent for families earning more than $70,000.

Globally the ability to own a personal computer has been and obviously still is out of reach for most of the population. But people are ingenious and ownership of technology may not be as critical as we might think. Public access points to the Internet are exploding around the world, from NGO or government supported telecenters to private sector Internet cafes that have popped up in every locale. The latter are turning out to be vital. Many people who have never seen a computer are seeing the results of searches on the Internet, which are printed and passed around ubiquitously.

Beyond computers are cell phones, and here individual ownership is growing by the millions per month. India will reach 500 million cell phones this year, China has an installed base of 250 million, Brazil has reached 40 million. And contrary to popular conceptions, the poor are very much savvy to information technology. In one of the poorest areas of India, where the $2 a day income is common, 85 percent of households own a television and more than 20 percent now have phones.

Going forward the most significant digital divide will be access to high-speed networks, usually wireless or mobile. A recent report from the World Bank found that 77 percent of the world's population now lives within range of a mobile network, an astonishing number when you consider that a few years ago, before the Internet and before cellular phones it was common to lament that two-thirds of the global population lived more than a two-hour walk from the nearest phone.

RELIGION

Will religion be the death of us? I ask this question in all sincerity. The final and most vexing divide is religion. It seems that human beings have always sought supernatural explanations for the unknown and mysterious. As we all know, in recent centuries people settled on a series of books, written hundreds or thousands of years ago as the final word on the search. And this has led to the greatest of all divides.

There are three problems. First, there is more than a single book, each claiming to be the final and only book. Second, these books were written by men who lived in pre-scientific, pre-rational enlightenment, pre-technological times. Were they written by educated people today they might look substantially different. In addition, the books and their sub-books were mostly written by people who lived years, decades, or centuries after the actual events they describe. Third, and most critically, the followers of each book claim, and indeed believe, that the precise words were inscribed or at a minimum specifically inspired by the god named in the book, and thus the followers suspend reason and rely on faith when assessing the truth or value of the book in question.

The followers of each of the major books have now divided themselves into "moderates" and "fundamentalists." The moderates tell you that the book in question is a "story." The writer(s) may have been inspired, but there is no need to believe that all elements of the story are true; rather one must allow the messages contained in the story only to guide one's own faith. Fundamentalists insist that the book in question is the single, only, complete, and unerring word of the god in question, that the events described in the book are true in every factual detail, and that this is to be accepted without question.

The fundamentalists of each book, enabled by the moderates, now insist that the most important game in the world is religious market share. In the case of the two dominant books, those of Christianity and Islam, this quest for market share has achieved a fever pitch, in large part because of the money and power that accrue to those with the biggest market share. Religion has thus shifted from a private affair in the stillness of one's heart or room, to a mega church, music blaring, gold chains dripping, suicide bombings, or millions of people on pilgrimage affair.

People have always been willing to kill and die for their particular book, but this willingness seems as high now as in the Middle Ages, and magnified by modern weapons, instant communications, and rapid travel. Moreover, the fundamentalists of each book have decided that it is critical at this point in history to merge their religion with their government, and henceforth to govern according to the book rather than to secular laws. But as Frank Herbert said in the *Dune Trilogy*, "When religion and politics ride in the same cart, the whirlwind follows." The move into governance has been accompanied by an altogether furious attack on science and on reason itself.

All of this strikes me as dangerous, perhaps as dangerous as anything threatening our future. It has obviously contributed to the terrorism and conflict that has characterized this century, though I hasten to add that of all the threats we face, terrorism is the most overrated (B. Friedman 2005).

Harris (2005, 15) argues that "We have been slow to recognize the degree to which religious faith perpetuates man's inhumanity to man." He suggests that we have to confront three myths to take this on, a task that he argues persuasively is urgent. The first myth is the idea that faith provides good things that cannot be had elsewhere. The second is that the terrible things done in the name of religion, like flying planes into buildings, are somehow the result of something other than that faith. And the final myth is that one should never speak of these things in a way that challenges the whole concept of faith or religion as it currently exists because religion is both fundamental to being human and divinely inspired and therefore not subject to discussion.

TURNING DIVIDES INTO PREFERRED FUTURES

This century and its predecessor have taught us that the great divides may slow economic progress, cause great misery, or even kill us. However it is now possible to see pathways to overcome these divides, pathways that come in the form of business and public policy partnerships, and breakthrough thinking.

Let's begin with the income divide and poverty. Radically new models are emerging that hold the prospect of ending poverty in the world. While that is an outrageous statement, it is a 15 percent vision, that is a vision we don't know fully how to accomplish but we try anyway because the vision is so important. Several ideas have come together in recent years, each exciting, each even capable of creating business revenue that can then be used to carry the vision forward. Jeffrey Sachs (2005) speaking on behalf of the UN Millennium project and an enlightened business community has laid out the vision itself, relating the story of John Maynard Keynes who wrote in the depths of the Great Depression of his dream of ending poverty in developed countries by the end of the twentieth century.

A key strategy against global poverty has been the financing method known as micro-credit (Yunnas 2003). People in poverty are beset by many problems, but credit is one of the central ones. In the vast shantytowns of the mega cities of the world, credit might be available, but from a local warlord or intermediary, at an interest rate of 600 percent. When a legitimate financial institution appears or is created to provide micro-credit, a loan of as little as $25 or $30 with an interest rate of 25 percent is sufficient to support local entrepreneurship. The rate, while high by developed world standards, is very low locally but high enough to enable the financial institution to profit and continuously make such loans.

Micro-loans are not the only story. Prahalad (2005) has provided the conceptual leap with a stunning idea that may not only break the back of global poverty but will also enable the global economy to flourish. Simply, there is a "fortune at the bottom of the pyramid." Prahalad lays out a multi-point program for redefining the global poor, even those on $2 a day, as a market rather than victims. To do so would require great innovation in product and service and partnerships with the poor themselves. The project by Nicholas Negroponte, the MIT Media Lab, and a nonprofit called One Laptop per Child, in collaboration with Quanta Computing, speaks to such innovation. They intend to debut a $100 laptop for the developing world in late 2006 or early 2007. A Chinese production of a $50–$80 computer would be a worthy competitor.

The whole point is that individually the poor are powerless, but as an aggregate market they are gigantic. If companies could catch this wave in the coming few years, it may be one divide that is narrowed more than we dare to believe is possible.

The education divide is also available for breakthrough business innovation. Mark Anderson's Project Inkwell is an entrepreneurial effort to bring desktop computing to every schoolchild in the United States and the world. Online learning via massively multi-player online role playing games has not yet entered the education market in a deliberate way, but the learning that takes place inside such virtual worlds, if planned and assessed, could be a tremendous education tool. Beyond that is use of wireless handheld devices for just in time learning. A person anywhere in the world ought to be able to ask their cell phone a question and receive an educational lesson at any time, either for a small fee or perhaps in exchange for listening to a 10-second advertisement.

Turning the digital divide into preferred futures lends itself to a variety of opportunities, most of which are imbedded within the projects to deal with poverty and with education. We have just begun to grasp the entrepreneurial energy that will be available when we move to nearly 100 percent of the global population within wireless range, and millions more people each month acquiring their own handsets or shared access. Stories of fishermen off the coasts of Asia, continuing to fish in their centuries old ways, but pausing offshore with their daily catch to place cell phone calls in order to learn which market needs which fish and where the prices will be best are only the beginning.

And finally there is religion. How can business deal with this divide when so many business people themselves subscribe to the same books and in particular to the same moderation or fundamentalism in their faith that makes the faith and its resulting divisions off limits for conversation? I do not know the answer to that. But I know the conversation must happen. We can begin with the obvious fact that all business is global. Religious divides and intolerance are incompatible with that. In addition, a knowledge value economy will depend on scientific research and discovery. This will happen best in a climate in which faith is open to question. Such discovery will not happen in a climate where faith is not to be questioned and is used to dictate public policy decisions.

One possible approach has been dialogues on the question of whether religion "will be the death of us." Reverend David Brown and I have led such dialogues. In them we encourage participants to explore whether humanity must move beyond religion, or, given the unlikelihood or undesirability of that happening, moving instead to a better way of doing religion. These sessions model a conversation about faith that is open, reflective, and forward-looking without being exclusive.

"What could possibly cause billions of people to reconsider their religious beliefs?" asks Sam Harris (2005, 224). He answers:

And, yet, it is obvious that an utter revolution in our thinking could be accomplished in a single generation: if parents and teachers would merely give honest answers to the questions of every child. Our doubts about the feasibility of such a project should be tempered by an understanding of its necessity, for there is no reason whatsoever to think that we can survive our religious differences indefinitely.

These great divides and the others that we have only mentioned may evolve in a variety of ways. If ignored, the divides may widen, resulting in hardship, turmoil, even bloodshed. If attended to constructively, the great divides may narrow and heal, with a resulting increase in creative energy in the world. As the Time Traveler character says in "The Toynbee Convector" (Bradbury, 1988, 10), "You see the point, don't you, son? To weave dreams and put brains and ideas and flesh and the truly real beneath the dreams."

CHAPTER 14

A Vision for the Twenty-First Century

Once time was divided into past, present and future, the past was mirrored in the reconstructed images of history. Foreshadowings of the future were seen in constructive images of the future. But our time knows only a continuous present. Between the present and cosmological time lies nothing, a vacuum. Qualitatively speaking time is not the same as formerly. The age old interplay between images of the future and the course of time has been abruptly broken off.

—Fred Polak 1973

SPACESHIP EARTH IS NOT AN OBSOLETE CONCEPT

Remember "spaceship earth?" The idea was simple. We are all crew, on a single ship, sailing through the void of space. What happens to any of the crew and the ship will impact all of us. Lately, a new cultural idea has taken root, and it is high contrast. It can be expressed as follows: "We are all in this, alone." There is constant talk of the ownership society, private accounts, personal responsibility in all things and never social responsibility, along with continuous efforts to identify enemies out there. The ideas have a certain appeal, but at a deep level they say you are alone, everyone is out to get you, and mere survival of the fittest is the goal. Ironically those who most strongly tout this line often claim not to believe in evolution based on survival of the fittest. But we are not in this alone, and spaceship earth is not an obsolete concept. We are all here, and it is a single planet hurtling through space.

TURNING REVENUE INTO THE FUTURE

This book is about turning the future into revenue. If you have stuck with it from beginning to end, you will probably have experienced it as kind of a strange trip. We began with descriptions of probable and possible futures and resulting revenue opportunities. Then we shifted abruptly to mental models and techniques for choosing preferred futures, and finally we confronted critical future challenges that threaten us. In taking the entire trip you may have discovered a hidden code. Turning the future into revenue is only half an equation. The other half is how to turn revenue into the future. This is the true result we want, after all. Revenue is of no value without a future. So we conclude with some thoughts on turning revenue into the preferred future.

The twenty-first century has started badly. It is hard to argue otherwise, despite many promising developments in science and technology, and in population dynamics. We have not gotten the twenty-first century that we all expected when the millennium was approaching. We have a challenge now—restarting the century.

IMAGES OF THE FUTURE

For many people the future image changed in the autumn of 2001, when it seemed that one view of the future came to an end and a new and less hopeful image emerged. Quite literally hope and the future were torn asunder. Have you noticed the degree to which our current view of the future is subject to the belief that things are bad, worse than they have ever been, and getting even worse by the moment?

Perhaps more interesting is to note how pleased many people are with this bleak assessment of the future. A few people seem positively giddy that things seem so bad. But what happens when a growing proportion of a society adopts a decaying view of the future? Does it matter?

In the early twenty-first century our images of the future have come to be dominated by large, impersonal forces, including globalization, turbulent economics, fast-changing science and technology, mass political and religious movements. Robert Heilbroner (1996) has suggested that these forces were generally seen as benign and positive in earlier historical periods but have recently come to appear potentially or actively threat-ening and dangerous. In both the most advanced industrial regions of the world and in the developing world the vision of the future has taken on this frightening tenor. Today's image of the future is marked by a new degree of pessimism.

While we don't know for certain, it is generally believed that through-out most of human history people believed that things would not change, at least not very much. The degree of change that occurred within a life-time, which averaged about 30 years, was so small that the world would have seemed stable. Then we entered a period of history roughly coincid-ing with the industrial age when people came to believe that things would change, faster and faster. Moreover, the expectation was that such change would be mostly for the better.

Today people continue to believe that things will change, but many now believe such change will be for the worse. What will be worse? You name it—the environment, the food supply, disease, overpopulation, global warming, international conflict, terrorism, business ethics, the economy, the behavior of young people, and on the list goes. As one person lamented to me after I had given a very upbeat and sunny speech on the future in the late 1990s, "I knew that things were changing, but I didn't know it was this bad."

It is not clear that such a negative image of the future has become dominant in our time. It is, however, clear that the future is seen as quite uncertain, and by many people quite likely worse than today. There are positive consequences of this more skeptical view of the future. The most important positive effect is a heightened vigilance against unconsidered technology, social inequality, and exploitation, as compared to a blind faith that things will always get better, all by themselves.

But there is a cost as well. The cost is reflected most significantly in a drift toward a growing proportion of people who adopt a future image marked by discouragement and stagnation, and ultimately hopelessness.

Contrast such a dour future image with the image of a visionary such as Buckminster Fuller, who argued that only in the 1980s and afterward had the world reached a level of technological, scientific, and imaginative knowledge, as well as sufficient connectivity, that it would now be feasible to take care of all humanity on the planet at a high standard of living, ever doing more and more with less and less, and thus preserving and enhancing the environment in the process.

Such an image seems both quaint and yet alluring in the early twenty-first century. Perhaps it seems quaint to think that a positive image of the future might have any validity or vitality in these cynical times. We are, instead, encouraged to fear the future, whether it comes in the form of overwhelming change, religious fanatics, or diseased chickens and ducks.

Fifty years ago Fred Polak raised an alarm. He proposed four critical theses:

1. The process of de-utopianizing then underway pointed to an underlying process.
2. The deep underlying forces of this process were upsetting a historical equilibrium and obliterating all thinking about the future.
3. The breakdown was a radical development, not simply a temporary disturbance in a historical pattern.
4. "In the absence of a diligent application of counter forces, the defunct condition of current images predisposes Western culture to breakdown. (Polak 1973, 223)"

We seem then to be caught in a loop. Fearful of the future, we avoid thinking about it. The future becomes a void that manifests as a lack of positive images of the future, particularly global futures, but also national, local, and enterprise futures. We count on our ability to muddle through as a survival strategy. But Polak was warning 50 years ago that such a void would lead to an abyss.

In contrast, we have seen that when it comes to your career or to the future of your business enterprise, the image of the future, particularly the preferred future, is the key leverage point for change. What will be the images of the future that will emerge in the coming decades of this century?

TWENTY-FIRST CENTURY DO-OVER

I suggest that we are in desperate need of a new vision for humanity in the twenty-first century, a vision as far from endless war as possible. We are in need of nothing less than a chance to start the twenty-first century all over again. The vision has eight parts.

1. Convert to the next energy era as soon as possible, even embarking on *Apollo* projectlike efforts to move more quickly. This era is beyond fossil fuels, and includes distributed renewable energy of many types, suitable to development in locations all over the planet. Thus the back is broken of energy oligarchies and all the regional and international conflict that comes with such concentration, and we attempt to minimize global warming as effectively as possible in the process.

2. Convert to the next transportation era as soon as possible, and particularly to the next automobile era. Such autos must be super-efficient, will include hybrids initially as a bridge to lightweight vehicles that run primarily on renewable bio-fuels and fuel cells, and must eventually be integrated with whole systems approaches to transportation that maximize choice and minimize adverse environmental impact. The next transportation era will necessarily include intense redevelopment of central cities to enable quality living with minimal need for long-distance movement to conduct daily life.

3. Bring broadband communications to affordable devices the last mile to all of Earth's inhabitants, enabling the emergence of full global community.

4. Accelerate the shift to no-waste, little energy, low-cost, cradle-to-cradle manufacturing of goods, eventually to include the possibility of molecular manufacturing and the shipping of bits rather than mass.

5. Accelerate the intelligent integration of a global labor system, where work is done where it makes the most sense, wages and benefits move to the middle, and a global middle class is born, while local capability for the production of basic necessities is maintained to allow for global emergencies and local commerce, and do all of this faster than two generations to minimize disruption.

6. Bring local economic development at the micro-credit scale and the macro "bottom of the pyramid" scale to the vast numbers of people who live on the edge of starvation today, and do this quickly and profitably for all concerned.

7. Build learning societies across the globe, in developing regions but also in developed countries that have begun to slip in their provision of advanced education.

8. Reawaken a hunger for peace rather than war.

YOUR MISSION: IDENTIFY FUTURE NEEDS AND MEET THEM BETTER, FASTER, CHEAPER

The interesting thing about the foregoing list is that I believe it is nothing more than an intelligent and rather simple business plan. The story is told of Henry Ford who was asked, just when he was first dominating automobile manufacturing, what he would do if it all came crashing down. He is reputed to have said without hesitation that he would find another human need and meet it better and faster and cheaper than anyone else and thus repeat his success all over again. The preceding eight point list is merely a list of human needs, and the only question is who will meet them well and fast and cheaply.

THE FUTURE IS SOMETHING WE DO

When I work with groups or speak to them, I am usually asked at some point the proverbial question, "Are you optimistic or pessimistic?" There was a time when I was more optimistic I must admit. Recently humans have demonstrated a startling mendacity along with a return to almost medieval belief systems that threaten the future. Still opportunity is everywhere, and as we have seen the great challenges themselves are opportunities. I take comfort in the words of my mentors, both those I knew in person and those I knew from a distance. In one of the final interviews before his death Buckminster Fuller was asked what keeps him optimistic. His answer was, "Just look at how the grass grows. Wow. . . . We're absolutely living in crisis second by second, man. Whether we are going to make it or not depends on the integrity of what we are doing. (Lenio 1983)"

Turning the future into revenue and revenue into the future is a matter of opportunity to be sure, but it is mostly a matter of integrity. See a need. Meet it. Do it in a sustainable way. Revenue will follow. And that revenue will lead to a future that we all prefer. In the end, you see, the future is not something that just happens to us. The future is something we do.

REFERENCES

Ackoff, Russell. 1991. *Recreating the corporation: A design of organizations for the 21st century.* New York: Oxford University Press.

America's best leaders 2005. *U.S. News & World Report*, October 31, 2005, 19.

Anderson, Mark. Strategic News Service. http://www.stratnews.com.

———. 2005. Strategic News Service, personal interview, November 3.

Asimov, Isaac. 1995. My own view. In *The encyclopedia of science fiction*, ed. John Clute. New York: St. Martin's Press.

Bacon, Frank R., and Thomas Butler. 1998. *Achieving planned innovation.* New York: Simon & Schuster.

Bailey, Ronald. 2002. Forever young: The new scientific search for immortality. August. http://www.reason.com/0208/fe.rb.forever.shtml.

Barker, Joel. 1992. *Future edge.* New York: William Morrow.

Bowlin, Mike. 1999. Clean energy: preparing today for tomorrow's challenges. Speech delivered at Cambridge Energy Research Associates 18th Annual Executive Conference: Globality and Energy: Strategies for the New Millennium, Houston, Texas, February 9, 1999. Quoted in Amory Lovins et al., *Winning the Oil End Game.* Snowmass, CO: Rocky Mountain Institute, 2005, 2. www.bp.com/genericarticle.do?categoryId = 98&contentId = 2000318.

Bradbury, Ray. 1988. *The Toynbee convector.* New York: Alfred A. Knopf.

Brain, Marshall. Robotic Nation. http://marshallbrain.com/robotic-nation.htm.

Brain, Marshall. Robotic Nation evidence (blog). http://roboticnation.blogspot.com.

Brin, David. 1998. *The transparent society.* Reading, MA: Perseus Books.

Broderick, Damien. 2001. *The Spike.* New York: Tom Doherty Associates.

Campbell, Colin, quoted in Adam Fenderson. 2005. Dr. Doom, October 2, http://www.energybulletin.net/9406.html.

Cascio, Jamais. 2005. Toshiba superfast recharge batteries. http://www.worldchanging.com/archives/002435.html.

Center for Bits and Atoms, MIT. Cambridge, MA. http://cba.mit.edu/.

Cohen, Adam. 2005. Europe executives offer gloomy assessment of economy. *Wall Street Journal*, December 14, 11.

Collins, James. *Good to great: Why some companies make the leap . . . and others don't.* New York: HarperCollins.

Collins, James, and Jerry Porras. 1996. Building your company's vision. *Harvard Business Review*, October–November.

———. 1997. *Built to last: Successful habits of visionary companies.* New York: HarperCollins.

Cool chips. http://www.coolchips.gi.

Coughlin, Joe. 2005. Disruptive demographics: Old age & new demands on the national transportation system. Lecture to FHWA Think Tank, July 12.

Dent, Harry S., Jr. 1995. *The great jobs ahead.* New York: Hyperion.

———. 2004. *The next great bubble boom.* New York: Free Press.

Drexler, Eric. 1986. *Engines of creation.* New York: Anchor Books.

Drucker, Peter F. 1999. *Managing for the Future.* New York: Truman Talley Books.

———. 1993. *Post-capitalist society.* New York: Harper Business Books.

———. 1999. *Management challenges for the 21st century.* New York: Harper-Collins.

———. 2002. *Managing in the next society.* New York: Truman Talley Books.

Dychtwald, Ken. 1990. *The age wave.* New York: Bantam.

Ehrlich, Paul. 1968. *The population bomb.* Cutchogue, NY: Buccaneer Books.

Elkington, John, and Mark Lee. 2005. Have you riven a ford lately. *Grist Magazine*, October 18. http://www.grist.org/biz/fd/2005/10/18/ford/index.html.

Engardio, Pete, and Carol Matlack, quoting Monika Queisser, Organization for Economic Cooperation and Development. 2005. Global aging, *BusinessWeek* online, January 31, 2.

Feynman, Richard. 1960. There's plenty of room at the bottom. *Engineering and Science*, February. Republished at http://www.zyvex.com/nanotech/feynman.html.

Fishman, Ted C. 2005. *China Inc.* New York: Scribner.

5-Minute nanosystems. Center for Responsible Nanotechnology. http://www.crnano.org/5min.htm.

Freitas, Robert. 1999. *Nanomedicine*, Vol. 1: *Basic capabilities.* Georgetown, TX: Landes Bioscience. http://www.rfreitas.com/.

Friedman, Thomas L. 2005. *The world is flat.* New York: Farrar, Straus & Giroux.

Friedman, Benjamin M. 2005. *The moral consequences of economic growth.* New York: Knopf. Quoted in Why the rich must get richer. *The Economist*, November 12, 87–88.

Gates, Bill. 2005. *Seattle Post Intelligencer.* http://blog.seattlepi.nwsource.com/microsoft/archives/GatesMemo.htm.

Gene Therapy News. November 2005. http://www.stemcellresearchnews.com/gene_therapy_research_news.htm.

Gibson, Rowan. 1999. *Rethinking the future.* London: Nicholas Brealey.

Global Business Network. Scenario thinking. http://www.gbn.com/SubjectDisplayServlet.srv?taxId = 111.

Grant, Sara. 2005. "The broadband explosion: Thinking about a truly interactive world. *Working Knowledge.* Harvard Business School, September 12. http://hbswk.hbs.edu/item.jhtml?id = 4990&t = technology.

Greenspan, Alan. 2005. Remarks by Chairman Alan Greenspan: Energy. Presented before the Japan Business Federation, the Japan Chamber of Commerce and Industry, and the Japan Association of Corporate Executives, Tokyo, Japan, October 17. http://www.federalreserve.gov/boarddocs/speeches/2005/20051017/default.htm.

Gretzky, Wayne, from his father Walter, in Wayne Gretzky and Rick Reilly. 1990. *Gretzky: An autobiography.* New York: HarperCollins, 88.

Guyon, Janet. 2005. "Making choices: The art of the decision. *Fortune*, November 14, 144.

Hamel, Gary, and C. K. Prahalad. 1989. Strategic intent. *Harvard Business Review*, May–June, 63–76.

Harvard Green Campus Initiative. 2005. http://www.greencampus.harvard.edu/.

Hainer, Bill, and Glen Hiemstra. 2000. *Strategic leadership: Achieving your preferred future.* Kirkland, WA: Positive Productivity.

Harris, Sam. 2005. *The end of faith.* New York: W. W. Norton.

Harrow, Lisa. 2004. *What can I do?* White River Junction, VT: Chelsea Green Publishing.

Hawken, Paul. 1993. The ecology of commerce. New York: HarperCollins.

Heilbroner, Robert. 1996. *Visions of the future.* New York: Oxford University Press.

Henry, Karen. 2005. FHWA advanced research potential partnerships—A Corps of Engineers' laboratory perspective. Speech to FHWA Think Tank Forum, Advancing Future Transportation with Breakthrough Innovations.

Hiemstra, Glen. 2000. Population explosion ends in a whimper. Futurist.com. http://www.futurist.com/portal/science/science_population_explosion.htm.

Hiemstra, Dr. Tracie. 2001. Balance and boundaries in our 24/7 world. Futurist.com. http://www.futurist.com/portal/creating_your_future/crf_balance_and_boundaries.htm.

Hirsch, Kenneth. 2005. A journey of transformation. Speech to American Institute of Architects. http://www.aia.org/liv_gov_testimonial4.

Hord, Shirley M., William L. Rutherford, Leslie Huling-Austin, and Gene E. Hall. 1987. *Taking charge of change.* Alexandria, VA: Association for Supervision and Curriculum Development.

Inayatullah, Sohail. 2000. Ageing futures—from overpopulation to world under-population. Metafuture.org. http://www.metafuture.org/Articles/AgeingFutures.htm.

Institute for Systems Biology. http://www.systemsbiology.org/Intro_to_ISB_and_Systems_Biology.

Jones, Richard. 2004. *Soft machines: Nanotechnology and life.* Oxford: Oxford University Press.

Jordan, Michael. 2005. *Driven from within.* Edited by Mark Vancil. New York: Atria Books.

Kaku, Michio. 1997. *Visions: How science will revolutionize the 21st century.* New York: Anchor Books.

Kara, Don. Sizing and seizing the robotics opportunity. http://www.robonexus.com/roboticsmarket.htm.

Knoke, William. 1996. *Bold new world.* New York: Kodansha International.

Kotter, John P. 1995. Leading change: Why transformation efforts fail. *Harvard Business Review*, March–April. Reprint 95204, 1–8.

Kurzweil, Ray. 1999. *The age of spiritual machines.* New York: Viking.

———. 2005a. *The singularity is near.* New York: Viking.

———. 2005b. When humans transcend biology. Seattle Town Hall Lecture Series, October 10.

Kusek, David, and Gerd Leonhard. 2005. *The future of music: Manifesto for the digital music revolution.* Boston: Berklee Press.

LaGesse, David. 2005. Engine of fun and profit. *U.S. News & World Report*, October 31, 26.

Lan, Jin. 2005. Personal interview, December 20. Jin Lan is the founder of Oc-taxias Company LLC, an international consulting company that acts as a bridge for those wishing to do business in China. http://www.chinaselections.com/.

Lean, Jeffrey. 2005. The big thaw. *The Independent*, online edition. November 20. http://news.independent.co.uk/environment/article328217.ece.

Lenio, Ted. 1983. A conversation with Bucky Fuller. *Aspen, The Magazine* 10, no. 2 (Fall).

Leonard, Andrew. 2005. Why "Made in China" is good news for the U.S. Salon.com, August 3. http://www.salon.com/tech/feature/2005/08/03/china/print.html.

Lindaman, Edward B., and Ronald O. Lippitt. 1979. *Choosing the future you prefer.* Ann Arbor, MI: Human Resource Development Associates.

Lippitt, Lawrence. 1998. *Preferred futuring.* San Francisco: Barrett-Koehler.

Loeb, Paul Rogat. 2004. *The impossible will take a little longer.* New York: Basic Books.

Lovgren, Stefan. 2005. Ted Sargent, quoted in Spray-on solar-power cells are true breakthrough. January 14. http://news.nationalgeographic.com/news/2005/01/0114_050114_solarplastic.html.

Lovins, Amory, E. Kyle Datta, Odd-Even Bustnes, Jonathan G. Koomey, and Nathan J. Glasgow. 2005. *Winning the oil end game.* Snowmass, CO: Rocky Mountain Institute.

Lynas, Mark. 2004. *High tide.* New York: Picador.

Markides, Constantinos C. 1999. *All the right moves: A guide to crafting breakthrough strategy.* Cambridge, MA: Harvard Business Press.

McCarthy, J. J., et al., eds. 2001. *Climate change 2001: Impacts, adaptation, and vulnerability.* Cambridge: Cambridge University Press.

McCarthy, Wil. 2003. *Hacking matter.* New York: Basic Books.

McFarling, Usha Lee, and Miguel Bustillo. 2005. 2005 vying with '98 as record hot year. *Los Angeles Times*, December 16. http://www.latimes.com/news/local/la-me-climate16dec16,1,664579.story.

Meyers, William. 2005. Conscience in a cup of coffee. *U.S. News & World Report*, October 31, 48–50.

Miller, Jody, and Matt Miller. 2005. Get a life. *Fortune*, November 28.

MIT Institute for Soldier Nanotechnologies. 2005. http://web.mit.edu/isn/.

Mishel, Lawrence, Jared Bernstein, and Sylvia Allegretto. 2005. *The state of working America 2004–2005.* Ithaca, NY: Cornell University Press. Excerpt quoted at http://www.epinet.org/books/swa2004/news/swafacts_international.pdf.

Monster.com. 2006. http://careersat50.monster.com/.

Nanoparticles, nanoshells, nanotubes: How tiny specks may provide powerful tools against cancer." ScienceDaily.com. http://www.sciencedaily.com/print.php?url=/releases/2005/11/051119105053.htm.

Nantero. 2005. http://www.nantero.com/index.html.

New microscope allows scientists to track a functioning protein with atomic-level precision." 2005. http://www.sciencedaily.com/releases/2005/11/051114111031.htm.

Oreskes, Naomi. 2004. Beyond the ivory tower: The scientific consensus on climate change. Science 3 306, no. 5702 (December): 1686.

Pacheco, Michael. 2005. Quoted in Michael Parfit, Future power. *National Geographic*, August. http://www7.nationalgeographic.com/ngm/0508/feature1/fulltext.html.

Parfit, Michael. 2005. Future power. *National Geographic*, August. http://www7.nationalgeographic.com/ngm/0508/feature1/fulltext.html.

Payne, Roger. 2005. The future of our oceans. *Future in Review 2005 Transcript.* Edited by Sally Anderson. Friday Harbor, WA: Strategic News Service.

Peak oil, by the Science Applications International Corporation (SAIC), a report for the U.S. Department of Defense. Quoted in Adam Fenderson. 2005. Dr. doom, October 2. http://www.energybulletin.net/9406.html.

Perkins, John. 2004. *Confessions of an economic hit man.* San Francisco: Barrett-Koehler.

Polak, Fred. 1973. *The image of the future.* Translated and abridged by Elise Boulding from 1953 work. Amsterdam: Elsevier Scientific Publishing.

Porter, Michael E. 1980, 1998. *Competitive strategy.* New York: Free Press.

Povejsil, Donald. 1989. Coming of age. *Inc.* April, 1989, 42.

Prahalad, C. K. 2005. *The fortune at the bottom of the pyramid.* Upper Saddle River, NJ: Wharton School Publishing.

Prahalad C. K., and Henry Mintzburg. 2000. *Mastering strategy: Complete MBA companion in strategy.* New York: Prentice Hall Publishing.

Prensky, Marc. 2001. Digital natives, digital immigrants. *On the horizon*, NCB University Press, 9, no. 5 (October).

Prensky, Marc. 2004. The death of command and control? Strategic News Service online newsletter, January 20.

Prewitt, Edward. 2004. The Agile 100. *CIO Magazine*, April 15. http://www.cio.com/archive/081504/overview.html.

Reiss, Spencer. 2005. Why $5 oil is good for America. *Wired*, December, 238–247.

Reynolds, Scott, Neil Ridley, and Carl E. Van Horn. 2005. A work filled retirement. Heldrich Center, Rutgers University, August. www.heldrich.rutgers.edu/Resources/Publication/191/WT16.pdf.

Rifkin, Jeremy. 2002. *The hydrogen economy.* New York: Tarcher/Penguin.

Ringland, Gill. 1998. *Scenario planning: Managing for the future.* London: John Wiley & Sons.

———. 2002. *Scenarios in business.* London: John Wiley & Sons.

———. 2002. *Scenarios in public policy.* London: John Wiley & Sons.

Roberts, Paul. 2005. *The end of oil.* Boston: Houghton Mifflin.

Russell, Peter. 1998. *Waking up in time.* Novato, CA: Origin Press.

Ryder, Tracie Rose. 1989. How can it look so good and feel so bad? Redmond, WA: Lincoln Global Productions.

Sachs, Jeffrey D. 2005. *The end of poverty.* New York: Penguin Press.

Sakaiya, Taichi. 1991. *The knowledge value revolution.* Translated by George Fields and William Marsh. Tokyo: Kodansha International.

Sandberg, Jared. 2005. Deciders suffer alone; nondeciders make everyone else suffer. *Wall Street Journal*, November 8, B1.

Schwartz, Peter. 1991. *The art of the long view.* New York: Currency.

Senge, Peter. 1990. *The fifth discipline.* New York: Doubleday.

———. 1994. *The fifth discipline.* New York: Currency.

Shell Global Scenarios. http://www.shell.com/home/Framework?siteId = royal-en& FC2 = /royal-en/html/iwgen/leftnavs/zzz_lhn5_2_0.html&FC3 = /royal-en/ html/iwgen/our_strategy/scenarios/dir_scenarios_28022005.html.

Simmons, Matthew R. 2005. *Twilight in the desert.* Hoboken, NJ: John Wiley & Sons.

Smith, Charles. 2005. Quoted in William Meyers, Conscience in a cup of coffee. *U.S. News & World Report*, October 31, 50.

Space Elevator. http://www.spaceelevator.com.

Sparks, Whitney. 2005. "Gary Hamel's idea hatchery. *BusinessWeek*, August 11. http://www.businessweek.com/innovate/content/aug2005/id20050811_693230 .htm.

Speth, James Gustave. 2004. *Red sky at morning.* New Haven, CT: Yale University Press.

Stephenson, Neal. 1995. *The diamond age.* New York: Spectra.

Sterling, Bruce. 1994. *Heavy weather.* New York: Bantam Books.

———. 1996. *Holy fire.* New York: Bantam Books.

———. 2002. *Tomorrow now: Envisioning the next fifty years.* New York: Random House.

———. 2005. Dawn of the carbon age. *Wired*, December.

Stock, Gregory. 2002. *Redesigning humans.* Boston: Houghton Mifflin.

Svensson, Peter. 2005. Virtual reality games are big bucks. *Seattle Post Intelligencer*, November 4. http://seattlepi.nwsource.com/business/247084_virtual jobs03.html.

The real digital divide. 2005. *The Economist*, March 10. http://www .economist.com/opinion/displayStory.cfm?story_id = 3742817&tranMode = none.

Thompson, William Irwin. 1985. *Pacific shift.* San Francisco: Sierra Club Books.

Toth-Fejel, Tihamer. 2004. Self-replicating nanomachines: A kinematic cellular automata approach. http://www.foresight.org/Conferences/AdvNano2004/ Abstracts/Toth-Fejel2/.

Vestergaard Frandsen. http://www.vestergaard-frandsen.com/.

Virtual Advisor. 2004. http://www.va-interactive.com/inbusiness/editorial/bizdev/ibt/tailorin.html.

The vision thing. 1991. *The Economist*, November 9, 81.

Voros, Joseph. 2005. A generic foresight process framework. Quoted in Maree Conway, Strategic planning revisited. *Foresight, Innovation and Strategy*, Ed. C. Wagner. Bethesda, MD: World Future Society, 270.

Weick, Karl E., and Kathleen M. Sutcliff. 2001. *Managing the unexpected.* San Francisco: Jossey-Bass.

Weisbord, Marvin, and Sandra Janoff. 2000. *Future search.* San Francisco: Barrett-Koehler.

Wheatley, Margaret J. 2002. *Turning to one another: Simple conversations to restore hope to the future.* San Francisco: Barrett-Koehler.

Whitman, Meg. 2005. Knowing it's time to buy. *Fortune*, November 14, 146.

Whole Foods Declaration of Interdependence. http://www.wholefoodsmarket.com/company/declaration.html.

Whyte, David. 1994. *The heart aroused.* New York: Doubleday.

Yunnas, Muhammad. 2003. *Banker to the poor.* New York: Public Affairs.

INDEX